THOMAS COOK

THE HOLIDAY-MAKER

JILL HAMILTON

SUTTON PUBLISHING

First published in the United Kingdom in 2005 by
Sutton Publishing Limited · Phoenix Mill
Thrupp · Stroud · Gloucestershire · GL5 2BU

British Library Cataloguing in Publication Data
A catalogue record for this book is available from the British Library.

ISBN 0-7509-3325-9

To Penny Hart, who has helped me so much
over the years.

Typeset in 11/14.5pt Sabon.
Typesetting and origination by
Sutton Publishing Limited.
Printed and bound in England by
J.H. Haynes & Co. Ltd, Sparkford.

Contents

Chronology

1808   Thomas Cook born in Melbourne, Derbyshire.

1834   John Mason Cook born on 13 January.

1841   Organises his first excursion by rail from Leicester to a Temperance meeting in Loughborough.

1845   Conducts his first trip for profit by railway to Liverpool from Leicester, Nottingham and Derby.

1846   Escorts a tour to Scotland.

1851   Promotes trips to the Great Exhibition in Hyde Park.
        The *Excursionist* published for the first time as Cook's *Exhibition Herald and Excursion Advertiser*.

1855   Inaugurates continental tour.

1863   Conducts his first party to Switzerland via Paris.

1864   John Mason Cook, aged 30, joins his father in business.

1865   Office opened in Fleet Street, London.

1866   John Mason escorts the first American tour.

1868   A system of hotel coupons introduced.

1869   Escorts his first party to Egypt and Palestine.

1871   Thomas Cook & Son becomes the official name of the firm.

1872/3   Organises and leads the first round-the-world tour – 222 days and 25,000 miles.

1873   New offices open at Ludgate Circus, London.
        The first edition of Cook's *Continental Time Tables and Tourist's Handbook* is published.

1874   Cook's Circular Note, an early form of the traveller's cheque, is launched in New York.

1878   A Foreign Banking and Money Exchange Department is established.

1879   1 January. John Mason becomes 'sole managing partner'.

1884   Thos. Cook & Son conveys a relief force sent to rescue General Gordon from Khartoum up the Nile as far as Wadi Halfa.

1892   Thomas Cook dies in Leicester aged 83.

Preface

Cook is a forgotten hero of his age. This book commemorates the 150th anniversary of his first overseas conducted tour in 1855. Driven by his religious faith, Cook founded a major industry, one that is now one of the world's biggest sectors. In the UK alone, it is the third largest industry, worth over £75 billion a year.

When Cook was born in 1808, the term 'tourism' had not been invented. Leisure in distant places was mostly an unknown experience – as was staying in hotels or eating in restaurants. Poor men made journeys only when necessary; poor women usually stayed at home. Yet, by the time Cook died in 1892, travelling abroad had become part of modern life. The number of travellers from England who steamed across the Channel to the continent via ports with railway connections grew from 165,000 in 1850 to 951,000 by 1899.

It was not until Cook started his cheap overseas tours in 1855 that workers, let alone women, had the opportunity to go abroad easily. His group packages gave them an umbrella under which it was safer to explore foreign places. Just how revolutionary this was can be seen by looking at the small numbers of women who had braved sailing boats in the previous four centuries.

Cook's career in travel began with the burgeoning of rail and steam transport in 1841; he died just as the combustion-engine era was about to take off. Since Cook's death in 1892 modes of travel have changed enormously, but not the basic methods, organisation and marketing that he championed. A printer by trade, he knew the potential of advertising, promotions and travel writing – even starting the first regular monthly travel newspaper in 1851. Nearly every trip was promoted in advance with posters and leaflets, and each tourist was given historical and practical information to animate places *en route* and destinations. The one thing, though, that would startle this man who left school at ten years old would be the university degrees in tourism and the many Professors of Tourism and Leisure Management. As degrees in different aspects of the travel industry have expanded, the Thomas Cook Archives in Peterborough have been mined by research students. Like them, I have relied heavily on this invaluable resource. This book, though, was neither commissioned nor subsidised by the famous travel agency that Cook started. It springs entirely from my interest in how he opened up the Middle East, especially the Holy Land and Egypt, to tourism.

Three times a week, when walking to the School of Oriental and African Studies in London, I walk past the site of Cook's former house in Great Russell Street, opposite the British Museum, and I never fail to recall Cook's tenacity and ability to keep going despite terrible reverses. The man who boasted that he had escorted over a million tourists without mishap witnessed the death of his only daughter at home because he personally misjudged the safety of a gas boiler. That was on top of having become estranged from his only son – but if he had lived longer he would have had the satisfaction of seeing that his name continued as a household word, synonymous with popular tourism; and that the Baptist chapel that he worked so hard to open in Rome in the 1870s is still well attended.

Jill Hamilton
Chelsea, November 2004

To travel is to feed the mind, humanize the soul, and rub off the rust of circumstance – to travel is to read the last new book, enjoy to its full the blessings of invention – to travel is to have Nature's plan and her high works simplified, and her broad features of hill and dale, mountain and flood, spread like a map at one's feet – to travel is to dispel the mists of fable and clear the mind of prejudice taught from babyhood, and facilitate perfectness of seeing eye to eye. Who would not travel at a penny per mile?

Thomas Cook, Excursionist, July 1854

ONE

Religion, Railways and Respectability

The prejudices which ignorance has engendered are broken by the roar of a train and the whistle of the engine awakens thousands from the slumber of ages . . .

Thomas Cook, *Handbook to Scotland*, 1846

Tourism is now among the world's largest industries, but little is known about its greatest pioneer, Thomas Cook, the father of tourism. He revolutionised travel, invented package holidays and brought mobility to the masses.[1] The sex, alcohol, overspending, indolent leisure and extravagance that are now associated with much of the holiday industry would horrify him. Few know of his preoccupation with God, Rome and the Holy Land, or of his determination to improve the lot of the working classes, let alone his abhorrence of beer houses, pubs and gin palaces. In the nineteenth century no priest, or minister, did more than this diminutive former preacher to shape Protestant attitudes to Palestine. By opening up Palestine to tourism, Cook deliberately offered the British people a way to reconnect with their religious roots. From 1869 onwards he brought the largest number of British to the Holy Land since the Crusader armies and private parties of pilgrims in the Middle Ages.

In 1976 a BBC documentary on Cook asked the question, 'But what made him do it? This strait-laced provincial missionary – what drove him on? What fired his abundant energy?' The following chapters attempt to give fresh insights into Cook – and, so that he, too, can have his voice, extracts from his voluminous writings are included in the appendix. His life gives a vivid picture of the influence of Nonconformity in England in the nineteenth century and the way it helped the slow march to a fairer society and

1

democracy. Success for Cook was integrated with the collective power of the Nonconformists, many of whose ancestors had suffered the rack, the dungeon and the scaffold both during and after the Reformation.

Cook's near-forty-year career was full of leaps and contradictions, but he himself changed little. He never lost his Derbyshire accent, his fidgetiness or the habit of walking with his hands thrust into his pockets. Sometimes, when listening, he put his hands together and twirled his thumbs over one another.[2] One writer described Cook in Paris 'answering questions and swallowing coffee with a rapid dexterity worthy of a Chinese juggler'.[3] Another writer, the Archbishop of Canterbury's sister, described him in 1871 as 'a home-staying, retired tradesman'. Failings in etiquette and his 'northerness' were compensated by his foresight, patience and the ability of a stage entertainer to hold a crowd and impart excitement.

Cook always felt that God was on his side. All his life he retained the traits of many Baptists – that is, a horror of self-indulgence, debts of any sort or extravagance. Faith sustained him when he was attacked in the press by upper-class critics trying to stem the tide of travellers to 'their' resorts. Ever resourceful, Cook actually prospered from their condemnation. When his 'hordes' began pouring into the tourist destinations of the more affluent, Cook looked to faraway places to find untrammelled havens. So, while more tourists went to places like Morecambe, Blackpool and Ramsgate, the middle classes were exploring the Continent and Middle East – with Cook.

Cook was impelled by religion. Devotion to God, prayer and the Bible fired his imagination and provided him with his daily strength. He also drew inspiration from two other features of the Victorian era – railways and respectability. Scope came from the spreading of the railways. Integrity came from Temperance, which epitomised the ideals of self-control and self-denial and fitted in with nineteenth-century prudery and decorum. To these can be added resolution and reliability. Finally, there was music. Often bands with drums and trumpets beat out rousing tunes on his excursions.

Cook's life was no fairy-tale rags to riches story of a man rising effortlessly from obscurity. In his case, nights filled with letter-writing, accounts and editing frequently followed days of sustained effort. Even when short of sleep, he often had to reverse mishaps, but somehow he coped with the misadventures of travel – missed connections, broken-down trains, fierce storms at sea, hotels with double bookings and lost luggage. When things went wrong Cook relied on the ethos of self-help so characteristic of the nineteenth century and religious stoicism. But his ability to remain unruffled meant that he could have prearranged trips to see stampeding elephants. Whether facing insurgent warfare or the perils of the Swiss Alps, customers felt safe.

His assets in the travel business were his career as a printer and his marketing skills combined with rigorous self-discipline, attention to detail and an ability to coordinate transport and ground arrangements. Sophisticated marketing, whether persuading people of the evils of alcohol or the advantages of taking a train trip, was at the forefront of all his businesses. With his own printing presses and the help of just a few apprentices, he could quickly turn out stacks of cheap-to-produce leaflets, posters and flyers. Today, marketing is a subject in the curriculum of universities, but Cook acquired his know-how first by selling cabbages, turnips and other vegetables at Derby market, then by learning how to attract converts when earning his living proselytising for the Baptists, and he finally perfected his skills during his near twenty years as a publisher of Temperance literature. He made sure that newspapers and leaflets heightened the anticipation about coming excursions, and that destinations were made more fascinating by guidebooks and itineraries with potted histories.

Cook's dazzling progress coincided with the most action-packed period of parliamentary change in England. He started out as an itinerant Baptist lay preacher at the age of nineteen in 1828, the year of the repeal of the Test and Corporation Acts. His time as a self-employed cabinet-maker began in the year of the Great Reform Act, which extended the franchise to all 'ten-pound householders'. He reached his goal of escorting trips to the Holy Land the year after the much-awaited passage of the second Reform Bill of 1867, which was also the golden moment of Nonconformity and Evangelicalism in English politics. Politics may sound a far cry from Cook sending thousands of holiday-makers off to criss-cross the earth's surface, but much reform, like Cook's early trips, was driven by the same ascendancy of religious ferment.

A leading anti-Corn Law campaigner, Cook promoted 'the poor man's bread', the Big Loaf and aid to the starving. He enjoyed the struggle in the 1840s tremendously. Born eight years into the beginning of the century and dying eight years before its end, he spanned the nineteenth century and was typical of those who were entrenched in Nonconformist religion.[4] At a time when reform was a key political slogan, Cook was one of the voices in the large groups of Nonconformist Liberals who cried out for education, the disestablishment of the Church of England, an end to church tithes and Free Trade.

While religion gave Cook drive and purpose, the Bible was the wellspring of his life, and, after he had taken the Pledge at the age of twenty-four in 1833, Temperance was the catalyst.[5] Cut-price package tourism became a social mission. Because travel freed people and widened their social circles, he wanted to help the poor to 'go beyond', get out of their rut, escape the confines of their own homes and fleetingly forget the dreariness of their lives by awakening their minds. Most people in his village seldom travelled further than thirty miles at the most, yet Cook took his name to the ends of the earth, turning it into one of the most easily recognised trademarks in the world. The phrase 'Cook's Tour' entered the English language. He made both scenic beauty and history, combined with trouble-free travelling, a saleable commodity.

The following chapters, while unveiling a little-known side of this 'pioneer of convenient travel', give an idea of the extraordinary extent to which religion, then one of the driving forces of the age,[6] dominated the lives and politics of so many. The contribution of Nonconformity in the nineteenth century, together with the mutual support given by its members, was enormous. Apart from Joseph

Paxton, nearly every helping hand extended to Cook in his first fifty years belonged to a Nonconformist.

Three of the destinations which Cook promoted with such fervour were well known because of the Bible: the Nile, so associated with Moses; the Jordan, which had become synonymous with Jesus; and the Tiber, which witnessed the expansion of the Christian Church. It was almost as if there was an invisible triangle connecting the three rivers which became part of his adult life. Five of Cook's most profound religious moments were near rivers and waterways. The first was when he was seventeen, when, near the River Trent in Derbyshire, he was plunged in the baptism bath in the Baptist Chapel in Melbourne, near his home. His second was at the age of thirty-five on the edge of the Grand Union Canal. His third was in 1869 while escorting the first package tour of English tourists to the Middle East, when he immersed himself in the Jordan in Palestine in the heart of the Holy Land where John the Baptist baptised Jesus. The fourth was the Nile, where he promoted trips as a tourist destination and explored places immortalised by Moses and Tutankhamen, and the fifth was setting up the first Baptist mission in history in Rome near the banks of the Tiber. Here he followed in the footsteps of Peter and Paul, who had made Rome into the cradle of Christianity.

It took Cook four careers and sixty years – as a carpenter, a printer, a preacher and a travel organiser – before he stood on the edges of the Jordan. By then this man, who had failed to acquire the finer arts of riding or ballroom dancing and who could not speak more than a few phrases in Arabic, could serenely lead a caravan of baggage camels, horses and donkeys, make himself heard and understood above all the noise and commotion, and, with only the help of men who knew no clocks and whose hours and minutes were regulated by the sun, the moon and the stars, get his tours to run with European punctuality.

TWO

A Nonconformist Childhood

Hedges so thick they seemed prehistoric had grown tall to shelter men and animals from the ferocious winter weather whose winds often blew low through the pretty little Domesday village of Melbourne, seven-and-a-half miles south-east from Derby, south-west of the Pennines. In 1807, winter arrived hastily after the long days of summer. There was snow in November. It melted away, but, as usual, from late November to early March, life was hard and there were few luxuries. Owning a pig was one of them. Happiness for labourers could often be measured by how many they owned.[1] When a man could not find enough for his family to eat, the pig would be sold. The money helped pay off debts and bought shoes, clothing and perhaps, in the spring, piglets and hens. Most labourers had a decent potato patch. Leeks, parsnips, turnips, cabbages, beans, peas, spinach, rhubarb, parsley, lavender, rosemary and other herbs were lovingly tended. There were usually a few apple and plum trees. Many men, permanently in debt, relied on pigs, extra harvest earnings and income from their wives' looms to make ends meet.

Nearly every dwelling had its loom. For centuries wool had been spun in farmhouses and village homes by women and children, but now the wool went directly to the huge newly built woollen mills just a little smaller than the large new sawmills. Beyond them was the land which yielded wheat, barley, fodder, turnips and the seemingly ever-damp grass for the flocks of sheep. Cared for by shepherds with their crooks and guarded by Border collies, they were the real wealth. Everywhere, the hedges, more than any building, gave a feeling of permanence and of man's unending struggle with the elements. Many had been grown to enclose open fields, commons and waste land and to absorb it into both farms and estates. Between 1750 and 1830 approximately 6.8 million acres in England were brought into private cultivation as a result of Enclosure Acts.[2] The soil was rich, renowned for its market gardens, yet scarcity coexisted with earthly abundance. Abject, hopeless poverty contrasted with the lives of the gentry and aristocracy.

Forebears of many labourers and tradesmen had been living near and around the area before the Civil War, before the Norman Conquest, back to the times when the Celts worshipped pagan gods, in circles of stones under the stars.

Horseshoes and little silver balls spelt out the names and date on the wedding cake, which was waiting to be cut. Soon the couple would come up the hill from the church past the tall holly hedges. The wedding of John Cook, a 22-year-old[3] labourer, to Elizabeth Perkins was taking place at the parish church of St Michael. John Cook's family had lived in Melbourne for at least four generations. After the Marriage Act[4] of 1753, marriage ceremonies could be performed only by clergymen of the Church of England, or by Quakers and Jews. Apart from the religious humiliation of having to marry in the church they defied, Nonconformists had the hardship of paying fees to the Anglican minister.[5] Elizabeth had not been taught to write, so she had to mark the wedding register with a cross. If the family tree in the Cook archives is accurate, she was just over twenty. It gives a date of 1788, but no source.[6] As John Cook had hesitated about entering the state of matrimony, her spinsterhood was underscored by her two younger sisters who had married earlier, becoming Ann Pegg and Alice Beresford.

After the wedding in the icy church in February 1808, just as the daffodils and early irises were pushing through the earth, the happy pair did not move in with John Cook's parents, William and Mary Cook, as was often customary, but rented the narrow picturesque tumbledown cottage at 9 Quick Close, on the highest crest of the hill of the village. If it had fallen down, it would not have been missed. In such cottages, the earth floors at the back 'heaved' in winter. From the street there was a panoramic view, but the house caught the winds and gales, which hissed rain down the chimney, rattled shutters and banged doors. It was a stiff climb up from the curving High Street with its pubs, chapels, shops, millers, brewers, maltsters, boot makers, grocers, butchers, bakers, blacksmith and flour dressers and dealers, though not as steep as the climb up from Melbourne Hall on flat ground near the lake.

Nine months after the wedding, on 22 November 1808, Thomas, the only child of the marriage, was born with a sturdy body and short legs that would remain spindly all his life. The birth was noted in the blank leaf between the Old and New Testament in the old family Bible which Elizabeth, as the eldest child, had inherited. Due to her lack of schooling, the words were penned in the neat hand of a stranger: 'On the 22nd day of November, 1808, at five o'clock in the morning, Thomas Cook was born in Melbourne.' As if to give symmetry to the pattern in his life, his birth coincided with the exhibition in London of the first steam locomotive and open carriage on rails by Richard Trevithick, the Cornish mining engineer, inventor of the steam engine.[7] Thomas's birth also coincided with another in Paris, that of Louis Napoleon (who would become Napoleon III), the son of Napoleon Bonaparte's brother, Louis, and Josephine's daughter, Hortense. The activities of Louis Napoleon would impact on Thomas's life, as would those of William Gladstone, who was born the following year, and of Giuseppe Garibaldi, who was born the year before Thomas.

War formed a backdrop to Thomas's childhood. With the exception of the period of the Peace of Amiens in 1803, the British had been waging war against the French since 1793.[8] Thomas's birth was at the height of Britain's long era of war, in the year that Wellington's soldiers began their fight against Napoleon Bonaparte's *Grande Armée* in the Peninsular War in Spain, the year that Napoleon – branded in English villages as 'Boney' the ogre – had reached his zenith.

The war brought an exotic touch to daily life in remote and inaccessible Melbourne. A proportion of the 122,000 French prisoners of war[9] were interned in the neighbouring town of Ashby-de-la-Zouch. With them came the sound of foreign tongues, the exoticism of the Continent and the constant reminder of the threat of invasion, something which had not been felt in England since the Spanish Armada. When Thomas was born, about 460,000 men had enrolled as volunteers in the home militia, including the volunteer infantry first raised in Derbyshire during 1803. As in the rest of Britain, each able-bodied man was trained in his spare time ready to defend hearth, home and country if invaded. In Melbourne, while there had been much improvisation with weapons, the brass band was so well equipped that there could have been rivalry about who was to beat the drum.[10] At the slightest excuse it struck up a tune, creating such an impression on young Thomas that he later used bands to give gaiety and style to his early tours.

In 1812, when Thomas was just three years old, a calamity with far-reaching repercussions altered the rural calm of the Cook family. John Cook died. There was little sign of God's Grace and no pennies or pounds for a gravestone. But despite few chapels being permitted to have their own burial grounds he was buried behind the Baptist chapel. The days after Thomas's father's death were crammed with people with red eyes, tears and the imagery of hell and the demonic.[11] Death was seen as the transition to a new life in Heaven, but the mourning period was long, gloomy, dark and anxious. There was scarcely money for food or rent.

That summer saw the preparations for the big 'waltzing ball' at Melbourne Hall. With its wild woods and deer parks, summer balls and winter shooting parties, it was a house where people came and went but seldom stayed for long – another world, one physically near by, seen every day, but closed to the villagers. Lady Melbourne was a formidable political hostess, so the house was animated by annual events in the Summer Season. Villagers were curious to know if her erratic daughter-in-law, Lady Caroline Lamb, who had been the celebrated mistress of Lord Byron, was at the house party.

Then things changed. Just after the harvest, banns were again displayed and read in Melbourne church. Black clothes were discarded, along with the grim mourning that weighed so heavily in the household. The curtains were opened and light was allowed into the downstairs room; the mood lifted from lamentations to celebrations. A new man, James Smithard, was to take the place of John Cook in the life of Elizabeth. This husband-to-be is listed in the church register as having previously married someone called Ann Hollingsworth in March 1802. Now, in September 1812, the bells of St Michael's pealed over and over again as Elizabeth's relations sat in the pews and benches to watch her stand beside the pulpit and again utter the words 'with my body I thee worship'. Friends who were reluctant to take part in *any* Anglican service yet again waited outside.

Afterwards, Elizabeth walked up the hill with her new husband. Smithard came to live in Elizabeth's crammed labourer's abode. Sleeping in the room where his wife's former husband had died only months earlier could not have been a romantic start to marriage. Barely nine months had passed before a half-brother, James, arrived. Another five years were to pass before the cradle was pulled out again, for Simeon in 1818, but Thomas remained his mother's favourite. Many stepfathers would have looked on a lively three-year-old as an intruder, but Smithard was a kind man. He later used some of his wages to pay school fees for Thomas, who was showing much promise. Perhaps, like his grandfather, after whom he had been named, Thomas might become a Baptist pastor. A few streets away from home, the school room was dominated by the squeak of white chalk on a large blackboard, the creaking hinges of desk lids, the choruses of boys chanting tables parrot-fashion and the stifled yawns of those taking dictation or copying out long lists of difficult-to-spell words. The rudiments of reading, writing and arithmetic were inculcated by three men of stern integrity and religious character – T. Pickering, John Smith and Joseph Tagg. Punishments ranged from standing in the corner to the cane. Good penmanship was essential and pages of fine, slanted writing were copied. Anyone could start a school, and many fell by the wayside, but sixteen years after Thomas had put down his slate Tagg's school was still listed.

At school Thomas showed little aptitude for intellectual pursuits, but his urge to learn and teach went deep, and pamphlets and books to help further his grounding in English were borrowed. The education of those fortunate enough to have any schooling was basic and hardly went beyond the three R's plus religious instruction. In many schools like Thomas's, the primer was the Bible. Teachers, avoiding the cost of extra books, could be confident that it would be the one book in the homes of most pupils. School began and ended with the reading of the Bible, often the Old Testament.

This narrow education, lacking any intellectual aspirations, could have been a handicap, but for Thomas the emphasis on the Bible was an advantage. Nobody could match him on either the Old or the New Testament. This would be of much use to him half a century later when taking tourists around the Holy Land. On the other hand, the travel articles he wrote in his own newspapers, most of which have a freshness and the indefinable air of the amateur, have sometimes been criticised as falling into 'the unctuous style of the sermon',[12] as his style was influenced by his Bible readings.

In the cloth-producing towns of England, such as Melbourne, tallow candles, lanterns lit by whale oil to read by, books, tin soldiers, paintboxes and most toys, apart from rag dolls, marbles and skipping ropes, were luxuries for most children. Bunyan's works were acceptable but novels were still frowned upon. The one book in most homes was the Bible or a cheap reprint with quaint woodcuts of John Bunyan's *The Pilgrim's Progress*, a book which added a dimension to both travelling and pilgrimages. Bunyan's prose, especially about the divided self, good and evil, love and hate, Heaven and Hell, had been kept alive in cottages and chapels. He was claimed as a former Baptist. His allegory was written during his six-months' solitude in a 'dark, dreary, dungeon', when he had been imprisoned yet again after English bishops were ordered to penalise anyone failing to come to Communion at their parish church. Thousands had been arrested.

During Thomas's second year at school, before the long summer holidays and harvest, the fateful battle of Waterloo was fought between Napoleon and Wellington, the 'Iron Duke' in Belgium during the weekend of 15–18 June. For a few hours Britain stood still to rejoice in a victory which had taken roughly twenty-five years. Up and down the country, guns thundered and bonfires were lit. Horrific stories of 50,000 human corpses, almost stripped bare on the battlefield, were imprinted on Thomas.

The expected upturn in England's fortunes following Waterloo did not materialise as foreign markets failed to buy sufficient British goods. There was fear of the Poor House, the Debtors' Prison or bankruptcy as the country plunged into depression. On top of this, 400,000 demobilised soldiers looking for work swamped the job market. A series of thin harvests led to bread riots and hunger for millions, while unemployment and inflation worsened the poverty among the ragged and hungry poor and food, shelter, blankets, clothes and a few shillings became a priority.

On 28 January 1817, before the Prince Regent opened parliament, reformers presented petitions with half a million signatures. Safely inside the House of Commons the Prince condemned 'those exciting a spirit of sedition and violence', but outside the crowd waited. Thousands hissed and booed as he drove up the Mall, stones flew and two bullets shattered the windows of his carriage. Committees found evidence of revolutionary movements in London and in the factory slums of Lancashire, Leicestershire, Derby, Nottingham and Glasgow. Unrest was aggravated by growing numbers of jobless men, pitiful wages, long hours, appalling conditions, child labour and near starvation. Repeated riots and demonstrations upset life in both agricultural and industrial districts. A month after this attempt on the Prince Regent's life, a nervous government suspended *habeas corpus* so that any person under suspicion could be thrown into prison without trial. Further restrictive acts, including the prohibition of seditious meetings, were passed. Times were dangerous and hard, but churches and chapels thrived and multiplied as they have never done before or since. As religion, in all its many aspects, was embedded in the life of nineteenth-century England and permeated many aspects, including politics, and was the mainstay of Thomas's life, a separate chapter is devoted to the background of his Baptist religion.

THREE

The Protestant Ethic

An *e* at the end of Melbourne was still optional, and in *Pigot's Commercial Directory of Derbyshire* it was still minus the *e*. Just as Melbourne was then spelt in two different ways, there were two main communities in the area, the Anglicans and the Nonconformists. No building in Melbourne competed with the church of St Michael, which, with its tall cliff-like walls, was so large that it had the air of being a small cathedral. After its completion in about 1120, St Michael's was used as a royal chapel by Henry I, then given by him to the Bishopric of Carlisle. It became a refuge for bishops when fleeing border incursions. For 700 years St Michael's had been the focus of the area. Now, though, it was no longer a symbol of unity in Melbourne. The Evangelical revival, with its new and reinvigorated Anglicanism, had conversely encouraged more villagers to attend the Nonconformist chapels. Each Sunday there were fewer villagers sitting in front of the fearsome old church columns with its capitals of a grinning cat, snarling dog and an ostrich.

Elizabeth's father, Thomas Perkins from Hinckley, in Leicestershire, had been a 'hell-fire' preacher, a man of boiling enthusiasms who electrified his congregation. With fire and brimstone sermons and talk of the Devil, he filled the hastily built chapel. Thomas Budge, a former Melbourne Baptist minister, described Perkins as a man who, 'in tones of thunder, hurled verses and paragraphs of the sacred writings like huge boulders to crush down all opponents'. Perkins was converted in the Leicestershire village of Barton-in-the-Beans by the 'Barton Preachers' – Evangelical revivalists, a splinter group started by a steward to Selina, Countess of Huntingdon. Selina, one of John Wesley's active supporters, had sold jewels to build sixty-four chapels and a training college for chaplains for her own Connexion, a sect of the Calvinist Methodists, distinct from Wesley's followers.[1] Perkins moved to Melbourne to 'spread the word' in 1760, the year that George III came to the throne. Ten years later he *walked* 180 miles to a meeting in Whitechapel, London, which resulted in the breakaway New Connexion of General Baptists.

This new branch of the Baptists, with their rousing meetings and loud, tuneful hymns, which injected a new vitality and self-reliance into everyday religion, was a result of the Evangelist Revival. Most of the Evangelicals, bar those who were Methodists, remained members of the Church of England, but the vibrancy and colour they brought into services also revitalised English Nonconformity. Perkins returned to Melbourne to become a co-preacher, a post which he kept for twenty-five years. Budge's history reveals a turn to his career. In about 1785, 'when somewhat advanced in life, he contracted a marriage which was thought . . . to be an imprudent one, and which led to his retirement from the ministry'. Then in 1792 he fell down a staircase and died. The cause of the accident was never recorded, but, as with many such falls, it could have been an excess of drink. Elizabeth, the eldest of three sisters, was six or seven years old when his coffin was dug into the chapel yard. By then the Baptist church had been established for 180 years. It had started in 1607 when John Smyth, a Cambridge scholar and ordained minister of the Church of England, had defected and fled to Holland where an increasing number of Dissenters were finding refuge from persecution. Known as the first Baptist, he defined the tenets of the new faith while in Holland, which had become a haven to thousands of those Protestants not conforming with the Thirty-Nine Articles introduced in 1571. Among those refusing to go along with the compromised Protestant religion in England was Thomas Helwys, a country landowner from Nottingham. While studying with the pious congregation of exiles in Amsterdam, Smyth and Helwys took up the concept of 'Believer's Baptism' instead of the christening of infants after birth. They took much from the Anabaptists, a spiritual movement of the fifteenth and sixteenth centuries based in Holland, which revolted against church hierarchy and found infant baptism unscriptural.

They believed that infants should be instructed in the Christian church but not made members of it. Faith, it was argued, required intelligence and should not be undertaken by a parent, but by each boy or girl. After being instructed in the basic doctrine of Christianity, each should decide personally to follow Christ. Young children were not of an age to make such a decision; for salvation to be effective, men or women must, by their own choice, believe. This was shocking to the Catholic, Anglican and other churches. A baby was often carried to church through rain, snow, sleet or wind because, if a christening was deferred and a babe died unbaptised, his soul went to limbo, lost with nowhere to go. A child must have the words 'Dearly beloved, for as much as all men are conceived and born in sin . . .' said over him and be sprinkled with holy water.

Smyth and Helwys set up the earliest Baptist church at Spitalfields, London, near Guy's Hospital in 1612.[2] Helwys died in prison; Smyth was a Pilgrim Father, sailing from Plymouth on the *Mayflower* in 1620. Eighteen years later the first actual Baptist church in America was set up on Rhode Island by Roger Williams.

The Baptists, like other Nonconformist religions, believed people needed to examine every line of the Bible themselves and not rely on interpretation by the clergy. Followers were encouraged to have a personal and direct relationship with God, with no priest acting as an intermediary.[3] The literates took pride in plodding through the hundreds of pages of the Old and New Testaments, and beginning again when they finished. For them, ignorance of the scriptures meant ignorance of Christ.

Church attendance increased in all denominations after Sunday schools had been started by Robert Raikes, the printer, prison reform campaigner and the proprietor of the *Gloucester Journal*. Seeing prisons crowded with people whose lives had been shaped by deprived childhoods, Raikes opened the first Sunday school in St Catherine's Street, Gloucester, in July 1780. Any child aged between five and fourteen was admitted, no matter what the state of their clothes. Raikes, the hero of the striving poor, helped to destroy illiteracy. Not until the Education Act of 1870 were elementary schools provided at public expense in England and Wales, and not until 1889 was schooling in England compulsory. The private and 'dame's schools', and the schools set up by charities, mainly the Church of England, were sorely inadequate. The Church, anxious not to lose control and fearful of schools not teaching the Anglican catechism, opposed all government grants. The first grant occurred in 1833 when £20,000 was shared by two religious societies, the National Society (for Anglicans) and the British and Foreign Society (basically non-sectarian but predominantly for Nonconformists).

On Sundays, children who slaved for six days in factories, farms and mines put on their 'Sunday best' and attended Sunday school. They were taught the Scriptures, the Catechism, the Psalms and basic reading. The monitoring method of advanced pupils teaching beginners, who, in turn, became teachers themselves, later grew into the pupil–teacher training system. Churches of all denominations brought the rudiment of literacy to the poor,[4] but it was the Nonconformists who were at the forefront of the Sunday school movement.

From the time when Henry VIII had dismantled papal authority over the Church of England and parliament had declared him 'the only supreme head on earth of the Church of England',[5] various splinter groups of Dissenters, Quakers, Baptists, Congregationalists,[6] Presbyterians and Unitarians[7] had become independent of the main church. Unitarians were the most extreme, denying the existence of Hell and rejecting the Trinity – the belief that God reveals himself in three persons, God the Father, God the Son (Jesus) and God the Holy Spirit (or Holy Ghost). While acknowledging Jesus as a teacher, they denied that he was a deity.

After the Reformation anyone not attending services in the Church of England could be prosecuted. This changed during the eighteen years of the Civil War and the Commonwealth, but was revived after the death of Oliver Cromwell in 1858 and the abdication of his son Richard the following year. The restoration of King Charles II in 1660 made life difficult again for Dissenters.

The iniquitous Corporation Act of 1661 cemented Anglican supremacy. Members of municipal corporations and officers of state

16

had to show proof of having recently taken communion within the Church of England. The following year, the term 'Nonconformist' was used to describe the Dissenters who risked fines and a possible prison sentence and left the Church of England rather than conform to the terms of the Act of Uniformity. This ensured that all clergy and teachers conformed to the Book of Common Prayer and the Thirty-Nine Articles printed in it as an appendix.

Next, the Test Act of 1672 was rushed through parliament. It excluded Nonconformists, Catholics and Jews from any government post, civil or military, unless they submitted a sacrament certificate that they had taken Holy Communion at a Church of England service. Among other restrictions put through during the reign of Charles II was the banning of all religious assemblies of five or more persons other than those living in a house. Anyone breaking this was subject to a penalty of £20 on each person, or imprisonment if this was not paid. John Bunyan was one of the thousands who ended up behind bars. Just how draconian these laws were can be seen by looking at the history of the Quakers. During the four decades after George Fox, a Puritan, set up the 'Friends of Truth' in 1646, about 21,000 Quakers were fined or incarcerated in England, many of them more than once. At one time there were as many as 4,200 behind bars, where about 450 died.[8] The Quakers were against war, oaths, paid ministers, gravestones, black in mourning[9] and all fixed ceremonies, addressed everyone as 'thou' and refused to doff their hats. They also denied that the sacraments of baptism and the Lord's Supper were instituted by Christ. They were the most independent and daring of the Dissenters.

When James II came to the throne in 1685, he attended mass in public and showed his inclination to overthrow both the constitution and the Church, but when William Penn, the English Quaker and founder of Pennsylvania, returned from America, his influence on the king was so great that in 1686 1,200 Quakers and all men and women imprisoned on account of their religious convictions were released. Nothing, though, disguised James's pro-Catholic stance. Public outrage turned into rebellion, and before Christmas 1688, James II threw the Great Seal of State into the

Thames and escaped across the Channel to France. William of Orange, and later his wife and cousin Mary, crossed the Channel from Holland. After they had been crowned as joint sovereigns of Britain, the life of Dissenters improved. Just as William's 'Grand Alliances' in Europe were based on the defence of Protestantism, his reign was a milestone in the growth of religious liberty[10] – aside from Catholics. The introduction of the Toleration Act of 1689[11] granted freedom of worship to Baptists, Congregationalists and Presbyterians (but not Unitarians and Quakers). They could pray publicly behind unlocked doors, providing that the meeting place was registered with the diocesan bishop or Court of Quarter Sessions. Fines and prison for non-attendance at Anglican services, executions and burnings at the stake became memories of a harsher age. In 1727, after George II succeeded, an Act was passed allowing Nonconformists to build chapels and meeting houses.

However, like Catholics, the Nonconformists were still obliged to pay church tithes, register their assemblies with the nearest bishop, archdeacon or justice of the peace[12] and marry in Anglican churches. Because of the Test and Corporation Acts they remained second-class citizens in relation to Anglicans,[13] and continued to be blocked from civil or military posts. Sometimes this ban was circumvented with 'occasional conformity', when a vicar signed a make-believe statement, but, on the whole, they were barred from the professions, universities and parliament. Talented Nonconformists gravitated towards commerce.

All Nonconformists, whether poor labourers or factory owners, were forced each month to pay the much-hated church tithes or the church rates. Income for the Church was gathered from the whole population. Members were forced to pay twice where Anglican churchgoers paid once. Nonconformists were obliged to contribute to the leisured comfort of the vicar and his family and the whole structure of the Church of England, with its vast and ill-distributed wealth. (Of 10,478 benefices in 1836, 7,890 provided incomes between £50 and £400 a year, 297 below £50, 2,107 between £400 and £1,000, and 184 over £1,000, including 118 over £2,000.[14]) The income of the Archbishop of Canterbury and the Bishop of

Durham was £19,000 per year, while that of the Bishop of Winchester was a lavish £50,000. The Baptist, Methodist, Unitarian and Congregationalist chapels in Melbourne relied solely on the voluntary subscriptions and donations of its congregation. As in other grand chapels, the Baptist chapel in Melbourne had galleries, raised seats for the choir and for the preacher in the pulpit. These alterations had been part of the major rebuilding project in 1756 when an increasing number of converts had called for a larger chapel. Some female members of the congregation had sold their wedding rings to contribute to the cost.

On top of grievances about church tithes there were objections to restrictions on burials and the laws which obliged Nonconformists to be married in Anglican churches. Education, too, was a sore point. Most schools were run or dominated by the Anglicans. Taking the sacrament as a member of the Church of England was still a requirement to enter Oxford or Cambridge, the only two universities in England. But dissenting academies brought a high level of scholarship to Nonconformism.

Benjamin Disraeli in his novel *Sybil*[15] divided the nation into the rich and the poor: 'Two nations between whom there is no intercourse and no sympathy; who are as ignorant of each oth'rs habits, thoughts, and feelings as if they were . . . inhabitants of different planets.' He had temporarily forgotten that the manufacturing and trading *bourgeoisie* had created a new stratum, the non-landed urban middle classes, who longed to be part of the gentry.

In spite of the hat-touching and servility, England was frequently less 'class conscious' than 'church-and-chapel conscious'.[16] With their numbers boosted by recent converts, the Nonconformist spire-less chapels had a disproportionate number of people from the lower end of communities. Belonging to a chapel could be an indication of humble origins. The Church of England was bound by silken chains to the Establishment[17] and so identified with the upper classes that it was later referred to as 'the Tory party at prayer'. The radicals were often Dissenters or anti-clericals.

In England in the nineteenth century, the numbers of Presbyterians were declining because they tended to merge with the Unitarians, who had been given a boost by the poet Samuel Taylor Coleridge, a Unitarian convert who became a part-time preacher at Nether Stowey near Taunton. Robert Southey was another convert. The expansion of the Nonconformists continued throughout the first half of the century with the Baptists and Congregationalists increasing, though not as rapidly as the Methodists. Each denomination had a separate doctrine, creed and dogma, but, as they had all been alienated and excluded from civil and military life for so long, there was a feeling of cooperation between most chapels. Faith also had the benefits of a club. A busy social life revolved around each chapel and members gave each other mutual help, especially in finding jobs and in business. Thomas is an example of someone propelled not just by his beliefs, but by contacts made through his beliefs.

In contrast, in the Anglican church there was much division. Squires and yeomen, accustomed to the timidity of the poor, expected weavers, labourers and cottagers to know their place at the rear of the church. Such partitions, accepted as a natural part of God's will, were parodied in the jingle 'God bless the squire and his relations and keep us all in our proper station', or in the hymn 'All things bright and beautiful, all creatures great and small . . . the rich man in his castle, the poor man at his gate . . .'. Scrubbed and groomed, with waistcoat, watch-chain and silver-topped cane, the richer, established men, usually so upright in their saddles, lounged in square box-pews in the front of the church. There were always empty pews. One parishioner, Joseph Dare of Leicester, in a report had said, 'We do not go ourselves to a place of worship because our clothes are not fit; the rich tuck up their fine things and sit away from us, as if we were filled with vermin.'[18] He added that a large number were absent, preferring a day of ease, while others stayed in bed 'while their *body-linen* is being washed, and to rest their limbs, as the work is too much for the food they get'.[19]

Separating Church and Dissent was a wall-like barricade. Vicarages were usually elegant and many incumbents were the younger sons or poorer relations of the upper classes. The pace of their social life could be intense. A refrain of the Evangelicals had been a call for them to desist from hunting and other pursuits unbecoming to their cloth. Vicarages usually had good cellars and curates did much of the routine work. Richard Church, Dean of St Paul's, in *The Oxford Movement*[20] described the 'country gentlemen in orders, who rode to hounds, and shot and danced and farmed, and often did worse things'. Vicars usually scorned the ministers of the Nonconformists in their 'little Bethels'.

Anthony Trollope[21] described the Anglican clergy preaching 'in their black gowns, as their fathers had done before them; they wore ordinary black cloth waistcoats; they had not candles on their altars, either lighted or unlighted; they made no private genuflexions, and were contented to confine themselves to such ceremonial observances as had been in vogue for the last hundred years. The services were decently and demurely read in their parish churches, chanting was confined to the cathedral, and the science of intoning was unknown . . .'. Trollope could have also been describing the Baptist chapel in Melbourne. But the Baptist cleric, rejecting many elements of Anglican usage and ceremonial considered to bear too close a similarity to the pre-Reformation Catholic Church, wore no surplice; the chapel had a plain interior, and there was more emphasis on the Bible, not the authority of the church, being the source of religious truth.

FOUR

A Spade! A Rake! A Hoe!

Thomas finished school at the age of ten, perhaps as a consequence of his brother Simeon's birth, and started labouring with mattocks, trowels, scythes and spades in the vegetable gardens run by John Robey. Wearing patched baggy breeches, thick knitted socks pulled up over the knee, hat pulled down over his face, he heaved sacks, propagated plants, watered, spread manure and dug for six days each week. As Robey often suffered from the effects of too much drink, Thomas would be overloaded with work. However, it introduced him to the habit of travelling. He went off in all weathers, hawking vegetables and plants to nearby villages, crying out, 'Peas! Beans! Seeds! Plants for sale!' and even walking as far as the Derby market eight miles away.

Getting around was always on foot, in the saddle of a horse, a mule or donkey, or in a cart. Mostly it was on foot. A horse cost more to keep than a man. A normal day's ration for a horse was up to twelve pounds of hay, oats, bruised barley or Indian corn – and grass. Sometimes Thomas took a cart to Derby, now full of potteries because the Trent provided the constant water supply needed for the steam-driven factories.[1] Ever since the end of the eighteenth century, both the population and the potteries on the banks of the Trent had been growing. The smell, though, was awful. Since the invention of the new bone china – cheaper to manufacture than porcelain – there were smoky buildings where bones were boiled, burnt and crushed to make bone-ash to mix with clay.

A year after the future Queen Victoria was born in London in 1819, Thomas's stepfather, Smithard, followed his predecessor to the grave. With three young children on her hands and funeral expenses to pay, Elizabeth was miserably poor. In one of Thomas's reminiscences he later recalled[2] that 'after his [Smithard's] burial my mother took me into her bedroom and laying her hands on my head said "Now, Tommy, you must be father to these two boys."' In eleven years, Elizabeth, from having been considered a spinster on the shelf, had been married and widowed twice. An avid student, Thomas could not enrol at the charity school in the town, started by a sister-in-law of Selina, Countess of Huntingdon, as his mother, like so many parents, was about to rely on his income. This habit of parents using the earnings of children to supplement the family spending on food, rent and clothes later became one of the obstacles to comprehensive elementary education in England. Had Thomas not attended the local Sunday school over the next six years, his education would have been woeful. From 1822 to 1828, he was in turn a scholar, teacher and superintendent.

Thomas knew that his life was, and always would be, hard. It could have been worse. Inadequate though his pitiful wage of a penny a day was, labouring made him strong and there was occasionally a surplus of vegetables to take home. But one legacy from this job was a deep wound to his right leg, after falling on broken glass, which would cause him severe pain in old age. The village of Melbourne was on the edge of the coalfields, where injuries were horrific, but his mother always protected him from going down the mines. Some village boys and girls were already part of this grim workforce. At least labouring meant that Thomas worked in the fresh air, not in dark tunnels.

Factories, hungry for fuel, consumed coal at tons every second, so coal mines were a combination of rabbit warrens and the pits of Hades. The mines caused the tall trees to disappear, felled in the haste to find more and more pit props. In parts of Derbyshire and Leicestershire more wealth now came from what lay beneath the soil than from what sprouted from it. As factory chimneys and dreary rows of red-brick streets increased, fewer fleeces were spun in homes. It is sometimes said that Thomas was employed on the Melbourne estate. This confusion arose because Robey, like the majority of farmers in the area, was a tenant or sub-tenant of the Melbourne family.

Traditionally many wage-earners and piece-workers in Melbourne had combed and spun wool and pulled threads through stocking-frames, but new machines in factories were forcing them to put away spinning wheels and wooden frames and take[3] up the intricate art of blonde lace-making, even though it did not pay as well. These part-machine-made laces, which were finished off by hand, were used for furnishing fabric, long trailing veils and dresses.

Britain, fast becoming the workshop of the world, improved its trade, but not conditions and wages. As a result, agricultural labourers repeatedly packed up and went off to find jobs in towns or to emigrate to the United States or Australia.[4] Others, found guilty of crimes – some serious, others petty or political – were torn from their families and sent as convicts to Australia.

There was no disappointment when George IV's coronation was deferred owing to the trial of the 'vilest wretch on earth', Princess Caroline, whom he proceeded to divorce on the grounds of alleged adultery on her journey to the Holy Land. The postponed coronation of 1822 coincided with Thomas's new job. When fourteen years old, he swapped scythes and spades for a hammer, chisel and saw and started a five-year apprenticeship as a carpenter and wood-turner to John Pegg – a prominent name in the annals of the Melbourne Baptist church. Tradition dictated that such trainees lived with their employer, so he moved in with Pegg. It is often said that Pegg was his uncle, married to his mother's sister, Anne, but Thomas, in his reminiscences, never said that he was a relation. He just states that the John Pegg was married to 'Mary'. Years later Thomas described Pegg's drinking in the *Temperance Mirror*: 'The turner sought his relaxation and enjoyment night after night in a snug corner in the village public-house, where much of his time was wasted and his means so dissipated that, notwithstanding a good business, he lived and died a poor man.'[5]

Again the labour and hours were arduous. One of his challenges was splitting ash planks with a handsaw into pieces to make farm-stool shafts. In this job, as in his last, the man in charge of Thomas was more than partial to a jar or two of strong brew, leaving Thomas with extra burdens when he was drunk or hungover. Thomas's horror of drink dates from this experience, but there is also the possibility that perhaps he, too, at some early stage of his life may also have been inclined to drinking, and, as said earlier, that it may also have caused his grandfather to fall down the stairs.

Much traffic passed through Melbourne. Since ancient times its inns – the White Lion, Three Tuns, Sir Frances Burdett, New Inn, Bull's Head, King's Head, Lamb, Melbourne Arms, the Swan and the Old Pack-Horse Inn – had been a stopping place for coaches and the pack horses on the 'miry and almost impassable'[6] highway between Derby and Leicester.

Of all the residents of the Lamb family who lived at Melbourne Hall, Lady Caroline Lamb was the most gossiped about. In 1825 it was the house to which she was banished because she had been causing trouble in London. Her affair with Byron had ended in 1813, but she was still 'passionately infatuated' with him and behaved in such a notorious manner that she became the most famous jilted lover of the nineteenth century. The Lamb family wanted William to commit her to a lunatic asylum. Instead, they sent her for a short time to Melbourne Hall. Lady Caroline would be seen walking out of the gates into the village itself.

The villagers were accustomed to seeing her in the muddy lanes wearing thin shoes, strange dresses and weird feathered hats, leftovers from the days when she had been part of the *haut monde*. She did not mind walking in the rain, getting wet in thin clothes or being splashed with mud. When children made fun of her, jeering and laughing, she snapped at them and lost her temper. One of the visitors during her banishment to Melbourne was the Duke of Devonshire. When his magnificent coach passed through the village, little did Thomas foresee that in just over twenty years this kindly man would impinge on his life.

An entry in the Minute Book of the Melbourne Baptist church for 18 December 1825 states that Thomas and three others 'were proposed for baptism and fellowship'.[7] The minister at the time was the Revd H. Joseph Foulkes Winks. An articulate pulpit man and prolific printer who enjoyed chewing on his pipe, he became a father figure to Thomas. Indeed, it is difficult to overestimate his influence.

Thomas looked up to this articulate minister, who opened up books and ideas to him. As the overriding ambition of Winks was to spread 'the word', he had set up a press in a room over a granary owned by John Earp's family.[8] Magazines and books were now the vehicles in which to disseminate religious news and views. Winks earnestly wanted to supply Baptist Sunday schools and churches with cheap literature, Christian magazines and books for children.

It seems that Thomas picked up the rudiments of printing – the key to his success – from Winks. There is no other time when he could have studied the complicated trade[9] and learnt to proof-read, something helped by his diligence at spelling. Trainees, 'printers' devils', were given the most unpalatable tasks. Their duties included placing each metal letter of every line either with their fingers or instruments similar to tweezers. In contrast to the delicate job of setting up the type was the pulling and heaving of the mighty presses, returning foundry type to their cases, cleaning up the mess and carrying huge stacks of printed paper.

Winks's kindness then extended in many directions. Horrified at the sight of beaten horses straining and slipping, often in vain, to pull loads along icy roads or up steep hills, he championed animal rights. Already, in 1824, what was to become the Society for the Prevention of Cruelty to Animals (the 'Royal' was bestowed by Victoria in 1840) was backed by both Wilberforce and later by Lord Ashley, better known by his later title, the Earl of Shaftesbury, and for campaigning for legislation to prohibit the worst forms of child labour and cruelty to animals. Winks was particularly active in helping to abolish cock fighting (banned in 1849), bull running (banned in 1835), dog fighting and badger baiting. He earned the nickname 'Gibbet Parson Winks', as he campaigned against the use of the gibbet – the wooden structure from which criminals were hung. Yet, despite all his good works, he was a bit of a dandy. Ten years later, when he had his best coat stolen, the ultra-Tory *Leicester Herald* remarked that it had been made in Birmingham for fashion but that his waistcoat had been made in Leicester for cheapness. Another newspaper in Leicester, the *Herald*, was equally critical, commenting that, after Winks had been elected to the council, he 'struts past his old acquaintances with his beak pointing upwards, like a bantam cock'.

FIVE

A Long Way from the River Jordan

It was a long way from the Jordan. In the iron-cold stillness of that February morning in Lent 1826, clusters of friends and relations waited in groups outside the Baptist chapel in Melbourne. Three months earlier, just after his seventeenth birthday, Thomas had made the decision to go through the ritual of total immersion.

Thomas was small. His most arresting features were his serene but dreamy expression, ready smile, bushy eyebrows and dark brown eyes that were once described as 'black and piercing'. His thick dark hair showed no signs of its future balding, nor were there indications of his becoming 'that fussy little bald man',[1] as he was described by a detractor when in his sixties. His physical stamina and will to persevere, which would later enable him to escort tourists up hills and mountains with ease, were not yet obvious. Despite his restless and fidgety nature, he cultivated a talent for listening – but never for too long. This, together with an ability to remember minute details, would keep him in good stead all his life. Constantly on the go, he was continually doing something.

It is not difficult to imagine the scene there in the middle of England that chilly February morning. Thomas, like the orator and the audience, was transported far away to a sunny New Testament scene beside the Jordan, below Jerusalem, where Jesus was baptised. Inside the chapel, many of the congregation found that it reminded them of the ritual of immersion. In the silence they imagined the same sandy stretch where John the Baptist had baptised Jesus Christ. After Jesus' resurrection he commanded his disciples to baptise in the name of the Father, Son, and Holy Spirit (Matthew 28: 19–20). Because there is no life without water, water is central in the customs of many religions. The Jordan is mentioned on 170

27

occasions in the Old Testament, but only about fifteen times in the New Testament, where it refers to the activities of John the Baptist, Jesus and the disciples.

The Jordan is distinct from any other river on earth. There are many rivers which are more impressive, but the Jordan was the place of the spiritual awakening of Jesus, which led to Christianity. At the baptism of Jesus, John the Baptist had said, 'Behold the Lamb of God who takes away the sin of the world' (John 1: 29).

The uniqueness of the Jordan for geographers is due to it being one of the few major waterways which do not mingle with the vast sheets of water which spread tentacles of liquid around the earth. It is unlike the waters of the Trent, which like all British rivers empty into the sea. Rising from many headstreams and mountains of melting snows in Syria and Lebanon, it flows through the oval-shaped blue Sea of Galilee (Lake Tiberias), then narrows through a funnel, squeezing its water in a valley flanked by two clay banks. It then meanders south for 200 miles. Just before its waters reach the Dead Sea, the plains turn into grotesquely shaped hills of desolation, then the waters flow through Qasir al-Yahud, a West Bank area just north of the Dead Sea where John the Baptist urged his followers to turn away from their sins.

The next dramatic landmark is below the Wadi Qelt, the Wilderness of Jesus' temptation. This rocky valley, five miles long and 100 yards wide at the bottom, is hemmed in by walls of rock rising 700 sheer feet. One side is broken by a raised area, fertile and green, with a Roman aqueduct flowing along it. The other side is now dominated by the Greek Orthodox monastery of St George of Koziba and St John, founded in 420, which clings dramatically to a rock face. Outside, the monastery is alive with rock doves and Mediterranean swifts hurling themselves out of the numerous eaves, filled with festoons of hanging bats. The monastery houses many relics, including part of John the Baptist's skull. Lastly, the river empties into the Dead Sea, the lowest spot on earth. The water goes nowhere. Nor does it ever flood. In the torrid heat and weird geological mysteries of the Jordan Valley, 1,286 feet below sea level, the water evaporates, leaving salt behind.

There in Melbourne's Baptist chapel, which exhibited the best proportions of Georgian architecture, Thomas and his fellow worshippers stared at the Baptistery in front of the pulpit, a deep bath sunk below the surface and usually hidden by the hinged covering boards.[2] It had been filled with water. In front of him was the vision of the Jordan's crystal-clear waters 4,000 miles away. Thomas, steeped in the old 'hell-fire' school of the Nonconformist faith, readied himself to plunge, fully clothed, into the icy water.

All eyes were on Winks. His slight build, fine features and posture made him appear taller and more important than an ambitious former draper's assistant. Born in Gainsborough, Lincolnshire, in 1792, after the French Revolution, he had somehow managed to get some extra education and become a Baptist lay preacher at Killingholme. Then aged thirty-one, he made his mark on Melbourne. His acquired learning did not veil his lowly childhood. Reciting from the Letters of St Paul, he[3] delivered his message with a fierce eloquence: 'As Christ died and was buried, and rose again the third day . . . the rising again out of the water declares us *to be risen to a new life* . . .'.

Winks's message was full of hope. Minute by minute Thomas's faith was becoming more intense with the approach of the act of immersion. Slowly, he took off his coat and velvet cap and readied himself to become 'newly risen to a new life'. Lowering himself, he entered the depths. The day was icy. It had snowed only a few weeks earlier. Already outside there were a few snowdrops, violets and wood anemones to herald the end of winter. Soon the cowslips would follow.

As though inducted into some infinite scheme, with his head submerged, holding his nose and mouth closed, Thomas was at one with the water. This was the moment when, for a few seconds, by re-enacting a ritual, Baptists shared a precise experience with Jesus and John. By going through the ceremony he was keeping alive a tradition which had not stopped for eighteen centuries. On that Sunday morning Thomas was immersed three times as Winks recited, 'I baptise you in the name of the Father, Son, and Holy Spirit.' Then the words of Mark 1: 4–12 came booming, filling the chapel.

Shivering and gasping for air, Thomas scrambled dripping from the bath. 'Glory be to thee, O God! Glory to thee!' He had been saved.

The bystanders broke into a rousing hymn. Whether the organ had at that time been installed is not known. Many chapels were then austere and more often than not devoid of musical instruments. Silence and a brief eerie gloom descended. The ritual allowed Thomas to feel that he was an integral part of an ancient tradition. He belonged. The nullity, the void, were gone. From that very moment he never ceased to be an 'earnest, active, devoted young Christian'.[4]

Thomas would have to stay in wet clothes until the congregation broke bread and mouthed more prayers.

A journey from Derbyshire to the Jordan would be roughly 3,000 miles as a crow flies, but 4,000 miles by boat via the Atlantic and Mediterranean to the nearest port, Jaffa. No ships went directly to the Holy Land, as passengers had to transfer from liners to smaller boats at Alexandria or Constantinople. A further two or three days by donkey or horse would then have to be endured on unpaved roads that were impassable when the winter rains came. High costs, too, not to mention the discomfort of such an expedition, added to the feeling of distance. In any case, there was no longer the slightest need for Christians to make pilgrimages, as people were told to look for the Heavenly Jerusalem and not seek its rival, the Earthly Jerusalem. Salvation could be found within.

Thomas's visits to the Trent increased. When he could sneak away, well before dawn, he would tiptoe from his warm bed and go either to its banks, or to its brook, which meanders through Melbourne. He would sit for hours under the low branches of the mighty alders with their black fissured trunks, which leaned over the deep waters of the river. The muddy banks usually smelled swampy. Fishing, though, was a sport of the rich. Fishing rights were the prerogative of landowners, who frequently leased out the rights, so most stretches of the river were out of bounds. Poaching laws limited the lower classes to hunting rabbit, hare, wildfowl and, in some places, fish. Frequently, Thomas would start work at two or three in the morning, so he could have a few hours to go fishing late in the afternoon.

The fast-moving currents pulled the water in wondrous patterns. In the summer, Thomas would sometimes join the local boys and swans drifting in the water, as he enjoyed bathing, but he was not a powerful swimmer. Luckily, there were the rope-like stems of the ivy above the protruding roots of the gnarled old alders offering their branches as life-savers to help them ashore.

SIX

Lay Preacher

These years in Melbourne of self-education moulded Thomas's personality. Elizabeth opened an enterprising 'village shop' at Quick Close selling books, probably religious ones, and earthenware. She had been illiterate when married, so becoming a bookseller was a surprise. Either she had acquired the ability to read herself since Thomas's birth, or, more likely, Thomas was the force behind this enterprise. It may have been an outlet for some of the pamphlets printed by Winks, who left shortly before the shop opened.

Winks moved to Loughborough, a picturesque town in the heart of England, renowned for hosiery, shoes, church bells, bell-ringing and the world's largest bell foundry. Lower-priced machines allowed him to start an up-to-date printing works and become an official printer to the General Baptist Association. Large sections of the public were becoming literate, and a new era of information was born, together with popular romances, magazines, newspapers, religious tracts and Bible stories. The question of whether Thomas followed his mentor to Loughborough remains unanswered. The *Encyclopaedia Britannica* (1911 edition), and Fraser Rae's book on the Cook firm published in 1891, both say that Thomas was a printer at Loughborough, but this is not mentioned elsewhere.

Having cast his grandfather Thomas Perkins as hero, Thomas was keen to perpetuate his work by spreading the Word. The vision of this proselytising preacher had been reinforced by Winks and Elizabeth. But Thomas lacked the qualifications to be ordained. Criticisms about the lowly status and illiteracy of preachers and their unedifying noises in the pulpit had led to higher standards for the education of Baptist ministers. Despite improvements during the Evangelical Revival, in 1811 Lord Sidmouth had complained of

32

dissenting ministers who had not been able to read and write. He tried to put through a bill requiring Nonconformists to produce a 'certificate of fitness' from six reputable householders recommending a man as fit to preach. The outcry was so loud that Sidmouth was forced to withdraw his bill, but it had drawn attention to the need to raise standards. Despite this, in 1828, when the Midland General Baptist Church wanted to put fresh efforts into home missions, Thomas's lack of schooling was overlooked.

His attempt to begin a career of lay preaching, district visiting, Bible distribution and impressing religion and morality on an unsettled population coincided with a triumph for both the Nonconformists and Catholics. It was a crisis with the Catholics which opened the door. Fearing a rebellion in Ireland, the Duke of Wellington, who had become prime minister that year,[1] demonstrated that staunch Tories were moving with the times by putting through the repeal of the Test and Corporation Acts. Following this act, in April 1829, much to the joy of the 60,000 Irish Catholics in Liverpool and 40,000 in Manchester, the Catholic Emancipation Act[2] was passed. The next month, in May, the first Roman Catholic took his seat in the House of Commons. Such was the feeling against Catholics that the king sobbed as his gouty hand signed the bill and some Protestants attributed the bad weather in the summer to its passing.[3] It was the beginning of the lessening of divisions between members of the Church of England and members of other religions.

Thomas realised that to qualify as a missionary or preacher he needed to be a practised speaker. In the early hours with his friend John Earp he would climb through the chapel windows and rehearse, 'each in turn became preacher and audience'.[4] This pulpit style was later used by him when herding tourists.

After diligently studying theological dogma Thomas was appointed an Evangelist. An 'impressive service, in which he was solemnly set apart for the work',[5] was later described in the *Home Mission Register*. But an entry in the Melbourne Baptist Minute Book on 28 October 1828 showed there were reservations:

It was agreed that Brother Nailor should send a letter to the committee of the Home Mission, on behalf of Brother Cook, as a recommendation, so far as regards his piety – and as a suitable person for the important work as an Evangelist, so far as we judge him fit, whatever other qualifications are requisite we as a Church not knowing the extent of the work devolving on a person in that station we leave the case to the discretion and judgement of the Committee.[6]

Thomas's job was to 'carry the gospel of salvation through faith in the Lord Jesus, to the ignorant and neglected'. In the wake of Captain James Cook hundreds of uncivilised corners of the world had been changed by the Bible and the British flag, but now there was an emphasis on spreading 'the word' locally in Britain.

When the blossom appeared on the apple and pear trees, about the time of his twentieth birthday, Thomas, with 'deep regret', left Melbourne and became a Village Evangelist for the Baptist Missionary Society. At £36 per annum it was not a profitable calling, but he was doing God's work. Rain, hail and shine, he strode out across fields silently rehearsing his speeches and sermons. Summer turned to autumn, and to the long dark winter. Undeterred by falling snow, or by the difficulty of negotiating muddy paths, he went on. A hat, some well-worn clothes, writing paper, quills, ink, prayer book, the Bible and a rug in his shoulder-bag were his only possessions. It was usual then, when walking over dark fields at moonless nights, to use a lantern, but for Thomas this was an unheard-of expense. For him the long dark nights, on the move or in lodgings, were often candleless. His habit of rising to catch the first glimmer of morning light so he could read would stay with him all his life.

Thomas's duties were to hold meetings, conduct services, find converts, preach the Word, distribute pamphlets, help out at Sunday schools, sell Bibles and Testaments. Superhuman joy could be reached through a conversion experience. As a lay-preacher he was poised to snatch people from temptation. He urged them to see 'the Light!' and replace the nullity and void in their lives with Him. The Nonconformist chapels provided moral cement to shape the long days of the labourers, underpaid piece workers and factory employees toiling under miserable conditions. The number of drunks, gamblers, dissolute wife-beaters and the generally depraved would have been higher if it had not been for the efforts of the chapels.

Preaching was a precarious existence, attracting hecklers and mobs delighting in hissing and throwing objects at do-gooding busybodies and, above all, at those speaking about salvation. Wesley and his co-preacher, George Whitefield, founders of the Methodist Church, had raised the levels of oratory but had withstood stones, rotten eggs and the dead cats of hecklers. Preaching would empower Thomas all his life, as did the habit of taking risks and stretching physical endurance.

At this stage, he could have provoked unwanted responses as he was bold and had a certain nonchalance. This, though, was balanced by an earnestness which rang through everything he said. Hiding his shyness, like a confident actor he developed a hearty platform manner. Defiantly, he would try to match the words of the hecklers such as when he later condemned hissing as 'Gooseism and Snakeism', telling an offender to 'return to Jericho until his beard is grown. Let us have no more of his puppyism and cowardly sidewinds'.[7] This independence provoked one Baptist minister in the area to criticise Thomas:

> Calling on Mr. Taylor on one occasion, he was treated kindly and accompanied on the road some distance; but regarding him as a kind of innovator on established order, he said to the young missioner before parting – 'Young man, I advise you to give up this work at once; you have a cold already, and if you continue the work you will not live long.' But Mr. Cook did not give it up, and, though more than sixty years have passed since then, he is still living.[8]

Thomas's itineraries were brisk and took him through the counties of Rutland, Lincolnshire, Northamptonshire and many new industrial areas where conditions were still grim. So far efforts to improve the lot of children had been ineffective, and movements to improve factory conditions still had a long way to go. Robert Owen had fought strenuously for the second Factory Act of 1819, which forbade the employment in cotton mills of children under the age of nine, but there was no adequate provision for inspection to check if factories were implementing improved conditions. Droves of pauper children were handed over to the mill-owners to work long hours in shifts and sleep in apprentice-houses. Days could well last from 5a.m. to 8p.m. with only brief breaks.[9] It was not until 1833 that a Factory Act set up inspectors.

There was a battle ahead to relieve the plight of wretched children in rags, starving orphans on the streets, tenants sinking in debt and squalor and widows without sustenance. Apart from the alms from the church, the poorhouse or, with luck, a better job, there was little hope. William Blake called for the building of a New Jerusalem 'among these dark Satanic Mills'. His epic *Jerusalem: The Emanation of The Giant Albion* portrayed a world of spiritual freedom, a new land.[10]

Lord Ashley fought for reform and lent his weight to various bills, resulting in the 1842 Mines Act and later the Factory Act, known as the 'Ten Hour Bill'. The Mines Act prevented women, girls and boys under ten from working underground; the 'Ten Hour Bill' limited the hours of women and young persons in the textile industry to ten hours a day for five days a week and eight hours on Saturday.

Far from Blake's 'Satanic Mills' was Barrowden, in Rutland, north of Peterborough in Northamptonshire. This quintessential sleepy brick-and-stone English village with its duck pond, two greens, mill, tannery, church and chapel became Thomas's new home. A water mill mentioned in 1259 was now the site of a new mill, behind which was a large tannery, where cow hides were made into rugs, parchment for drums and glue. Thomas lodged in a farmhouse belonging to a Baptist, Henry Mason, a widower with five sons and one daughter, and described[11] as a farmer, grazier and maltster. The eldest, Marianne, a Sunday school teacher, kept house. When she met Thomas in 1829 she was already twenty-two, an age which then put her 'on the shelf'. The courtship dragged on for four years. This was not caused by awaiting permission, as legal consent for marriage was then required only up until the age of twenty-one, and she had been older than that when their romance had begun. Indeed, she was eighteen months older than Thomas.

Photographs show that Marianne was petite, light-haired with blue eyes and thin lips. Her slightly severe appearance was due to sharp features. She was later described as possessing a 'better business brain than her husband' and being a 'smallish very dapper lady who gave one the impression that she was all there'.[12] An interest in religion, especially the Bible, remained prominent in her life. She had learnt to read and write at the same time as taking the art of managing a large household in her stride. Capable though she was, she was shy and hesitant. The mannered correspondence between Thomas and her in their few surviving letters does not reveal a loving relationship, but over the years they developed an affectionate dependency on one another.

Years later Thomas described his debut as a preacher: 'After I had been one year in the service of the village Missionary Society, I made a tour through the principal parts of the Midland Counties, and held meetings in most of the General Baptist Connexion' in dozens of towns and villages, including Barlestone, Nailstone, Market Bosworth, Hugglescote, Ibstock, Measham.

During these years he found that, like Bunyan's roads, his were crowded with moving figures and adventures. The twelve-arched thirteenth-century bridge over the Trent at Swarkestone, the longest stone bridge in England, was crossed and recrossed. At some venues he was greeted with open arms, at others hooted and pelted. For some, heckling, jeering and rough handling were a sport.[13] The easiest places were those where there were already New Connexion Baptist chapels, like Hinckley, set up in 1770, the home town of his grandfather. Thomas must have been suffering from the toughness of his campaigning and constant travel, as the Baptist minister there, the Revd James Taylor, told him 'to get back home as soon as possible'. Years later, Thomas wrote that this minister 'had the impression that I should not be long-lived if I continued in that work'.

Another centre which he enjoyed was Barton-in-the-Beans, the rich bean-growing area of Leicestershire, a place which had influenced the New Connexion of General Baptists. The town of Billesdon with its academy, run by William Creaton the minister and headmaster, was also high on the list of the places he liked to visit.

SEVEN

Another New Career

In 1829 a shadow fell over Thomas's career. From £36 per annum, his salary was reduced to just £26 on 'account of the great kindness of people among whom he laboured giving him so many presents, and, we judge, inviting him so frequently to their social board'.[1] Preacher though he was, the only figures that Thomas produced have nothing to do with the converts he brought to the church, but the meticulously measured distances he travelled. In 1829 he noted that he clocked up 2,692 miles. Each day he calculated the distance covered, carefully writing down the figure in a pocket notebook. Over 2,000 of those miles (2,106 to be precise) were walked. A further 500 miles were as a passenger in horse-drawn carriages, stage-coaches or horseback. This careful cataloguing of mileage might also have been to impress his mother, who had earlier undertaken walking tours of England in search of converts.[2] The newly introduced railways are not mentioned in Thomas's notes, as there were then no railways in the Midlands. The Stockton to Darlington railway, Britain's first railway, was only four years old.

Rails started criss-crossing the landscape after the inauguration of both George Stephenson's *Rocket* in 1829 and the Liverpool to Manchester train service[3] the following year – the most expensive train built since Stephenson had invented the locomotive in 1814.[4] Immediately, it became the fastest line in the world and was also the first 'inter-city' railway line linking two large industrial centres. While some companies such as this one made huge returns for shareholders, the promises of many other companies proved hollow. Railway shares were so risky that they were parodied by Lewis Carroll in 'The Hunting of the Snark' with the line, 'You may threaten its life with a railway-share'.

39

For three years from 1829 discontent from France crossed the Channel. The English monarchy was at its lowest ebb. When George IV died in July, after his funeral *The Times* wrote, 'There never was an individual less regretted by his fellow-creatures than this deceased King . . . What eye wept for him?'[5] His brother, William IV, sixty-four, was more popular, having kept the habits of a brusque, hard-swearing, hard-drinking sailor.

As a general election had to take place following the succession of a new sovereign, there was a new government, with Earl Grey as prime minister – remembered for the aromatic tea named after him. When disturbances spread in which even moderate orators attacked the absurdity of the electoral system, Grey began the moves which would result in passing one of the most significant pieces of legislation in British history, the Reform Bill. The hurdles, though, were many. On 8 October 1831, after the Archbishop of Canterbury and twenty other bishops in the House of Lords had voted against it, anti-clerical riots broke out across the country.[6] In Bristol crowds burned not only the bishop's palace but another hundred buildings to the ground. The army savagely attacked the crowds, leaving a death toll of over a hundred.

Political stirrings were voiced by churchmen, but new preachers like Thomas had to be careful. He did not, though, have to exercise caution for long. Before his thirty-second birthday, he faced the fourth change in the way he earned his living. Job shortages and general distress were heightened by an epidemic of cholera – which had replaced both smallpox and the plague as the major killing disease – of unprecedented severity.[7] This was seen as a judgement of God upon the nation, and there were cries to shut down theatres and ballrooms, to smash card tables and to sack parsons who hunted. When one MP called for a general fast as an act of penitence for the state of the nation, Henry Hunt, the rabble-rousing MP who had been imprisoned after the Peterloo riots, asked the promoters if they were aware that one-third of the people of Britain fasted almost every day in the week.[8]

Like those of thousands of men in England then, Thomas's nerves were quickened by the economic downturn. The Baptists announced that there were no longer any funds to pay an itinerant preacher. This may have been a convenient excuse. Should he further his schooling and become a minister like Winks, who had already moved from Loughborough to Leicester to give more scope to his dual career as a clergyman and publisher of children's literature? But at twenty-three Thomas let his heart rule his head. He set up shop as a carpenter in Barrowden so he would be near Marianne Mason.

Mastery of his trade put Thomas in a better position than the thousands of unskilled unemployed, but customers were slow in coming. In the middle of November 1832 he relocated to nearby Market Harborough, the twelfth-century market town dominated by the Anglican church of St Dionysius. From then onwards the county of Leicestershire was to be his home. No doubt, the appeal of Leicestershire was partly because of its reputation for religious tolerance. Nearby was Lutterworth, the home of John Wyclif, the 'morning star of the Reformation'; George Fox, the founder of the Society of Friends or Quakers, was also born nearby in Fenny Drayton.

Market Harborough, which then had a population of only about 2,500 but at least six places of worship, was on a road to Leicester, and the Royal Mail coach from Manchester to London stopped there each day at 9.30p.m. at the Three Swans in the high street.[9] Day and night countless drivers of coaches and carts halted to refresh themselves and their horses while collecting boxes of hats and carpets. All trade was welcome, as the carpets and worsteds factory belonging to John Clarke and six straw hat makers, the main employers in the town, were then feeling the effects of the slump depressing trade everywhere.

Thomas's rented house in Adam and Eve Street, backing onto Quakers' Yard, was, like his workshop, surrounded by one-up, one-down labourers' cottages. To establish himself in a new town would have been a brave or a foolish thing to do without either cousins, uncles or membership of a chapel. For a worker migrating from town to town, belonging to a chapel could be the ticket of entry and offer instant relationships with people with common aims. Religious affiliation often turned members into a particular community that fought together so each could 'better oneself'. Politics once again was becoming a subtle component of chapel life, something which was soon to gain momentum and, from the late 1850s, carry the Liberal Party into the next century.

No newcomer who settled in such a town was ever truly part of it. Outsider though Thomas had been in Barrowden, he had been on the fringe of acceptance by being engaged to the daughter of a well-respected family. Here in Market Harborough, as in most small towns, groups of suspicious neighbours instinctively excluded, and even rejected, outsiders. The experience of these snubs would harden Thomas for the many which lay ahead.

At last in 1832 – over a year since the bishops had opposed it – the political struggle which had begun after Waterloo came to a head. The Reform Bill, which Grey called 'that most aristocratic measure', was passed. Bonfires were lit up and down the country. The anomalies were still huge,[10] but the Rotten Boroughs were no more. Less than 15 per cent of adult males had the vote out of a population of 24 million, but there would be forty-two MPs for the industrial towns and each county was to have two MPs. With the number of voters still limited to about one in eight adult males, the increase was only from 400,000 to somewhere between 600,000 and 800,000. While it broadened the class and backgrounds of those who could take part in the ballot, there was still a wide gulf between MPs and the people who elected them.[11] The aristocracy continued to dominate politics, with landowners filling most seats on both sides of the House, but now at least some MPs now lived in the areas they represented.

Because of the repeal of the Test Act, some of the newly elected MPs were Nonconformists and there were a few dour self-made MPs, marking the end of the old order. But there was a wait of thirty-five years before there was one in the Cabinet – when John Bright, the Radical Quaker, celebrated political orator and Anti-Corn Law League founder, became president of the Board of Trade in 1868. One reason for the small number of Nonconformists participating was because the majority were ineligible to vote as they lacked the necessary property qualifications. Only in such places as Birmingham, Leicester, Manchester, Salford and Sheffield, where there were enough members of the chapels with incomes large enough to bring them into the '£10 householder categories', were there noticeable differences in the type of MPs.

Much campaigning to better the lives of the working classes came from Manchester, then the mecca for change and also the home of many intellectual agitators. One was Friedrich Engels, author of the ground-breaking *Condition of the Working Class in England*[12] and devotee of Karl Marx, whom he helped financially. Another was John Shuttleworth, the Nonconformist textile manufacturer and a founder of the *Manchester Guardian*, who campaigned to transfer the seats of Rotten Boroughs to the new manufacturing towns, demanding that Manchester and Sheffield had two MPs and Salford[13] and Wigan one MP each, instead of none.

Among the new style MPs was Richard Potter (grandfather of Beatrice Webb), a Unitarian cotton manufacturer in Wigan and typical of the new politicians from industrial areas. Another was the member for Sheffield, the social reformer, Temperance and anti-slavery campaigner, James Silk Buckingham, who was the force behind the first free public library in England.[14] He was also the author of *Travels in Palestine through the Countries of Bashan and Gilead, East of the River Jordan*. Conceited, charismatic and clever, he had an exotic reputation that had been enhanced by an engraving of him, turbaned and bearded with a jewelled dagger in his colourful waistband, in the frontispiece of his book, *Travels among the Arab Tribes*.[15]

The danger of travelling across the Holy Land was reinforced by Robert Curzon's *Visits to the Monasteries of the Levant*, published in 1849.[16] He was twice captured by bandits. Curzon said that the West wanted to possess the Holy Land and predicted that in so doing it would destroy the very thing it desired. His book was not as graphic as those by Silk Buckingham who epitomised two things close to Thomas's heart: the Holy Land and Temperance. In 1834 Silk Buckingham had persuaded his fellow MPs to appoint a select committee, mostly Evangelicals, to 'inquire into the extent, causes and consequences of the prevailing vice of intoxication among the labouring classes . . . in order to ascertain whether any legislative measures can be devised to prevent the further spread of so great a national evil'.[17]

EIGHT

A New Life in an Old Town

The turning point for Thomas came, once again, from his local Baptist minister. The new incumbent in Market Harborough changed the course of his life, just as Winks had done in Melbourne – and like him he had lived for a few years at Loughborough, about twenty miles away. Francis Beardsall, a pioneer of the Temperance movement, converted Thomas to the cause of combating the use of Britain's 'oldest drug', alcohol.

The Temperance movement had started a few years earlier in the dark mills of Lancashire when 'the Seven Men of Preston' signed a pledge to abstain 'from all liquors of an intoxicating nature'. Under the leadership of the weaver and cheese-maker Joseph Livesey,[1] the movement snowballed. Like so many related movements – anti-slavery and Free Trade, for instance – it would bring into the fore such self-made men as John Horniman in tea, James Barlow in cotton, W.H. Darby in shipping; Cassell, Saunders, Chambers and Collins in publishing; George Eskholm in brass manufacture and Charles Watson in ventilation systems.[2]

At a meeting a year later in Preston, in 1832, Dicky Turner, a reformed drunkard, stuttered that 'nothing but tee-tee-total will do'. Livesey replied, 'That shall be the name!' Temperance soon became one of the biggest mass pressure groups in the history of the British Isles[3] and a major cause in Victorian Britain. With it went Nonconformity, preaching and tuneful hymns. Due to the widespread public concern about drunkenness, parallel organisations, such as the London Temperance Society,[4] had been started in many other places. Their aim was to reduce drinking by moral persuasion, by parliamentary acts and prohibition. Worthy, competent, patronising, necessary and ever-so-slightly dull, these organisations spread and multiplied.

The long-standing members of the Baptist chapel, a severe group as Thomas was to discover, had agreed that Beardsall could be both their minister and the representative of the British and Foreign Temperance Society as long as it did not interfere with his pastoral duties. A survey, some fifty years later, shows that Beardsall was at the forefront of a powerful trend for pulpit Baptists. It listed 1,000 out of 1,900 Baptist ministers as total abstainers.[5]

A few days before Christmas, when many homes were being decorated with holly and mistletoe, and women were preparing festive fare, decisions were made by many not to pour brandy over the Christmas pudding. Thomas was one of them. On New Year's Day, January 1833, six weeks after arriving in Market Harborough, two months before his wedding, he signed the Pledge. Initially, the Temperance campaign was only against spirits. Wine, ale, beer or port were allowed in moderation. Before long, though, they too were added to the forbidden list. But far from being negative, Temperance was a complex organisation with much popular appeal. Members realised that social gatherings would fill the void of the pub and also strived to promote all forms of learning.

The old Church of England vicar, the Revd Richard Carey,[6] officiated at the Mason–Cook marriage on 2 March 1833, in the thirteenth-century stone Anglican church of St Peter's, Barrowden. Thomas promised to endow his bride with all his worldly goods, which then consisted of nothing but his carpenter's tools, his prayer book and his Bible. One of the witnesses who signed the certificate was Marianne's uncle, Henry Royce. Later, his grandson, the motor and aeronautical engineer Sir Frederick Royce, brought fame and money to Derbyshire with his Rolls Royce factory.[7]

After the newly weds set up home in Adam and Eve Street, Thomas worked as 'a wood and brass turner', specialising in toys and Windsor chairs.[8] A boy was born on Plough Monday ten months after their wedding, on 13 January 1834. Just as Thomas had been named after one of his grandfathers, so now was the new baby. He was christened John, after John Cook, and also given the surname of Marianne's father, which was generally used not as a middle name but as part of his everyday name. A moral fastidiousness was instilled in John Mason from the cradle. The solemnity of home with its daily prayers and Bible readings was reinforced by the imposition of quietness in the house on the Sabbath, when the family sat through at least two services.

A second son, Henry, was born the following August. However, before the second wedding anniversary, grief descended on their new household. Henry, an alert, happy little baby, named after Marianne's father, died when four weeks old. It was their first great loss and something from which neither would really recover. Morbid thoughts of death were not alleviated by prayer and Marianne wept over the tiny grave. Tennyson's lines epitomised such grief :

You'll bury me, my mother, just beneath the hawthorn shade,
And you'll come sometimes and see me where I am lowly laid . . .[9]

Shortly afterwards she overcame her 'nervous disposition' and opened up their house 'for the accommodation of Temperance travellers'.[10] The need for good, clean accommodation for the growing band of professionals, the commercial travellers, was the result of increased trade from the Industrial Revolution. Inns were often dirty, noisy and expensive.[11]

Evenings for Thomas were filled with Temperance meetings and his new role as a superintendent at adult education classes run at night by the Baptist Church. Classes for workers outside the academic setting was part of the Adult School movement; inspired by the Sunday schools, it had been growing for over fifty years. Many organisations, especially the Temperance movement, began to provide tuition so that artisans could acquire the accomplishments essential for advancement. Attempting to educate the deprived and convert sinners swallowed many of Thomas's hours, leaving few to spend with either his family or his own business to ensure a satisfactory income. Children were taught to accept the dominant position of their father, but John Mason's strained relations with his father can be traced back to this time.

Preston always kept its position as 'the Jerusalem of the teetotal movement' in the face of a proliferation of offshoots. The British Association for the Promotion of Temperance in 1835 was followed by the National Temperance Federation, the Temperance Society, the Irish Temperance League, the Church of Ireland Temperance Society, the Royal Naval Temperance Society and countless others. Some groups, such as the Bible Christian Church, went further and also denounced animal food. William Harvey, a Bible Christian and Mayor of Salford, was prominent in the United Kingdom Alliance for the Total Suppression of the Liquor Trade, the most powerful of all the prohibitionist pressure groups.

After Thomas attended a Temperance lecture in Market Harborough Town Hall given by John Hockings, known as the 'Birmingham Blacksmith', before Christmas 1836, Temperance became his 'guiding star'. Abstinence was now a lifelong mission. Fired with zeal, he was one of seven men in the drawing room of William Symington, who, following the men in Preston, pledged 'to abstain from ardent spirits and to discountenance the causes and practice of Intemperance'. Religious-like rituals unified followers. For example, in Market Harborough there were seven men – not five or eight – who took the pledge, reciting the same words. Symington, who became president, was the first of the group to take the pledge; Thomas, who became secretary, was the last.[12]

Symington, a tea and coffee merchant and an active member of the Congregational chapel, lived above his shop in the high street. Coming from Lanarkshire, the birthplace of the movement, he had an advantage over newer converts. When Thomas became the secretary and Symington the president, they began a close friendship which lasted for fifty years. Little deflected them from their passionate drive to rescue people from the evils of drink. Their offices became the meeting places of a lively group of young men full of ideas to change the world and ways to entice drinkers away from pubs.

Market Harborough, notorious for having the most discordant anti-teetotal mob, kept its place for a few years as one of the strongest small towns in the Temperance movement. Before long, though, it was eclipsed by Leicester, where Thomas Cooper, the

Chartist, did much for the cause. Meetings in the town hall[13] and Thomas's house were often targets for the burgeoning anti-Temperance brigade. It was the same in thousands of other towns in Britain. What was happening in Market Harborough reflected what was happening in other parts of the British Isles. Before long members of the Society of Licensed Victuallers were outnumbered – but not overpowered or weakened. They managed to limit legislation against drink. Far from stifling the movement, their intransigence hastened its growth. But drunkenness continued. For a large number of people, the only refuge from depression and misery was the bottle. A copper or two, obtained by pawning the last rag, could buy oblivion. According to the reformer George Sims, 'Drink gave the poor the Dutch courage they needed to go on living,' but excessive drinking could not be condoned because it shattered such a large number of lives. Women and children were the greatest victims. Many social problems were related to alcohol.

Group celebrations, from weddings to burials, frequently degenerated into drunken commotions. For many workers, the long-awaited pay day could be the start of prolonged drinking bouts or 'randies' and bare-fisted fights over grievances. Pay day, with wages being frittered away by jovial men downing drink after drink, was often followed by days of despair when wives had not enough to pay the baker or the butcher. Wife-beating was not uncommon. In contrast, in some mining towns where Temperance flourished, women put on their second-best clothes along with starched stiff aprons on pay day and sat waiting for their men to return home and throw their wages, sovereign by sovereign, into their laps.

As the message of abstinence was one that many did not want to hear, Temperance associations devised ways to make life without the bottle attractive. It was an uphill struggle. English middle and upper classes served and drank wine at dinner. Working-class men consumed beer and cider, frequently home-made, while their wives and children drank weak tea, often with no sugar or milk. Pubs, with their gossip, conviviality, mirrors, woodwork and a roaring fire on chilly days, were the centre of village life. Rough taverns, too, with sanded floors and all sorts of games and pastimes, were also places where people could 'drown their cares' and slip away from the oppression of reality. The consumption of cheap gin, particularly by factory workers, increased. Tobias George Smollett, the Scottish doctor and author, described the sign over many spirit-bars in London, saying, 'Drunk for a penny; dead drunk for 2d; straw (to sober off on) for nothing.'

Innumerable booklets and posters highlighted the dangers of drink. One series was by the artist and cartoonist George Cruickshank, once a prodigious imbiber and son of a man who died an alcoholic.[14] He was famed for his witty and amusing caricatures of George IV[15] and illustrations for Charles Dickens's *Oliver Twist*. Dickens, though, who had little time for Evangelicals or Nonconformists, stressed in *Sketches by Boz* that the English vice of heavy drinking was caused by shocking living conditions. Sneering at the efforts of 'well-disposed gentlemen, and charitable ladies', he added that the cure should be directed 'against hunger, filth, and foul air'; then, and only then, would 'gin-palaces . . . be numbered among the things that were'.

During the previous century, to counter the importation of foreign brandy, legislation had sent the distillation of spirits in England spiralling upwards. Then the numbers of drinking establishments had increased with the Duke of Wellington's 1830 Beerhouse Act, which allowed any 'householder desirous of selling malt liquor, by retail, in any house, may obtain an excise license on payment of two guineas, and for cider only, on paying one guinea'. Beer-houses could open from 4a.m. until 10p.m. every day – except when divine service was held on Sunday and other holy days.[16] Politicians thought that if milder drink, such as 'malt liquor' and other ales, were promoted, the consumption of others would fall. The result was 30,000 new beer-houses – and people continued to drink gin.

John Mason's 'pathetic'[17] childhood was intimately described in a scathing article in the Tory magazine *Blackwood's* that was too libellous to have been published during Thomas's lifetime. This public display of self-pity and anger dramatised John Mason's early years by graphically describing how he had hungered for attention and a decent education. The article put the blame on Thomas because of the 'narrow means at home' and Thomas using the time which he might have spent with his family on either activities.[18] These circumstances prevented 'a lengthened or elaborate education: the scholar still at the hornbook was already earning wages; at fourteen he left school altogether, and what he knew in after-life (and he knew much) he had acquired for himself. He was broken to harness almost as an infant, and we hear of him, a child of eleven, marshalling troops of other children at a school-feast.'

Some of the criticism was true. Thomas was home day after day, but not really part of his son's life until he was older. The article, though, fails to state that John Mason was sent to a Dame's School and then to a larger school in Leicester[19] or that he must have had adequate food because he was taller than his father, well-built with good posture.

John Mason's immense muscular strength, gained from pulling the presses in the printing office where he set type, was also described:

for those were the days before the adaptation of steam and the labour entailed severe physical exertion. But to use his strength was a joy to him: he thought nothing of walking six miles every day to and from his work, or of sitting up the whole night through to strike off a thousand or two double-royal posters, which without rest or pause, he would himself distribute next morning through the neighbouring towns.

The description could have fitted Thomas himself. They were hardships similar to the ones he had endured, and many parents then imposed the same rigours on their children that they had experienced themselves. As Thomas included his son in some activities, it seems that the author of the article was unduly biased. Reputable magazine though *Blackwood's* was, there is also a question mark over the veracity of all the facts. It states that at the age of six, in 1840, John Mason went to Melbourne to see his grandmother by making a circuitous four-day journey by himself, taking two omnibuses, a canal boat, a train and a cart. The first day he walked from Market Harborough to Kibworth; the second he walked from there to Leicester; the third he was at West Bridge station and caught a train to Long Lane (now the town of Coalville), a terminus near to the Leicestershire collieries, part of the Leicester and Swannington line, which went via Leicester; then he went by canal to Shardlow, where he caught a horse-drawn omnibus to Derby; on the fourth day he caught Green's carrier's cart to Melbourne.[20] Contrary to the article, it seems that his father may have accompanied him part of the way. Thomas later wrote that his sole railway journey had been from Leicester to Long Lane.

Then, overnight, there was a new era with the first queen on the throne since Queen Anne. In May 1837 Victoria celebrated her eighteenth birthday. On 18 June 1837, while holding a drawing-room at St James's Palace, remembering that the day was the twelfth anniversary of Waterloo, her uncle King William IV, said, 'Let me but live over this memorable day.' A day and a half later, Victoria was queen. Lord Melbourne, who had been prime minister since 1835, showed tact and wit in introducing her to her new duties. He almost fell in love with her as an uncle might with a niece, and she in turn idolised him – but briefly. Even before her second anniversary as queen she began finding him dull. He was completely displaced after she sent a marriage proposal to her cousin – her mother's nephew – Albert of Saxe-Coburg, who had no time for him or his right-wing views. One of the many imaginative decisions of this German prince would later affect Thomas's career.

NINE

Total Abstinence

Champions of Temperance were dismissed by many as interfering busybodies and were often the targets of physical assaults, sneers and stones from those who relaxed with a jug or two. Cook later wrote, 'my house in Adam and Eve Street[1] was violently assailed, and brick bats came flying through the window to the imminent danger of Mrs. Cook and myself'.

Violent heckling, hissing and booing in the streets sometimes assailed Thomas. Once, the large bone of a horse's leg was hurled at him. Picked up from a pile of bones in the narrow street, it crashed into his neck. Stunned for a moment, Thomas fell to the ground. His old itinerant preaching days had taught him that the meek did not get results. Not a man to 'turn the other cheek', he managed to get up and chase his assailant. Finally, at the entrance of the Talbot Hotel yard, the attacker was caught and later convicted and fined in the magistrates' court.

Committed abstainers stuck to their pledge not to drink any form of alcohol during their own life, and promised not to provide it to others – something which put aspects of Thomas's life in conflict. His father-in-law, like many farmers, was also a brewer, and most employers, including Thomas in his wood-turning workshop, provided their workers with beer by brewing a sack of malt, usually barley. Cutting this off caused much resentment among Thomas's workforce of three. His half-brother Simeon, who was living with him as an apprentice, enjoyed his beer and the companionship that went with it so much that he ran away, breaking his indenture. While Thomas drew in men and women to sign 'the pledge' and kept drinkers away from the notorious drinking club in the town, known as 'The Tenth', temptation soon pulled them back into old ways.

53

Discord then came from the chapel itself. The kinship network of the Baptist chapel had helped Thomas's Windsor chair and toy workshop, but it also soured his relations with its members. In a row over an unexplained business deal between him and a Mr Knowles, they took Knowles's side, even though he does not appear to have been a member of the congregation. The episode was dealt with as 'Disciplinary Action' by the senior members of the Market Harborough chapel. The Minute Book for 24 August 1837[2] contains a reprimand over some of Thomas's financial dealings:

> That in Mr. C's transaction with Mr Knowles we think he acted totally unbecoming as a tradesman and a Christian professor. That we are sorry to be compelled to believe on unquestionable evidence that he has been disgracefully inattentive to his word . . . J. Buckley [John Buckley the new minister] and Wm. Bennett shall visit him and endeavour to bring him to proper state of mind, and that he be suspended from the privileges of the Church till the next regular church meeting, when the matter shall again be considered, and if possible decided upon.

Thomas's expulsion from the church on 8 October lasted for five months. Upsetting though it was to have accusations of being duplicitous, this setback coincided with a burst of activity against drink and the beginning of his publications promoting the cause of Temperance. So great was his success in putting together pithy words for pamphlets and newspapers in his modest print works that the house at Adam and Eve Street became the retail outlet for the South Midland Temperance Association. He was co-editing two monthly magazines which both sold for a penny, the *Monthly Temperance Messenger*, first issued in November 1839, and the *Children's Temperance Magazine, a Cabinet of Instruction and Amusement for Little Teetotallers, edited by a Father*, which ran for eight years from January 1840.[3] Like his gardening magazines, no copies of the children's magazine have survived, but one envelope from a grateful reader shows their impact:

> The person to whom this letter should go
> Lives in Adam and Eve Street, Market Harbro':
> He neither drinks Ale, nor Brandy nor Wine,
> Nor anything else on the Publican's sign;
> He edits a book on the Teetotal plan,
> And tries to reform the world if he can;
> But lest you should not find him out by his book,
> He is a Wood Turner, and named THOMAS COOK.

The following year, Thomas recorded that he was publishing 'near' 100,000 tracts and distributing 100,000 more. He was also carrying on with his wood-turning business. None of these activities, though, were bringing in enough money. A newspaper cutting from the *Harborough Advertiser*[4] quotes a resident as saying that Thomas was then apparently 'hard up, and he came to my mother and asked her to give him some work. My mother said, "You can make me a music stool!" . . . That relic, a four-legged music stool, is now in my possession.'

To embark on any new enterprise in those years was full of risks. In Leicester in February of that year, one of the worst winter months ever recorded, Poor Relief had to be paid to a quarter of the people.[5] One American wrote that 'in Lancashire the mills were on short time; in Leicester wool spinning was at a standstill – everywhere the workers were degraded by poverty, low wages and the cruel bread-tax which takes food from their mouths to swell the incomes of the land-owners; or by poor-rates to feed the millions who have been made paupers by this very taxation system.'[6]

Two years earlier, the People's Charter had been issued by a group of reformers, the Chartists, who would, now and again, clash with Thomas. He knew one of its founders, Thomas Cooper, well. Cooper, who had been born in Leicester, had become leader of the Leicester Chartists before spending two years in prison in Stratford for sedition,[7] and moving to live in Lincoln. Like Thomas, he strove against wrongs and injustices. The politico-religious sermons of Cooper became a feature of Chartist meetings in Leicestershire.

Methodism and Nonconformism helped the spread of Chartism. Many of the leaders, including Cooper and J.R. Stephens, had been raised in Methodist or other Nonconformist homes. Using methods similar to the old-style Methodists, they marched to Chartist hymns with such lines as 'The Charter springs from Zion's hill' sung to familiar tunes. Such phrases as 'Jesus Christ was the first Chartist' were used, as for many members Chartism was a way of bringing Christian teaching into reality.

The Charter denounced the Reform Act as a sell-out to the aristocracy and upper middle class. Their Six Points demanded universal male suffrage, annual parliaments, equal electoral districts, the abolition of property qualifications for MPs and their payment and voting by secret ballot. Other aims were to promote education and to guarantee 'the free circulation of thought through the medium of a cheap and honest press'.[8] Later, although the Anti-Corn Leaguers competed with the already well-established Chartists, on the whole they attracted different classes of workers.

Thomas was finding that distributing Temperance tracts, pamphlets, periodicals, pledge cards and medals[9] of the South Midland Temperance Association to the growing numbers of societies was costly. Even though the financial responsibility remained with the Association, difficulties arose because of lack of capital. He said that he would continue to take risks, but 'something must be done, and done soon, or myself, and your printer, will be sufferers to a serious extent'. Six members put up £5 each. However, two months later, in April 1841, it was agreed that 'a Committee be appointed to make arrangements with Mr. Cook for the future management of the Tract Depot, in order that all responsibility may be taken from the Association, and that Mr. Cook carry it on, in future, on his own responsibility'.[10] Thomas was, at last, in charge of the repository completely.

TEN

'Excursions Unite Man to Man, and Man to God'

Hurrah for the Trip – the cheap, cheap Trip!
Thomas Cook, *Excursionist*, July 1854[1]

The introduction of the postal service in 1840 is a landmark in modern communications. In January that year, a month before Victoria's wedding to Prince Albert, the 'penny post' was launched, allowing anyone to send an envelope anywhere. Purchasing an adhesive[2] penny stamp and gluing it to a letter became the rage and letters as we know them began to be shifted daily across the British Isles. In the first year 168 million letters were posted; ten years later this figure was an incredible 347 million, which included tens of thousands of subscription magazines and newspapers from Thomas Cook's outlet. The following year Thomas himself would make an impact on communication. Like so much in his life, it came about through either the chapel or his crusade against drink. As secretary of the district association embracing parts of the two counties of Leicestershire and Northamptonshire, he thought nothing of walking fifteen miles to Leicester to a Temperance meeting, and he did just that on 9 June 1841. Spring had already turned to summer, and the day was warm. Carrying water, bread and a waterproof cloak, he allowed four hours for his hike. Meetings were a regular part of his life, but this one was of particular interest. Lawrence Heyworth from Liverpool, a well-known railway and Temperance man and director of the Midland Railways, was to speak and preside.

Thomas, in a similar way to many men of this era, used a stick shod with iron when walking across the hilly countryside, so his brisk step was accompanied by a rhythmical click. He was still slight in figure, his hair still dark brown and thick, and even in the hot weather he seldom discarded his waistcoat and jacket. The cost of a coach or omnibus fare was out of the question, as was a horse. Carriages flew past, but, accustomed to privation, he felt no envy.

When about halfway on the long hike and passing the Congregational church at Kibworth Harcourt,[3] Thomas had a flash of brilliance, which he later often recalled, saying that his 'mind's eye has often reverted to the spot'. His idea was that an excursion by train for Temperance supporters would be 'a glorious thing' so that 'the newly-developed powers of railways and locomotion could be made subservient to the promotion of Temperance!'

Dismissing the caution with which many people looked on trains, Thomas dreamt up the idea of a train trip. The idea developed as he strode over the last six or eight miles. But such an outing by train was not really extraordinary. Trains had first concentrated on freight, but by the early 1840s railway mania was gripping the nation. Nine years earlier the *Annual Register* (1832) had reported that 'the bulk of the half a million third-class passengers who are carried on this railway in the course of the year are strictly the working classes, weavers, masons, bricklayers, carpenters, mechanics, and labourers of every description, some of whom used formerly to travel by carts, but the greater number on foot'. Thomas was in the habit of finding counter-attractions, events and entertainment to entice men away from alcohol, to get men and boys off the streets and out of pubs or ale houses. Like other temperance reformers in Britain and America, he and his committee arranged diversions such as picnics[4] in parks, coffee houses, reading rooms, libraries and excursions accompanied by fiddles, hornpipes or a brass band.

Trains were often in the news. Newspapers had hyped up anticipation about the launch of the royal train, which would take the Royals from Slough to Paddington in London at the speed of fifty miles per hour. Prince Albert, always behind the advancement of technology, was anxious to counter the prejudice against railways and had requested the Great Western Railway to build an ornate state carriage with a crown on the roof. Carriages were then cheerless with bare boards and small apertures for windows, while the trains were shunted here and there with interminable pauses and delays at lonely sidings.

The hesitation towards railways was evoked by (the painter) J.W. Turner's evocative canvas *Rain, Steam, and Speed, the Great Western Railway 1844*, in which a train races through a foggy landscape into an uncertain future. Elation at such power, coupled with a fear of its underlying strength, was a widespread response.

At the meeting Thomas managed to grab a few minutes on the dais and suggested that the group engage 'a special train to carry the friends of Temperance from Leicester to Loughborough and back, to attend a quarterly delegate meeting'. The chairman approved and the meeting roared with enthusiasm. Next morning Thomas proposed the scheme to John Fox Bell, the resident secretary of the Midland Counties Railway Company, who answered, 'I know nothing of you or your association, but you shall have your train.'[5] This positive reaction was not surprising, as rivalry between companies had increased. The slow transition from trains just carrying goods to transporting both goods and people had suddenly changed and companies were competing for customers. The Midland Railway Company, eager for ways to increase traffic, 'realised at once the advantages'.[6]

Monday 5 July 1841 seemed to have become an undeclared holiday, as about 500 passengers[7] responded to notices from the Temperance meetings and to the many posters and handbills put out by Thomas. As they arrived at Campbell Street Station,[8] Leicester, the mood of anticipation was high. Apart from the novelty and thrill of hurtling along at breakneck speed over huge iron structures, the excessive excitement at travelling just twenty-two miles in one day reveals just the idea of how long it had taken for the idea of railways instead of coaches to take off.

The train surged forward. A wave of excitement communicated itself from the passengers to the well-wishers on the platform, who were anxious not to miss the excitement. They too added to the holiday atmosphere. Bridges *en route* were jam-packed with people trying to get a peep at the modern travellers speeding past below.

The passengers, who had purchased tickets for the not inconsiderable sum of one shilling (children half price), were, according to the *Leicester Chronicle*, crammed into a train 'consisting of one second-class carriage and nine third-class [tub] carriages, each crowded with respectably-dressed, and, apparently, happy teetotallers. . . . They had with them the Leicester Independent band in uniforms, and two flags' to divert them from the third-class carriages, which were roofless and seatless, differing little from cattle trucks.

The cast-iron engine, which was enveloped in clouds of smoke and making a terrifying noise, made everyone feel that they were taking part in something very up to date. Most people had seen trains before, but now this marvel of technology was part of their lives. Thomas wrote that 'people crowded the streets, filled windows, covered the house-tops, and cheered us all along the line with the heartiest welcome'. He also mentioned something which would become a signature of his tours – music. On board there was 'an excellent band . . . headed by their district officers and flags.' There is no mention of the travellers in the open carriages being hit by sparks, grime and soot, but, if the wind was blowing the wrong way, that was what happened. Like wind, rain and snow, they were one of the hazards.

As the train pulled into Loughborough, it was greeted by the bugle, drums, trombones and trumpets of another brass band, and more thronging crowds waving banners. There was also much hymn singing and stirring speeches on the importance of abstaining from intoxicating drinks. Just how highly organised the Temperance movement was is seen in the references in descriptions of the day to bands, district officers and flags. The Loughborough flag was white satin trimmed with deep lace and white rosettes and its motto was 'Do not drink wine nor strong drink'. Derby's blue silk and red silk-fringed flag, with the prodigal son on one side and a mechanic on the other, was supposed to show the advantages of teetotalism.

A journalist then described the excitement of the crowds in Loughborough:

they proceeded in procession towards the market-place, and were met by a number of the Catholic teetotal society, with a banner, near the barracks. The number of spectators was immense; the Nottingham road from the canal nearly to the barracks being one crowd of human beings. A number of the dragoons at the barracks had got astride the roof, and being stripped to their shirts and their wide white trousers, their fine proportions appeared swelled to those of Patagonians. The windows were also crowded with fierce mustachoid faces, one of which, in particular, attracted our attention. This soldier, like those on the roof, was stripped, his head was clothed with a queer red woollen nightcap, his mustachois were black and large, and he regarded the moving, joyful crowd beneath him with the imperturbable gravity of a Turk.

Loughborough was well known to Thomas as it was the town to which Winks, once so close to him, had lived before moving to Leicester. Thomas later described the jolliness of the excursion:

We carried music with us, and music met us at Loughborough station . . . and cheered us all along the line with the heartiest welcome . . . the whole affair being one which excited extraordinary interest, not only in the county of Leicester but throughout the whole country. . . . All went off in the best style . . . and thus was struck the keynote of my excursions, and the social idea grew upon me.

As the band[9] played the national anthem, Mr Paget, who had opened his large grounds and gardens at Southfields for a gala picnic, 'came forward to receive the leaders of the procession'. When Paget welcomed the throning line of marchers, another precedent was set for future trips: local celebrities at stations to meet his tourists. Social standing in those days brought awe and influence. Marshalling people and supervising arrangements were other elements perfected on that historic day, which would become integral to Cook's future tours. For him 'arrangements' was a cherished word – arrangements for banners, arrangements for bands, arrangements for posters and arrangements for dignitaries.[10]

The day-trippers who had come by train – including seven-year-old John Mason Cook and Thomas's half-brother, Simeon – were joined by members from Derby and Nottingham. The number of participants was put at 3,000. Much to Thomas's joy Simeon had forsaken drink and become a member of a teetotal choir, 'able to render a plaintive song in a pecularlary [*sic*] pathetic manner'.[11]

The *Leicester Chronicle* described throngs of people in Loughborough 'lining the streets and filling the windows as they passed by'. Once in the market place the crowd paused to raise their voices and sing, then they marched and held up placards as they were applauded by amazed onlookers. The mood was raised by Cook's zest for life, his sense of style and all the props that would give a carnival atmosphere.

A stylish picnic lunch under the trees – something which would be a hallmark of thousands of tours – was laid out on white tablecloths. There was good bread and Yorkshire ham and later a high tea of cakes, crumpets and sandwiches. To compete with the fellowship, conviviality and companionship that is so associated with drinking in alehouses, groups played innocent games, such as 'kiss in the ring', 'tag', 'drop the handkerchief' and 'blind man's bluff', then they dispersed themselves into new groups for dancing followed by a cricket match.

'Hip, hip, hurray' was chorused over and over again after each speech given by the various ministers present. The Revd J. Babington of Cossington made remarks on the evils of drunkenness and the benefits arising from total abstinence. He had signed the Pledge after hearing an address by Thomas and told of his brother, a surgeon at a London hospital, who 'invariably found that persons who were brought into the hospital, who had been accustomed to drunkenness, were the most difficult to cure'.

Next was the speech given by the Revd Mr Boot, Baptist minister from Wolverhampton, who said 'that Teetotalism was good for the body, the pocket, and the mind. It was good, too, for the drunken man – and it was good for the drunken man's wife.' Cheers greeted his words about the 'great benefits that would accrue to every class of society from the universal adoption of the Total Abstinence principle'. He added that he hoped the time was not far distant when all intoxicating drinks would be confined – as they were once – to the apothecary's shop. The Revd Mr Robinson, Primitive Methodist, hoped too that the time was not far distant when 'the Teetotal banner would be hoisted in the midst of the burning sands of Africa, and also in the frozen regions of the north'.

Minister after minister spoke. Thomas, who was chairman, raised some laughs by asking people to 'hold up their hands to show who were pledged Teetotallers' – for he could not yet pretend to distinguish by the face a Teetotaller from those who were not – especially when he saw so many with suspiciously rosy cheeks. A regular forest of hands was held up. 'Surely', said the Chairman, 'there must be some mistake, or else the police must have kept every drunkard and every "moderate" man out of Mr. Paget's park!' He then announced that a meeting was to be held in the Baptist school-room on Tuesday evening, and that a lecture was to be delivered on Thursday evening by Mr Higginbottom, surgeon, of Nottingham. The calendar of activities for those in Temperance was certainly crowded.

Eventually, the exhausted party assembled on Loughborough station with much jollity, were jammed into the return train and at 10.30p.m. alighted at Leicester Railway Station. The air of exuberance of the outing contrasted with the often stunted lives of many of the farm labourers, local factory workers and home-based frame-work hosiery knitters. The day had lifted them temporarily away from their dismal homes, many of which were pestilent, back-to-back hovels where occupants were prey to epidemics, vermin and sloth.

Thomas had the advantage of his trading beginning when the outdated medieval structure of holidays was in its closing stages. In many factories Christmas was the only recognised full day off work other than Sundays. Christmas and Good Friday were also the only full holidays which the Factory Act of 1833 prescribed for children under the age of twelve in the textile mills. Some manufacturers took advantage of a loophole under which, if children consented, they could work on those days. The same trend affected offices. The

Bank of England closed on forty-seven holidays in 1761, forty in 1825, eighteen in 1830 and just four in 1834 – Good Friday, Christmas Day, May Day and 1 November.

But as the national income grew, improved hours and holidays could not be withheld indefinitely. The most important innovation was the weekly half-holiday. By the 1850s the building trades in some towns stopped work at four o'clock on Saturdays, leading to the one-and-a-half day weekend. Thomas strove to fill this spare time and each year benefited from the introduction of more holidays, which climaxed in the Bank Holidays Act of 1871.

When Thomas started his tours there had been a few organised package trips on railways here and there, but nothing long lasting. Some had been money-making concerns but most were for clubs, such as the 'interchange of visits between the Leicester and Nottingham Mechanics' Institutes'. Fares for group bookings had now been for sale for five years and outings had been organised by some railway companies in 1818. Thomas's tours were the most enduring and most financially successful of the nineteenth-century travel entrepreneurs, but he could not claim to have invented train excursions. He later made clear that his was 'the first publicly advertised excursion known in the country'[12] and the first personally conducted tour, even though it was 'either the second or third train of the kind ever run on the Midland Railway'. When Thomas later wrote that the Loughborough outing had been 'the starting point of that series of excursions and tours', he also acknowledged the invaluable help of printing and advertising. In his *Guide to Leicester* he wrote, 'Advertising is to trade what steam is to machinery.' Indeed, he applied the same principle as with publishing: the more you do, the cheaper it is per copy. Later he wrote, 'I now see no reason why a hundred may not travel together as easily as a dozen . . .'[13] The major cost of each train trip was the coaling and the 'steaming up', so the idea was to pack it with people.

Comparing Thomas's career in travel with that of the inventor of the modern post, Sir Rowland Hill, shows how many started but soon ceased business. Hill organised the first ever seaside package trip but he did not manage to sustain it even though seaside holidays had begun to flourish in the late eighteenth century, and already Brighton, Weymouth and many other new resorts were well established. But, like many other tour operators, Hill was left behind. It was Thomas whose trips grew into an on-going enterprise. He was the pioneer who battled 'against inaugural difficulties' and placed the 'system on a basis of consolidated strength'.[14]

ELEVEN

Leicester: Printer of Guides and Temperance Hymn Books

Within two months of the Temperance train outing to Loughborough, just as the hollyhocks were coming into flower, Thomas and Marianne packed up their home in Market Harborough. A new life was in front of them in the ancient city of Leicester, the 'Metropolis of Dissent'. It was a suitable place for the Cook family to live, especially as two-fifths of the local churchgoers attended seven Baptist chapels each Sunday. Famed for its Radicalism and Free-Church/Puritan/Quaker/Nonconformist heritage[1] and its hosiery and shoe trade, Leicester 'was spread over an unusual extent of ground in proportion to its population'.[2] It retained a pleasing variety of architectural styles – medieval, Tudor, Georgian and Regency – and the open-air market place still occupied the whole of the south-eastern quarter of the walled town, as it had since the tenth century. Factories and warehouses were spreading but did not yet impinge on its trees, gardens and wide new streets. Houses for workers were superior to those in Nottingham, most with four rooms[3] and with yards and some even had little gardens.

William Baines, a Congregationalist draper who had not paid the church levy, was imprisoned for seven months.[4] Outraged, his pastor, Edward Miall, openly vowed to confront the issue of church rates, become a champion of religious liberty and fight to separate church and state. Miall and the organisation he set up, the Anti-State Church Association, which in 1853 became the Liberation Society, moved to London, where he brought out a newspaper, the *Nonconformist,* to fight for the disestablishment of the Church of England. The same year as Baines was sent to prison, four more parishioners in Leicester who refused to pay fines for non-payment of rates were saved when an elderly lady stepped in to pay them.

In contrast to this, five years earlier the power of Nonconformists had created a new era, a new age with a radical council. In 1835 the Municipal Corporations Act converted the old corporations that had controlled English town life since the Middle Ages into 179 new municipal boroughs. Leicester, as other towns, started planning council elections. In 1836, as in many industrial cities and towns in England, Leicester turned over to the rule of Nonconformists. A Nonconformist lord mayor was supported by Nonconformist councillors, aldermen and town clerk. Now any male householder whose house was rated could cast a vote in council elections, a number greatly enlarged because of the repeal of the Corporations and Test Acts. Precise records of the religious affiliation of members, though, are either limited or have not been examined, so in most areas there is no certainty as to whether the elections brought in a similar dominance of Nonconformists in other places. Only in Leicester, Manchester, Salford and Birmingham, where the Nonconformist element was well recorded, have scholars analysed and published the composition of the borough councils, let alone the number of the MPs in the parliament after the Reform Act in 1832.

Most of the thirty-eight new council members in Leicester had been a mixture of Nonconformist Radicals, Liberals and Whigs. No longer was the town directed by the landed gentry. Only four Tories remained. The first mayor, a Unitarian, belonged to the chapel called 'the Great Meeting', as did the following seven, so the chapel earned the name the 'Mayors' Nest'. The Act of Toleration of 1689 had excluded Unitarians and Quakers, but that had not prevented the Unitarians of Leicester building it in 1708. The same defiant spirit now set out to reform the council.

In the same way that their Nonconformist ancestors, in contrast to Catholics, had created places of worship which were bare and unadorned, the new councillors stripped the town hall of the trappings of the former Tory Corporation. Wanting a total break with the past, they threw out much of what signified the pomp of

English civic life. During the Reformation their ancestors had rejected and thrown out rosaries, relics, incense, statues of the Virgin Mary, pilgrimages, the intervention of saints, making the sign of the cross, lighting candles, buying indulgences, venerating images, and so on. Out went the silver-topped mace and gilded goblets and baubles. Anything described as the 'paraphernalia and appurtenances which symbolised the dignity and extravagance of the old order' went under the hammer at an auction in the Guildhall – much at knockdown prices. It was hoped, too, that much of this would bring in cash to make up for monies lost during the previous corrupt council.

Two of the new-look councillors who had agreed to auction these historic objects 'at promptly one pm on 1st January 1836' were men who were catalysts in Thomas's life. One was a Baptist, the other a Quaker. The first was Winks, who had been pivotal in Thomas's life; the other was John Ellis, the tall, portly Quaker industrialist. Like the majority of men who had a far-reaching influence on Thomas's life from 1834 onwards, Ellis, or 'Railway John', from Beaumont Leys, was an anti-drink crusader. A farmer and factory owner who had purchased Belgrave Hall,[5] a mansion on the outskirts of the city, Ellis gave Thomas his first openings in major railway excursions. In Leicester, as in most other places, the men behind Temperance were mostly Nonconformist and/or Liberal – still an imprecise term. There were confusing and shifting alliances of Whigs, Conservatives, Peelites, Irish nationalists and Radicals for the next forty years.

An ambiguity over the use of the word 'Liberal' confuses the situation. At this stage there were only two political parties, the Whigs and the Tories. Before a clear two-party system emerged, there was *no* unified national Liberal party of any sort in Britain, even though there were local associations, each with its own ideology. 'Liberal' was an expression used to describe political leanings, as an adjective. It became a paradigm in political life, an inadequate umbrella used by a range of politicians, such as Radicals, anti-trade union Whigs like Lord Melbourne, fanatical Free Traders, or reformers, such as Ellis, Potter or Silk Buckingham.

'Liberal' meant different things in different places. The Liberal Party finally came into existence in the summer of 1859 at a meeting at Willis's Rooms in St James's organised by a group of Radicals, Free Traders, Peelites, Gladstonian Liberals and Old Whigs to combine to oust the government of Lord Derby. A large number of Radicals pushed for the disestablishment of the Church of England, for the redress of other Nonconformist grievances, for the widening of the franchise, for the limiting of the power of the House of Lords and Free Trade. The Conservative Party had been formed earlier in 1835. But it was not until 1868, nine years after the Liberal Party had been formed, that the first Liberal government was elected, with Gladstone at its head. Although Gladstone was a High Churchman and an Old Etonian, the party he led for twenty-five years was predominantly a party of religious Nonconformity – and remained so until the end of the century.

After the first Leicester elections, some of the tight-knit feeling between the Nonconformists was lessening. For centuries, the struggle against the Anglican monopoly in the council had given them unity, but without a common cause the Nonconformists were no longer in agreement, and two groups were fiercely against each other. On one side there were the 'Improvers', led by William Biggs,[6] one of the town's largest hosiery manufacturers. They insisted on improvements to beautify the appearance of the city at the same time as installing and maintaining sewers, drainage and water supply. Leicester needed, they said, an imposing town hall, a wider high street and more recreational grounds for the working class. Opposing the 'Improvers' were the 'Economists', or 'Economy Party', led by Joseph Whetstone, chairman of the Finance Committee of the Council, who wanted to trim expenditure down to what was essential and to give priority to drains. The Public Health Act was still in the future,[7] and life expectancy was low in Leicester, as in other places, because of appalling sanitation, scarce drainage, the lack of fresh-water reservoirs and indifference to the accumulated rubbish and the factory effluents which polluted the River Soar. When delivering a fiery talk in Leicester, Biggs referred to the 'merchant princes' of nearby Derby as 'the Medici of their day'. Biggs, like other men who owned large modern mills with mounting exports, helped finance the Anti-Corn Law League, furthered Free Trade and was sympathetic to Nonconformist men who fostered similar causes. He was soon singled out by Thomas.

Aware of the need to attract votes, Biggs allowed the newly formed Leicester Temperance Society to use his hosiery warehouse for Thomas's 'great tea meeting which comprised 1000 guests', many of whom came from afar. Within weeks an advertisement appeared in the *Leicester Chronicle* saying that he was 'a *Bookseller and Stationer*' specialising in 'all kinds of Periodicals, Unstamped Newspapers and Books of every description . . . Printing and Bookbinding in every department executed to order'. His printer's shop at 1 King Street also sold pens, stationery and a few commemorative medals.[8] Time and money, though, were in short supply. While setting himself up in Leicester, for four years Thomas also arranged what he called 'amateur performances', Temperance railway outings. Destinations depended on where the new track had just been laid.

Thomas wrote that 'a succession of trips, uniting Leicester, Nottingham, Derby, and Birmingham, all at that time connected with the Temperance movement, engaged my attention for two or three years'. There were also outings to and from Rugby and other nearby stations. Thomas wrote that the fares for all these local trains, except for Birmingham, 'were 1/- for adults, and 6d for children under fourteen years of age. Return fares to Birmingham were generally 2/6, and for children half-price'. He added that these trips 'were generally very successful. Most . . . were in connection with the Temperance movement, and I had no personal pecuniary interest in them beyond the printing of bills.' He was, though, preparing the way for commercial sightseeing trips by providing classic tourist destinations on his itinerary, such as Mount Sorrel and the old spa town of Matlock, situated amidst romantic scenery on the Derwent.

As well as being a tour organiser on a non-paid basis for Temperance causes, Thomas occasionally climbed up onto rostrums and took up his old role of preacher. Three total immersion baptisms were performed by him on 28 July 1844 in Smeeton Westerby, a village south of Leicester near Foxton Locks on the

Market Harborough to Leicester stretch of the Grand Union Canal. Leicestershire has plenty of inland waterways and is rich in meandering rivers, like the Soar and the Welland, so why a rivulet had been chosen is not known. But when some troublemakers broke down the embankments, an alternative venue was found. The General Baptist Repository[9] recorded that at 'On Lord's Day, July 28th, three persons, one male and two females, were added to our little flock by baptism. The sacred ordinance was performed in the canal, about a mile from the chapel . . . in front of a crowd estimated at from 800 to 1000 who listened with marked attention to an address by Mr T. Cook, Leicester, who afterwards immersed the candidates.'[10] Thomas remained active as a preacher, delivering yet another address to the Sabbath School at Smeeton a week later.

William Biggs, who served Leicester as mayor in 1842, 1848 and 1859, was also secretary of the local Liberal Association. After he led his party in winning the town's two parliamentary seats from the Tories in 1838, the two new members were chaired through the town in a procession of about 20,000 people. This was the first time in history that non-Tories had won seats in Leicester.

Ellis was also typical of the Nonconformists in the new council. Blunt but charitable – his daughters[11] tirelessly ran a local school and helped Leicester's poor – he was chairman of the Midland Railway Company between 1849 and 1858 and the Liberal MP for the area for four years from 1848. A pioneer in passenger trains, he had recruited George and Robert Stephenson (of *Rocket* fame) to build the Leicester to Swannington railway in 1832, the third railway to be opened in Britain.[12]

There was now a line all the way to London from Leicester – the population had grown to a staggering 48,167, of which about 3,000 men and women were employed in the hosiery factories, and 600 in the more recent shoe and boot industry. The city, according to the *Temperance Messenger*, contained 700 spirit and beer shops and public houses, 'great numbers of dying drunkards . . . [and] a greater proportion of prostitutes than any town beyond the precincts of the metropolis'. Other urban evils included a high mortality rate, slum dwellings and bad drainage – a problem exacerbated by the flatness of the area.

Living in the heart of a city did not mean that Thomas forgot his four years in the market garden in Melbourne or the rural pleasures of growing vegetables and flowers. He started the *Cottage Gardener*, a 'periodical of considerable size, which attracted great interest'.[13] Since the Royal Horticultural Society had been formed in 1804, various magazines had been launched, including the *Gardener's Chronicle* in 1841 and the *Horticultural Register*.[14] The most influential of the garden writers, John Claudius Loudon, a self-made Scot, carried on the *Gardeners' Magazine* for seventeen years.[15] Although too expensive for most gardeners, it did inspire local magazines, such as Thomas's in Leicester.

Gardening was a consuming pastime in the new suburbs, and most people tried to follow the latest fashions. Contrarily, Thomas promoted the charm of small, simple productive gardens with honeysuckle, wild roses, strawberries and vegetables. The *Gardener* was not mentioned in *Botanico-Periodicum Huntianum* nor acknowledged as a predecessor in the better-known magazine called the *Cottage Gardener*, founded in London by George William Johnson in 1848. Alas, no copy of Thomas's magazine, nor his *Garden Allotment Advocate*, survives.[16] Anxious to prop up the new allotment movement, Thomas also helped found the Leicester Allotment Society and in 1842 made a vain appeal for money for members to purchase potato seeds at cost price.[17] As well as doing everything he could to help the poor grow their own food, on another occasion, to alleviate the hunger in Leicester, he bought cheap potatoes in Northamptonshire and sold them at cost price. But his supplies were not up to the samples so he could not compete successfully with the established potato merchants, and his efforts came to nothing.

Just before Christmas 1842, Thomas gathered the information and printed the *Leicestershire Almanack, Directory Guide to Leicester and Advertiser*, priced at one shilling. Its 170 pages were packed with precise information, including the names and addresses of the Dissenting chapels and the times of services.

His output would soon rival that of Winks, who had become a printer and distributor of Baptist publications, as well as being the unpaid minister of the Carley Street chapel.[18] Thomas said that his own works printed and distributed 'at least half a million tracts on Temperance and kindred subjects' plus Baptist devotional works and hymn[19] books with such words as:

> Six hundred thousand drunkards march
> To wretchedness and hell
> While loud laments and tears and groans
> In dismal chorus swell.
>
> *The National Temperance Hymn Book and*
> *Rechabite Songster of 1843*, published by Thomas Cook

In addition, Thomas printed 'the *British Building Societies Record*, edited by Mr McArthur', and the *Temperance Gazette* for 'Mr Kendrick of West Bromwich'. He also began a registry for servants, a registry for lodging and boarding houses and a guide to Temperance hotels in Britain. Laying aside his hammer and tools for good, he somehow found the capital for the presses, inks and stocks of paper, so he could become a full-time professional printer. His skill in layouts, typography and printing generally was exceptional.

Lack of money made thrift and long hours of work necessities. Just as his family home doubled up as a boarding house or Temperance hotel, John Mason's schooling did not prevent him from earning his keep. His fees of a few pence per week were paid to a preparatory school, but he was also a 'printer's devil' and helped with the laborious end-of-month job of rolling, wrapping and addressing hundreds of periodicals.[20]

While juggling his Temperance activities and promoting train outings, Thomas relied on subscriptions and from printing magazines and books. The numbers of periodicals and sheets which had the stamp of 'T. Cook, Printers, Granby Street, Leicester' on them was growing. He was also producing the *Temperance Messengers*, the *Children's Temperance Magazine*, the *Anti-Smoker* and *Progressive Temperance Reformer*.

But it was not all work. In the summer of 1843, Thomas wrote about an excursion of teetotallers to the Peak of Derbyshire and parts of Yorkshire where he could 'breathe uncontaminated air'. This took place just before the family and shop moved to 26 Granby Street in the centre of Leicester, advertised as a 'Temperance Commercial Boarding House' and a 'Cheap Printing Office'. One advertisement reminded readers: 'Commercial Gentlemen, Visitors &c are respectfully informed that Thomas Cook has opened his Establishment as a Temperance Commercial Boarding House, where Refreshments may be had at any hour of the day, and good sleeping Accommodation is provided. Thomas Cook is the general Wholesale and Retail Agent for Dawson's Celebrated Turkey Aroma, the best substitute for Coffee ever invented. Agent for the Temperance Provident Institution.'

Thomas's mother, influenced by her favourite son, gave herself more options by turning her back on the country for the bustling metropolis of Derby, where she ran a Temperance hotel. Putting her two widowhoods behind her, she married for a third time, becoming Mrs Tivey. Her grandson, John Mason, came to stay with her, often for extensive periods.

Gambling, like drink, was seen as evil. Baptists did not even allow raffles, let alone lotteries, to be held to raise funds. To entice children away from the annual races in 1844, Thomas arranged what he called a 'Monster Excursion of Juveniles' for children attending Sunday schools to travel from Leicester to Derby. John Mason wrote, 'My public career as a Personal Conductor commenced in 1844 as a small boy with a long wand assisting the guidance of 500 other children from Leicester to Syston by special train – for five miles; then a two mile walk across fields to Mount Sorrel Hills for an afternoon's picnic and back the same route to Leicester.' Thomas invited Sunday school teachers to take their schools to Derby, where their counterparts would 'open their school-rooms and provide tea for those of the same religious denominations'.

As at least 5,000 children and teachers booked, the event had to be spread over two days. On the first day 3,000 children were conveyed in every kind of vehicle that could be mustered, including a number of new coal wagons: 'The ordinary rolling-stock was inadequate to the occasion; and, with the wagon supplements filled to their utmost capacity, we still left behind 1,500 little enthusiasts for a second day . . . [all] were conveyed the thirty miles and back for one shilling adults, and sixpence children, all scholars coming under the latter classification.' Other Sunday school outings followed. These coincided with restrictions imposed by the Railway Act of 1844, pushed through by Gladstone, then still a Tory and vice-president of the Board of Trade. Monopolies and the duplication of tracks were discouraged and each company had to run at least one train a day in each direction which stopped at every station – known as the 'Parliamentary'. Most importantly, Gladstone imposed safety standards, limited fares to no more than one penny per mile, and stopped passengers travelling in open 'tub' carriages, like cattle. Other facilities, such as lavatories, though, were not generally introduced for forty years.[21]

One of the most significant occurrences for Thomas in that eventful year in Leicester was the visit by Silk Buckingham, who addressed a Temperance meeting. In his fiery talk, Silk Buckingham lashed out at beer-houses and contrasted the drunkenness of Christian nations with the sobriety of the Muslim countries.[22] Thomas valued him as his chief adviser for future tours to the Holy Land. These 'Eastern Tours' would take twenty-four years to materialise, but his path to Egypt and Palestine had begun that night in Leicester.

Thomas enthusiastically reported Silk Buckingham's talk in the Temperance newspapers which still flew from his presses, including the *National Temperance Magazine*. He also made time to produce a new magazine, the *Anti-Smoker*, which he described as 'the first periodical organ of anti-tobaccoism the world ever knew'. But the tobacco leaf was becoming as much the national food as beef and beer,[23] so his magazine limped on for just three issues, finishing in mid-1843. Despite accepting defeat and putting his energies elsewhere, Thomas seems to have avoided those who smoked heavily, such as Winks. Through their involvement in the Baptist chapel, their paths must have crossed, yet there are no records of them together in Leicester. This split may have been caused by Thomas's lonely fight against smoking while Winks was wedded to his pipe. 'The barbarous habit' began after Sir Walter Raleigh's return from Virginia, USA. By the end of the eighteenth century the odour of tobacco-tinctured saliva and stale tobacco on clothes was even more familiar,[24] as smoking came to be listed among the accomplishments of a gentleman together with dancing, riding, hunting and card-playing.

In 1845, with courage and a little temerity, Thomas advertised a commercial tour. From being a gardener, carpenter, preacher, publisher, printer and boarding house proprietor, he was now setting up a tour business with a trial trip to the thriving port of Liverpool. Although the fare did not include food or lodgings – a selection of hotels and inns was advertised in the handbook, but no accommodation was booked in advance – it was really the inauguration of Cook's Tours and would be a dress rehearsal for hundreds of thousands to follow. The 1841 Leicester to Loughborough trip had initiated him as an excursionist but that, like all the other tours until 1845, had been on a non-profit basis. Train trips would now augment Thomas's income. Soon there would be more expenses, as, at last, ten years after the death of baby Henry, Marianne was pregnant.

TWELVE

1845: The Commercial Trips, Liverpool, North Wales and Scotland

It was terribly wet during the summer of 1845. But on 10 August, as dawn slowly broke over Leicester Railway Station, the clouds rolled back. The railway platform was jammed with about 300 men, women and children bedecked in their best clothes, most young, gay and so excited by the trip, a carnival atmosphere and much laughter. Only a few looked anxious or weary because of lack of sleep. Thomas had sternly warned that 'parties will have to be "wide awake" at an early hour . . . Promptitude on the part of the Railway Company calls for the same from passengers.' Most eyes were turned to the left, eager to catch sight of the much-anticipated train. Just before 5a.m. a flutter of smoke could be seen on the horizon, and the railway engine came roaring towards them. Coming into the station, it drowned all conversation as it squealed to a halt, releasing gusts of steam.

For many people waiting on the station, this round trip to Lime Street, Liverpool, would be their first long railway journey. Liverpool with its huge docks was then the port for ships sailing to North America and the glamorous gateway to nearby North Wales. Each customer had paid a fare of fifteen shillings for first class, or ten shillings for second class; there was no third class, as the journey was too long to have people in open carriages. Thomas was reaping the reward of his reputation from years of shepherding people in the cause of Temperance. Organising the trip, though, had swallowed up months of his time, as some companies had turned down the idea of low-priced fares for group bookings.[1]

On top of the basic ticket, many customers purchased four-shilling supplementary tickets either for the special steamer excursion from Liverpool, which was to sail under the Menai Bridge and up the Straits to the medieval fortress castles of Caernarvon and Bangor in North Wales, or for the exhausting side trip of climbing Mt Snowdon. Thomas was overwhelmed at the response to all the advertisements. The idea of the trip 'created such a sensation that at Leicester the tickets issued . . . were in many instances re-sold at double those rates. The rolling-stock of the company was not adequate to the demand, and a second trip [with 800 passengers] had to be improvised a fortnight later to satisfy the public.'

At Liverpool that historic morning the passengers climbed one by one into the stationary train. Nobody pushed or rushed. Among those shepherding the crowd was ten-year-old John Mason. Then the doors were slammed, the whistles blew and the carriages were moving, pulled by the steam engine with surprising velocity to Nottingham and Derby, where more passengers boarded, making a total of 1,200. The train ran via Normanton, through the Yorkshire and Lancashire valleys to Manchester, and then over the Manchester to Liverpool line, a distance of about 170 miles.

On this occasion, as so often in the future when people travelled to special events, they wore their Sunday best. Some even dressed as if for a carnival or wedding, even though soot from the engine blew back into the carriages and caused smudges on clothes. A side effect of up-to-date, fashion-conscious passengers was of female dresses taking up extra space. Having purchased a ticket, people expected to have a whole seat on a train, and not have to share it with the voluminous skirt of a woman sitting beside them. As seats were narrow and hard, fashion caused much inconvenience for passengers on this and other long journeys. Full skirts, worn over a large number of starched and horsehair petticoats, took up a lot of room, as did the new crinolines. Sleeves, too, were puffed up and could intrude.

During the Welsh tour sightseers often outnumbered the town's permanent population. As well as the thrill of being in infrequently visited destinations, the passengers also discovered the inconveniences. A group of over a thousand English men and women arriving *en masse* was like an invasion. In Caernarvon, 'intense interest was excited amongst the Welsh people by the appearance of so large a party of English ladies and gentlemen. We spent a night and a day amongst the mountains . . . the great feat being to gain the summit of Snowdon' – scaling the highest peak in England and Wales at 3,560 feet could be perilous.

It was over 500 years since Edward I had led his ruthless incursions against the Welsh, but they had preserved so much of their culture and language that Thomas had difficulty in hiring an English-speaking guide. But he rejoiced in a silent message in the ruined castles and monasteries, writing that he felt 'gratitude that the tyrannies they sheltered are no longer oppressing us, and regret that with all our increased facilities for amassing wealth, we have no charities in the present time, at all comparable to them'.[2]

A second excursion was arranged for 800 passengers the following fortnight. Again there was a 'monster' train, a steamboat excursion and a trip to take visitors to the wild areas of the barren but beautiful summit of Snowdon. And again they ascended on foot – as Thomas called it, by 'Shanks's naggie'.

Thomas's profit is difficult to gauge. It seems that the trip was a shared project with the Midland Railways, which took much of the responsibility, and that Thomas's task may have been to find the passengers and produce the handbook. Unlike a year later, he may not have been financially responsible. In the newspapers it is the Midland Railways that was given the credit for organising the trips, not Thomas.[3] Travel from Leicester to Liverpool then meant buying three tickets from three competing railway companies – the Midland, the Manchester & Leeds and the Liverpool & Manchester lines. Now Thomas produced one ticket to cover the whole journey – rather as happens nowadays. He later said that these two trips to Liverpool were the first excursions with tickets with the 'division of the fares through the Railway Clearing House'. He appears to have received a commission of 5 per cent from each of the four railway companies that had issued the reduced-priced tickets for the complicated journey. Out of this he had to deduct advertising and printing costs, including the expenses of organising the journey.

Thomas's reputation from four years as an 'Excursion-Agent' now paid dividends. He knew the difficulties of travel, understanding the need of reconnoitring a route, issuing guide books and finding destinations which were exciting or romantic. Aware of competitors, Thomas usually managed to add an extra dimension, such as history, which he soon discovered made places saleable. With the skill of a showman, he wove historical facts into his guide books, livening up the itineraries, descriptions of destinations and lists of hotels and boarding houses.

On his second trip, from the heights of Snowdon, Thomas looked out across the haze 'towards Ben Lomond and Ben Nevis' and the magic world of Walter Scott and Robbie Burns. Scotland, the romance of it all! The tartan, kilts, wild scenery and bagpipes beckoned. Military music was part of many cultures, but the Highlanders had the tradition of pipes and ballad singers exciting warriors to fight. Gaelic battle songs, Scottish bagpipers and bands playing regimental marches, such as 'Cock o' the North', were now penetrating into England. Scotland had become, like the Lake District, a fashionable destination. Unable to go on Grand Tours to the continent because of decades of war, such large numbers of English people were flocking north each year that Sir Walter Scott had remarked, 'Every London citizen makes Loch Lomond his washpot and throws his shoe over Ben Nevis.'[4]

Much of the vogue for Scotland then emanated from the legend of Ossian, which was related in a lengthy poem of that name and was almost a cult in Europe at the beginning of the nineteenth century. Even Napoleon Bonaparte recited its lines. The poem was either written by an ancient Scottish bard or forged by the Scotsman Macpherson. Its lack of authenticity did not detract from its romantic image and it was sometimes connected with prestigious visitors to Scotland such as Dr Johnson, James Boswell and Felix Mendelssohn.

Thomas made a resolution to get to Scotland the next year or 'know the reason why'.

THIRTEEN

Scotland

The vision of the picturesque Highlands remained with Thomas. In 1843 he had followed the dramatic events in Scotland when 470 ministers, wanting independence from government control, had resigned their livings and formed a new denomination, the 'Wee Free' church, the free Kirk – it was a battle for the soul of Scotland. During Christmas and New Year 1844/5 Thomas saw the changes for himself, when he made his much-longed-for trip north after a sales tour in Lancashire to promote his new *National Temperance Magazine*. In contrast to Preston, where he had been shown the spot where Dicky Turner had first uttered the word 'teetotal' – he arrived in Edinburgh for Hogmanay, which was celebrated with uproarious joviality.[1]

The ecclesiastical reorganisation in Scotland overlapped with the tourist renaissance started by Victoria and Albert, who could be called the first media royals. Victoria's book *Leaves from a Highland Diary* is full of rapture for the Scottish landscape, the Scots and Scotland itself. Albert shared her affinity. It also reminded him of the mountainous scenery of his native Saxe-Coburg. Memories of 'Bonnie Prince Charlie' and Culloden were still vivid, as was that of the 'Butcher of Culloden', Prince William Augustus, Victoria's great-uncle. But Victoria's love and understanding won over the hearts of the Scots.

A new awareness about the need to preserve wild scenery had been raised by Jean-Jacques Rousseau, who urged readers to appreciate nature and to look in forests, not gardens.[2] These efforts to appreciate unexploited nature were duplicated by William Gilpin, a Hampshire clergyman, schoolmaster and amateur artist who invented the word 'picturesque' and helped to open the eyes of the

British to the wild areas of Britain. His books, *The Lakes*, *The West of England and the Isle of Wight* and *The Highlands*,[3] made people look more deeply at the beauty of the countryside in its untamed state. The Highlands became a cherished destination for upper-class tourists. Thatched cottages, wild gardens, orchards, enjoyment of the open air, walking in the woods and going on picnics all took on new meaning. Many English people, reared on Sir Walter Scott's novels and picturesque engravings, turned to Scotland, to salmon leaping in swift rivers, lochs, islands, moors, white Highland cattle, men baring their knees in kilts playing fiddles or bagpipes – and to tartan.[4]

The popularity of tartans, which had become internationally fashionable during the Napoleonic wars, had been boosted again in 1822 by George IV's state visit to Scotland, organised by Scott. George's standing in Scotland had been enhanced by much 'Highland' regalia, and at the Caledonian Ball he demanded Scottish reels: 'None of your foreign dances!' Vain about his slender legs and an enthusiastic reader of *Waverley* and *Rob Roy*, at the levée at Holyrood House he wore a kilt over flesh-coloured pantaloons and posed for Sir David Wilkie[5] in a much-reproduced oil painting. It was as if he tried to compensate for the absence of any reigning British monarch coming north of the Border since Charles I.

Back in Leicester, Thomas was both advertising a trip which was the first of its 'kind ever made from England to Scotland' and preparing his *Handbook of a Trip to Scotland* with 'such information . . . will be found most useful for those who avail themselves of a privilege which no previous generation ever had offered to them – an opportunity of riding from Leicester to Glasgow and back, a distance of about 800 miles, for a guinea!'

Earlier criticism led Thomas also to include a few swipes against the upper classes: 'A few years ago a "visit to a watering place" was a luxury beyond the reach of the toiling artisan or mechanic; his lot was to waste the midnight oil and his own vital energies in pandering to the vitiated tastes of the sons of fashion . . .'[6]

Posing the question, 'But what does it amount to?' and quoting critics who said that 'it neither fills the belly nor clothes the back', he said that travel 'provides food for the mind; it contributes to the strength and enjoyment of the intellect; it helps to pull men out of the mire and pollution of old corrupt customs; it promotes a feeling of universal brotherhood; it accelerates the march of peace, and virtue, and love; – it also contributes to the health of the body, by a relaxation from the toil and the invigoration of the physical powers'.[7]

Tactfully he did not advertise two things: that the trip would take place the very year that potatoes failed in the Highlands;[8] that it coincided with the centenary of Culloden, the battle on Drumossie Moor, on 16 April 1746, when 5,000 Scots had died supporting Bonnie Prince Charlie, Prince Charles Edward Stuart, grandson of James II. Lasting less than an hour, Culloden led to the virtual extinction of a way of life and the traditional ways and means of earning an income in the Highlands.

There were no easy connections to Scotland, as no railway line yet crossed the border with England. So the organization of the trip was extremely difficult for Thomas. Newcastle upon Tyne was then the northern limit of the English railways, and there was no through line from Leicester to Newcastle. Approaches to railway managers were met with nothing but rebuffs and he had 'great difficulty in persuading the companies to accept' his proposals.

The apathy of the railway managers was unexpected, as railways were competing for trade and most were looking for ways to increase their traffic and returns to shareholders. Thomas found similar resistance with his efforts to get passages on the ships going north. The General Steam Navigation Company's initial refusal to carry a large number of passengers from Newcastle to Leith caused him to later write despairingly, 'Failing to make my way into Scotland by the East Coast route, I turned to the West, and after some difficulty succeeded in effecting a railway arrangement to the Port of Fleetwood; a steamboat from there to Ardrossan; and railway from Ardrossan to Glasgow. This trip was advertised for Midsummer, 1846 . . . I offered to guarantee £250 to the General Steam Navigation Company, for the conveyance of passengers from Newcastle to Leith and back, but they would not accept . . . I then arranged to take passengers by that route to Ardrossan, and from thence by Rail to Glasgow.'

The two steamers which regularly plied on the west coast, the *Queen* and *Consort*, did not have adequate cabins for the anticipated 500 to 1,000 passengers, so Thomas tentatively booked a larger boat which had more first-class cabin accommodation. Bookings, though, failed to come in. Unable to guarantee a fixed number of passengers, again he switched to two steamboats which regularly ran between the two ports.

Then, at the eleventh hour, many last minute bookings were made, so there were suddenly 350 passengers. Most believed that their ticket *included* a cabin. But when they boarded they found they had the choice of staying out on the deck, with waves washing over it, or paying a surcharge to the purser for the use of a cabin. Bad weather exacerbated the lack of cabins and a large number of the passengers were forced to stay shivering and crowded outside during the wet and cold night as a result. Complaints and litigation would hound him for months. Remembering the importance of keeping up appearances and putting a good face on things, Thomas hoped the fuss would die down and tried to dismiss the matter, just saying that the sea voyage was 'disagreeable to some of the party'. Yet the misery and inconvenience suffered by many of the passengers were things that would not go away so lightly. It was written up by a member of the party under the derisive heading 'The "Pleasure" Trip to Scotland' in the *Leicester Chronicle* of 4 July 1846. The main grievances were about the lack of provision of tea at Preston station and the extra charge of ten shillings for a cabin:

More than twenty carriages, containing about five hundred passengers, left the Leicester Midland Station on Thursday morning . . . from Fleetwood, where the greater number embarked the same evening for Ardrossan. From the handbill published by Mr Cook, the bookseller (the getter-up of the trip), it was made to appear that the passengers would be allowed the privilege of leaving the train at Manchester, Parkside, or Preston, at any of which places they might re-unite with it on his return on

Friday, July 3rd. What authority Mr. Cook had for making this statement, we know not, but the reverse was the fact; for after leaving the Midland Railway at Normanton, where the passengers were certainly afforded both time and opportunity for refreshment, the tourists were rigidly compelled to keep their seats as if they had been prisoners about to leave their country for their 'country's good,' instead of a body of respectable citizens who had paid their fares for a pleasure trip. This was particularly the case at the Victoria Station, Manchester, where policemen were placed to prevent the passengers from leaving the carriages – an injunction which was strictly enforced, and created much dissatisfaction among them. At Parkside, sixteen miles from Manchester, the same command was made, and with few exceptions, enforced. At Preston, where, according to Mr. Cook's handbill, tea was to be provided in the Exchange, at one shilling each, the train only stopped for a few minutes, to the no small disappointment of all who had anticipated the enjoyment of such a tempting repast.

The correspondent included a scathing attack in which he said that 'rather than subject myself to such rough and unceremonious treatment!' in future he would travel alone. He added:

Mr Cook is a *Temperance man*, an advocate for the principle of *Total Abstinence*, and it would seem as if he wished those whom he has so shamefully duped to practise *total abstinence* too . . . a toss overboard into the projector's *favourite element* would have been almost his due. Let us beware how he again attempts to gull the public in the matter of an Excursion Train.[9]

However, others forgot about the boat trip and enjoyed the journey through Scotland in a special train that took them to Glasgow. To celebrate their arrival, guns were fired as the train drew up, then a band escorted the travellers to the City Hall, to a large soirée. A similar ovation awaited them at Edinburgh, where they were met by a band of music and escorted through the principal streets, and the publisher William Chambers, another passionate advocate of Temperance, laid on a special musical evening. They did not get to the Highlands, but made various side trips instead, travelling on a steamer on the river Forth to Stirling, sailing on Loch Lomond and Loch Long and making a slow journey on the Ayrshire Railway to 'the Land of Robbie Burns' and the shrine to Lord Bute's former ploughman who had become Scotland's most quoted poet.

FOURTEEN

Corn Laws: 'Give Us Our Daily Bread'

Back in Leicester, Thomas was caught up in a wild, tumultuous movement, the Anti-Corn Law League, becoming one of a large number of socially aware Nonconformists playing an active and prominent part. The Anti-Corn Law League, a vehicle for Free Trade and many forms of political agitation, took on the character of two of its founders, John Bright and Richard Cobden, both fiery orators and propagandists[1] who denounced the privileged position of landlords.

Every Monday and Friday evening Thomas stood behind the middle window on the first floor at Granby Street using the skills in oratory he had learnt as a preacher. Shouting at the top of his voice, he would call out the prices of wheat and other cereals, then he would pause, waiting for the thunderous clapping, and call out through the roar, shouting even louder, to announce 'the state of the markets and other matters connected with Corn Law Repeal'. Thomas was such a vocal campaigner that, if MPs had then been paid, he could well have taken up politics as a career.

The crowds were constant. Over a thousand people thronged, sending up loud cheers as Thomas described graphic examples of the false claims of certain bakers. He enjoyed the applause. Appreciative crowds, especially those following him, were mesmerised as if he were the Pied Piper of Hamelin. Thomas and a new committee were formed to arrange meetings against the Corn Laws, to bring regularity to the price of bread and to keep it in line with the price of flour. It aimed to shame bakers to sell bread by weight. If that did not have any results, the committee threatened to resort to the law.

Among the immense multitude in Granby Street, throngs of shabbily dressed men took off their hats, waving them in the air as they cheered him. Thomas, eloquent and pragmatic, adopted theatrical-type cue boards to reinforce what he was saying. Brightly coloured placards announced the prices of corn, wheat and other cereals and their correlation with the price of bread. Some of the placards bore 'Down Again' as prices fell, or 'Up Again' if prices rose. His outbursts brought him nothing but adulation from the crowds, who from time to time shouted 'Hurrah!'

Apart from the deleterious effects of alcohol, Temperance supporters blamed the manufacture of spirits for an unnecessary demand on corn and other cereal crops, which should be used as food. Wheat, barley and corn prices were spiralling; agricultural protectionists were accused by the Free Traders of inflating the price of wheat. They said that it was the demand on cereals by the liquor industry, together with the duties on imported corn, that sent the price of bread to ridiculous heights.

In order to bring down the price of bread, the League fought vigorously for the repeal of the iniquitous law that kept the price of corn high. After it was set up in Manchester in 1839, the League spread like wildfire, fanned by urban discontent, the recession, a few bad harvests and rising prices. Unemployment affected labourers, poor tenants, wheat growers, textile workers, craftsmen and manufacturers. Some were not just hungry, but were malnourished and near death. In the late 1830s and the 'hungry forties', starving labourers set fire to farmers' ricks and there were clashes with the military. In the Potteries, the Black Country and the cloth towns of the west, men could no longer find jobs, and the high price of bread brought them and their families near to starvation. Radical action was urged at many meetings.[2]

Already adept at banging the drum against such issues as smoking, drink and the poor, Thomas now put the Anti-Corn Law campaign through his printing presses. While his *Cheap Bread Herald* spoke of the 'moral injustice' and 'class legislation' which only helped the landowners, Thomas addressed meeting after meeting with intense fervour. His speeches, forthright and to the point, were delivered with the passion of someone who had known the suffering of hunger as a child. Behind the impassioned speaker was his childhood persona: the hungry boy smelling the aroma of freshly baked crusty loaves, but being unable to taste them because his mother could not afford it. Similar misery and suffering had fuelled his horror of alcohol.

Since 1815, the price of corn and other cereals had been protected by the Corn Laws because it was argued that agriculture needed to be propped up. Wheat had trebled in price from 43 shillings a quarter (28lb) in 1792, the year prior to war against France breaking out. It rose to 126 shillings in 1812, the year Napoleon had marched across Russia to Moscow.[3] When prices had dropped after Waterloo, many farmers were ruined and rents could not be paid. While the Corn Law of 1815 safeguarded landlords, it both penalised consumers and caused political unrest. Cereal crops may have appeared not to be relevant to the warehouses in Lancashire piled high with unsold cotton goods, but both were the subject of tariffs, and both were arguments in the strategy of the Leaguers. This protection was implemented when foreign corn, including much from the United States, was prohibited if, due to a good harvest, the home corn fell to a specified price. In the following years import duties fluctuated dependent on the price of home corn.

The religious fervour of Leaguers was shown by the name of the newspaper, the *Free Trade Catechism*, and in such mottoes as 'Give us our daily bread', as the theme of many of the speeches. Free Trade was put up as a panacea capable of overcoming all economic and social ills.

Among the many arguments in the Anti-Corn Laws agenda was the suggestion that a high-rate of duty on imported grain would provoke foreigners to retaliate by boycotting British exports. Thomas proudly told how he was one of the agitators: 'I was intensely interested in the progress towards Free Trade; and in connection with the repeal of the Corn Laws I took a very active part in promoting interest and excitement among the people. I published a little paper entitled the *Cheap Bread Herald*, in which my main object was to accelerate the downfall of Protection.'[4] He further spoke of the havoc wrought by farmers keeping the price of wheat high and bakers who cheated with underweight loaves. Appalled at bogus claims and false advertising, he formed a committee to expose bakers and force them to price their bread honestly. His motivation was similar to that behind the soup kitchens he was later to organise:

> On such evenings there generally collected together about 1,000 people to listen to my statements from my public window of my house, and during most of the time I had the satisfaction of issuing exposing placards headed 'Down Again,' as prices continued to fall. A committee was formed to work with me, and very strenuous efforts were made to compel the bakers and breadsellers to sell bread by weight, and much excitement was created in the town. One Monday morning we sent out a number of men to purchase a loaf from every baker and breadseller in Leicester; the loaves were ticketed with the name of the shop where each was bought and the price paid, and in the evening, in response to an invitation by placard, at least 2,000 people assembled in the Amphitheatre in Humberstone Gate to witness a public Assize of Bread.

One by one, the loaves of bread from the shops, of all shapes and sizes, were carried up to the raised platform, where, by permission of the town clerk, the borough scales were waiting. Each loaf of bread was weighed. Loaf followed loaf. Now performing as a cross between the preacher that he was and the auctioneer he could have been, Thomas announced the weight of each loaf. The scales revealed the truth of his hypothesis. Bakers were found to be cheating their customers by not using enough flour. In some instances, 4lb loaves were little over 3lb. Whenever Thomas announced a large discrepancy, the audience roared and cheered. He added: 'The names of the dealers and their prices were all published, and great excitement was caused in the trade, but the magistrates were with us and enforced numerous fines – not only for the omission to weigh the loaves, but also for adulteration. An analyst was employed, and a number of fines were inflicted for adulteration.'

There may have been justice in the attacks on the Whigs by many members of the Corn League, such as Thomas, who liked to point out their folly, disunion and incompetence.[5] Indeed, he was not averse to attacking the Whigs as if they were Tories. Meanwhile, he fell foul of the law by failing to pay stamp duty on the *Cheap Bread Herald* for an issue which had included a paragraph referring to the French Revolution of 1848. As this was deemed as general news and the Stamp Duty Act specified that only papers and periodicals which did not carry general news were exempt from stamp duty, Thomas received an urgent summons calling him to London to face the Court of the Exchequer.

From London's Euston Station he walked south. Everywhere there were signs of dash and style: swift carriages with coachmen in top hats, phaetons, barouches, broughams, waggonettes, gigs, four-wheeled chaises and four-in-hands jostled beside horse-drawn buses[6] and hackney cabs. London, choking with traffic, poverty and riches, seemed to have more people and horse-drawn vehicles than anywhere else in the world. Behind the grandeur were tenements, open sewers, pickpockets, thugs, beggars, drunks, prostitutes and abandoned children running wild. Thomas could smell the Thames before he saw it. It also exuded the dank mists of winter, which, combined with the products from smoking chimneys, created murky smog.

In Kingsway he turned left into Fleet Street, where on the corner of Whitefriars Street, since it had moved from Manchester in 1843, was the office and nerve centre of the National Anti-Corn League. It was significant that it was in Fleet Street, the home of newspapers, as it was the first political lobby group to use modern media methods to further its cause – an example Thomas followed. From Fleet Street he walked to his appointment with the solicitor of the Inland Revenue at Somerset House in the Strand on the Thames. Buttoning up his waistcoat and holding himself tall, he walked along the Strand then turned left past the gatehouse into the paved courtyard to the eighteenth-century royal palace on the river front. Men with bundles of papers under their arms hurried down narrow, gloomy cream corridors. The old rooms were now divided into offices filled with members of the legal profession and Inland Revenue. Thomas defended himself: 'He took in my letter, presented it to the Board, and came out, stating that the Board, seeing that the objects I had in view were of a benevolent character, agreed to withdraw the summons on payment by me of a sovereign, which would not cover the expenses incurred. He told me that I was at perfect liberty to say what I liked in my paper about Whigs or Tories. I might denounce them all if I liked, but if I touched the revenue they would touch me.'

On his return walk to the station Thomas saw the graceful pale curve of Regent Street, with its domes, balustrades and shops, and Piccadilly. This sortie to London reinforced his resolve. Galvanised by his near-prosecution by the Inland Revenue, Thomas was soon on a rostrum again making 'an energetic speech' to help send a petition to parliament protesting against the use of grain in the distillation of liquor.

Thomas always stood firmly behind the Anti-Corn Leaguers, but he was no political radical, let alone aligned to any of the newly formed trade unions. Although the Anti-Corn Leaguers and the Chartists both revolted against the middle-class ascendancy established by the Reform Bill, there was much rivalry between the two organisations. The Chartists pushed for the fulfilment of the six points of the People's Charter of 1838 (see p. 56). From the time of their first national convention in London, marked differences separated the northerners (who were fundamentally anti-industrialist) and the men from the Midlands and London.[7]

Anti-Corn Leaguers were making such a major contribution to politics that their power was feared by the Tories and Protectionists. The subject of Protectionism versus Free Trade raised tempers, produced slogans and filled newspapers. So prevalent was the agitation that if the Corn Laws had not been defeated, it was rumoured that there could well have been a cataclysmic event as there had been in France. In 1846, Gladstone, then at the Board of Trade, prepared the bill for revoking the Corn Laws.

Just before dawn on 16 May 1846, at 4.15a.m., in one of the most symbolic nights in British parliamentary history in the Palace of Westminster, voting cut across parties, across class, across family. When the tellers counted the votes, the Ayes had it. Almost overnight Britain moved from Protection to Free Trade.

Paradoxically, the Irish Famine had been one of the excuses which Sir Robert Peel, the Conservative prime minister, used to bring about the repeal of the Corn Laws, but it did little to help the starving millions there, who needed charitable aid and money. As not enough people in Ireland could afford to buy Irish wheat, meat and dairy produce, its export to England continued – as before.

Trade restrictions remained an unremitting political issue into the next century.[8] Britain, according to many farmers and critics, had sacrificed the interests of agriculture to industry. Nobody was sure how far the legislation would affect trade. Would cheap goods and food flood through the newly unbarred ports? British farmers were assured of a certain amount of protection by the sheer cost of shipping grain combined with the hazards of rats and mice in the hulls of ships. At that stage there was no large surplus of foreign grain awaiting entry.

FIFTEEN

Bankruptcy and Backwards

The repeal of the Corn Laws that year had not brought the anticipated relief. Many people were still hungry and others, including Thomas, were surrounded by chilling circumstances. Misfortune appeared to be delivering him blow after blow, but this may have been a result of spreading himself too thinly. He was busy, organising trips, campaigning and producing pages on everything, from the evils of drink and smoking to the joys of cheap bread and travel. On top of this, some of the tourists on his first trip to Scotland were suing for compensation for their perilous night on the ship to Scotland. A further trip to Scotland the following year had failed to attract sufficient customers and had lost money. The final blow was the failure of the *National Temperance Magazine*, into which he had put so much effort. Whether its closure was a reflection of difficult times, or because readers had fallen away because of a fall in quality, is not known. In the very last issue of the magazine, in August 1846, he told readers of the 'painful and sudden reverses' which made it impossible for him 'to sustain his position. After ten years of ceaseless toil in the Temperance cause', he was forced to give in to 'those influences which have driven several Temperance publishers from the field'. His farewell message, written in the third person, had a desperate ring: 'Borne down by heavy responsibilities and legal oppressions, he has no alternative but to bid, at least temporarily, farewell to his esteemed friends and supporters.'[1]

The bleak picture of a debtors' prison painted by Dickens just ten years earlier in *Oliver Twist* (1837–9) remained. Those who failed to pay taxes, rent or debts usually pawned or sold their household belongings – everything from silver-plated hairbrushes to wedding rings – and, if they still failed to meet their creditors, they ended up in special jails. As in the workhouses, inmates often made potato sacks and baskets.

Declared bankrupts were now exempt from prison, so Thomas quickly made himself his own petitioner. Bankruptcy hearings for 'T. Cook, printer of Granby Street, Leicester' took place in Nottingham on 15 January and again on 12 February 1847. The records do not reveal any further proceedings. Thomas was discharged and his print works and travel company continued seemingly unaffected, and he did not move from his old address. He may have been bailed out by John Ellis. Chagrined and bothered though Thomas was by his bankruptcy, he was determined not to lose his base. Like many Victorians, he followed the homespun philosophy of another railway man, Samuel Smiles,[2] who promoted the values of hard work, thrift and progress. This author of *Self Help* was a former administrator on the Leeds and Thirsk Railway and South-Eastern Railway.

Thomas's personal setbacks did not prevent him appreciating that it was another year of triumph for Nonconformists. As with the repeal of the Test and Corporation Acts nineteen years earlier, they had again managed to chip away at the status of the Church of England. The Manchester Act 1847 reduced the number of bishops in the House of Lords from forty-three to twenty-six – a reduction that was seen as a stepping stone for the Dissenters in their long campaign against discrimination.

Well before Christmas optimistic sentences flew from Thomas's pen: 'The year 1847 opened more auspiciously for Scotland, and I had that summer three large excursions, the railways from York to Berwick to Edinburgh being available.' This sudden jump in trade was despite the discomfort of train journeys – well illustrated by Frederic Chopin's descriptions of his trips the following year. Henry Broadwood, the maker of fine pianos, booked a ticket for Chopin and three others for the arduous twelve-hour journey from Euston to Edinburgh: one extra seat for his legs, one for his new servant Daniel and one for his pianist/manager. In October, when returning to London, the rail link over the Tyne was still not completed on the east-coast route, so he was forced, as Thomas's tourists often were, to walk across the bridge at Berwick.

After one of these journeys north, Thomas, with a large party, followed the Queen and Prince Albert. Travelling across moors, around estuaries, sea cliffs, beaches and rocks, and on perilous routes by sea and land, his group were five days behind the Queen – sailing around Bute, along the Crinan Canal and from the Atlantic coast to Oban. From there, like the Queen, they went to the islands of Staffa and Iona, circumnavigating the island of Mull, and afterwards visited Glencoe and Fort William and went on the Caledonian Canal to Inverness. Being in the wake of a royal party set an example which would be repeated.

Thomas's empathy with the mysterious islands of Iona and Staffa matched that of Mendelssohn. The appeal of seeing the graves of warrior kings, ecclesiastical dignitaries and many a shipwrecked mariner was sadly contrasted with the poverty of the inhabitants. Mendelssohn's gift to the people there was his *Hebrides* Overture or *Fingal's Cave*,[3] a musical celebration of its wild shores. He wrote after his tour in 1829: '. . . many huts without roofs, many unfinished, with crumbling walls, many ruins of burnt houses; and even these inhabited spots are but sparingly scattered over the country. Long before you arrive at a place you hear it talked of; the rest is heath, with red or brown heather, withered fir stumps, and white stones, or black moors where they shoot grouse. Now and then you find beautiful parks, but deserted, and broad lakes, but without boats, the roads a solitude . . .'

Thomas tried to help the islanders in practical ways. After one trip he took up the cause of 'the Social Condition of the people of the Western Highlands and Islands of Scotland', saying that it was 'impossible for tourists visiting the Hebridean district to be indifferent to, or unmoved by, the symptoms of destitution and distress'. He argued that the large parties going to Staffa and Iona with him 'frequently evinced a kind and sympathetic regard for the isolated and suffering inhabitants of that interesting island, where learning and piety, thirteen hundred years ago, concentrated their sway and diffused their influence, and where still remain relics of ecclesiastical, monarchical, and chieftain greatness'.

Scottish history, from real life and from romantic novels, came to life for Thomas through places, scenery and such characters as Rob Roy MacGregor, Flora MacDonald, Bonnie Prince Charlie and the feuds and raids with Borderers, Lowlanders or Islemen. Novelty was found in everything, from the fauna with its Highland cattle to the exquisite flora, especially the dwarf Arctic birch,[4] which runs in and out of the heather, and the dwarf willow.[5] There were few railways in Scotland then, so, when not travelling in ferries, Thomas took tourists in coaches on the many roads that crisscrossed the country, extensions of the military routes built by the English after Culloden.

'The great Highland coach road between Inverness, Dunkeld, and Perth became a favourite route long ere the first sod of a railway was turned,' wrote Thomas. He also took tourists on the roads between Inverness and Aberdeen, the Deeside, by Balmoral, Braemar, Spital or Glenshee, Blairgowrie, Aberfeldy, and to all points of the Highland roads to Inverary, Glencoe, etc. He explained the arrangements:

Here were commenced my first great combinations of special tickets for circular tours, but still the privileges were restricted to the large excursion parties that I took from England, for whom I got very great reductions of fares, and before the termination of the decade now under review I frequently took to Scotland as many as 5,000 visitors in a season. From every part of England visitors came to the Midland Counties to join in with my Scottish excursion, immense numbers falling in with me en route. I had generally to take two, and sometimes three special trains from Newcastle. On the opening of the Caledonian line, I began to work alternately over the east coast and west coast routes, but the popular way was by Newcastle and Berwick. Every new season my plans had to be submitted to the committees that controlled Scotch traffic, but for a number of years I had no great difficulty, so popular and successful were the excursions.

SIXTEEN

1848: Knowing Your Place in Society and Respecting Your Betters

The year 1848, the year the potato crop failed in Ireland for the third time, was a year of revolutions. Crop failures throughout Europe from 1845 onwards, aggravated by industrial depression in towns, created a fertile atmosphere for revolt. Trouble erupted in Austria, Poland, Prussia, Hungary, Sicily, Spain, Portugal, Switzerland, France, Piedmont, Venetia and Greece. Britain was the only major European nation, except Russia, to escape some sort of rebellion in that dramatic year. But the government was nervous, and with renewed vigour it countered the efforts of agitators.

Times were again really bad for many, including Thomas in Leicester: '1848 was a blank in my Railway Excursions,' he wrote, 'owing to the unwillingness of Companies to negotiate.' He was suffering from his recent bankruptcy and the railway companies' decision to run excursions themselves. Many now employed excursion managers so they could bypass outside agents like Thomas, whose arrangements with the railways were not long term, so he had no comeback. Thomas's plans for the Scottish tours had been approved each season by the committees that controlled traffic in Scotland, so it had always been a hand-to-mouth affair. Nor did he have a monopoly of the trade, as there were now other excursion operators, some good, some inefficient, but all ready to take away his customers. Just as Scotland was the mainstay of his operations, in return dozens of Scottish hotels and boarding houses relied on his trade. Many of them, pretty little places covered in roses and honeysuckle tucked away in the hills, changed hands.

Now, after being a celebrated railway excursionist, Thomas had the indignity of going back to horse-drawn carriages. It would be several years before he got into his stride again. Unwilling to abandon his touring company, Thomas organised 'numerous Coach Trips to Belvoir Castle, Melbourne Gardens, &c. &c.', mostly in Leicestershire and nearby counties. Oddly enough, Thomas never took tours to Bosworth Field, where the final battle of the Wars of the Roses had ended with Richard III slain by Henry Tudor's army.[1]

Thomas's bumper coach visits to ancestral homes were a century, almost to the year, before their large-scale opening up after the Second World War. In the 1940s and 1950s, when the Marquis of Bath charged tourists a shilling to enter Longleat, or the Duke of Bedford a similar sum to enter Woburn, it was seen as an innovation. Long forgotten were the many stately homes that had earlier allowed visitors. The visitors, though, were usually not members of the working class. The Elizabethan home of the Devonshires, Chatsworth, in the 1760s had welcomed guests on 'two public days in a week', and the 'strangers' book' at Wilton, in 1776, listed 2,324 visitors. By the 1790s, Woburn restricted visitors to Mondays, yet other grand houses continued to receive visitors by the hundreds. Housekeepers pocketed so many tips from visitors that Horace Walpole joked that he was tempted to marry the housekeeper of Strawberry Hill, his stuccoed and battlemented pseudo castle at Twickenham.[2] Until the time of Thomas's day trippers, no entrance fees were fixed,[3] but, seeing the market potential of stately homes and gardens, Thomas blazed a trail. Increased numbers of paying visitors were a symbol of social change, something which many owners, even those who opened their houses and gardens, feared. The Duke of Devonshire, known as the 'bachelor Duke', was an exception.

A lonely man hampered by poor hearing, he became close to two architects, Jeffrey Wyattville and Joseph Paxton. With them he created magnificent settings for his newly acquired paintings and antiques at Chatsworth, in the heart of the Peak District National Park, reputedly the finest stately home in Britain. Like many avid collectors, the Duke enjoyed displaying his collections, so the powdered footmen of Chatsworth opened the stately doors to Thomas's tourists. With awe the visitors ascended the main staircase to the majestic statue of

Mercury and stood enthralled under the richly painted ceilings. Room after room, including the new long wing designed by Wyattville, was crammed with portraits in ornate gilt frames and one of Europe's finest collections of drawings. One sumptuous suite had, between 1570 and 1581, housed Victoria's ancestor, Mary Queen of Scots, for eleven of the long years of melancholy captivity imposed on her by her cousin Elizabeth. By visiting Chatsworth, once again, Thomas was following the footsteps of Victoria and Albert, who had stayed there in 1843. Lord Melbourne, who had also been invited, had left an unhappy man. Victoria had few minutes to spare to talk to him and found him duller than ever.[4]

More exciting than the house, for some, were Chatsworth's 105 acres of gardens. Here they could see tall palm trees and exotic lilies from South America inside Paxton's massive Great Conservatory – 'the great stove', at the time the largest glass building in the world. One water lily had such large leaves that a child could float on it.

Paxton, born into poverty in 1803 in Milton-Bryant near Woburn in Bedfordshire, had left school at fifteen. His first job, like Thomas's, was as a garden boy, but in the Horticultural Society's Chiswick Gardens beside the Duke's garden at Chiswick House. When Thomas first went to Chatsworth in 1847, Paxton had become the controller of most of the affairs of the Duke, having worked for him twenty-one years. Paxton seemed to bring prosperity to much that he touched – even his railway shares. Unlike thousands of unlucky investors in trains, he chose the Midland Railway and as the company grew he became one of its active directors under the chairmanship of Ellis. Meetings between Thomas and Paxton on the visits in 1847 are not recorded, but it is more than likely that they discussed arrangements. In just three years' time, Paxton would be the catalyst for Thomas as a tour operator.

Another obvious stately home to put on the new itinerary was Melbourne Hall. None of Thomas's family had lived in the village for over thirty years, but its hold on him had never ceased. Unlike Chatsworth, Melbourne Hall remained out of reach. Only the romantically landscaped grounds were to be open. Nobody could step inside the ancient house, but Thomas would be allowed to stroll through the gates, once closed to him. Again, the sun shone on 10 August when Thomas, leading nine horse-drawn carriages carrying 109 passengers, set off from Leicester. From the gentle rolling hills, they diverted past the wild expanses of Charnwood Forest with its rocky crags. The horses pulled the coaches up a steep hill to Mount St Bernard Abbey,[5] the first Roman Catholic abbey built in England since the Reformation. It had almost been a celebration of the passing of the Catholic Emancipation Act in 1829 and had been conceived as an act of reparation for the destruction of the monasteries in general at the time of the Reformation.

Unlike many Nonconformists then, who were intolerant of both Catholics and 'popery', Thomas did not hold an inveterate hostility. As he had not made any prior arrangements to visit the abbey, it seems that it may have been the result of last-minute urging by someone in the party. Even though the monks would not allow Thomas and his trippers entry, their excuse was music to Thomas's ears. A party who had visited the previous day had misbehaved with 'exhibitions of intemperance, insulting observations, and acts of willful damage to the property'.[6] With a little persuasion permission was given for the men with Thomas, but not the women, to enter the abbey. But the inspection was brief, as, by mid-day, the coach party had to be at Melbourne, where a 'powerful brass band of eighteen' was waiting to greet them in the centre of the town.

The excitement of the arrival in Melbourne, with loud music and speeches, heightened the mood of the visitors. In contrast, the visit to the gardens at Melbourne Hall was a timid affair with no refreshments and no repast. But Thomas could now wander beneath the leafy arches of the trees, walk through the world's longest yew tunnel, continue down the long parterres, sit beside the winged statues set in alcoves of more clipped yew hedges and gaze at the iron arbour with the fanciful title of the Birdcage.

Two weeks later, on 29 August, another stately home was on Thomas's schedule. A well-advertised 'Pleasure Party' arrived at the Duke of Rutland's Belvoir Castle, which dates from the eleventh century, not far from Melton Mowbray, famed for its pork pies. Thomas's visitors were allowed to tour inside the castle, and again they benefited from a threepenny guide, the *Hand-Book of Belvoir Castle*, from the presses in Granby Street. Packed with facts about history and architecture, the booklet also told visitors 'how to behave in the castle and grounds' and, in a patronising tone, instructing them to observe the niceties of polite society:

> It is very seldom indeed that the privileges extended to visitors of the mansions of the nobility are abused; but to the shame of some rude folk from Lincolnshire, there had been just causes of complaint at Belvoir Castle: some large parties have behaved indecorously, and they have to some extent prejudiced the visits of other large companies. Conduct of this sort is abominable, and cannot be too strongly reprobated. We are sure that Leicester visitors will not *knowingly* commit the slightest infraction on the rules of good behaviour, and all we desire of them is to observe the 'notices' which hang in the different apartments of the Castle; and in the promenades through the surrounding walks, to satisfy themselves with observations, and not damage in the slightest degree shrubs or flowers, or deface by writing, seats, walls, statues, or any objects of interest. A word to the wise is enough.

This invaluable booklet – '*Designed as a Guide to an Excursion Party from Leicester to Belvoir, Aug. 29, 1848; with a Description of the Route from Leicester, and Places of Interest in the Locality of the Castle.*' – was a forerunner of the extensive facts and helpful information which were to be a hallmark of all Thomas Cook tours.

The Duke, a public-spirited man who was the Lord Lieutenant of the county for fifty years, allowed the visitors to tour inside the house in groups of twenty-five – as long as they behaved 'with propriety and decorum'. To discourage tourists from bringing 'numerous basket accompaniments and annoyance of picnic parties', Thomas suggested they took refreshments 'on economical terms' at the nearby Belvoir Inn. Apart from wanting to avoid careless cooking and the tough meat so often served at such inns, strict Temperance men went out of their way to avoid contact with *any* establishments serving liquor. Yet, over and over again, as he ferried larger and larger groups through the front doors of giant, forbidding mansions, Thomas was compromising – and not just his Temperance ideals. Considering his principles on the rights of the working class, it is a shock to come across his forelock tugging – as seen in the sycophantic prose describing his upper-class hosts in his *Hand-Book of Belvoir Castle* – which far exceeded the usual deference to the aristocracy. Even if we remember that he aimed to establish regular paying visits to stately homes and that their owners looked with nervous anxiety at such intrusions, his words are over the top: 'This liberality on the part of the aristocracy of the country constitutes a pleasing feature of the present times, and is calculated to produce a good moral effect in binding together in one harmonious chain the different sections of society. May God speed the day when the sons of toil shall live happily in the enjoyment of the just rewards of their labour, and the rich shall live at ease in the undisturbed possession of the wealth and greatness to which they have a legitimate claim!'

Apart from tours to stately homes, there were also events such as excursions to see Isambard Kingdom Brunel's famous *Great Britain* steamship when in 1846 she suffered a major mishap, being stranded after running ashore on the rocky coast of Ireland at Dundrum Bay. The grounding was caused – it is said – by deviations in the ship's compass resulting from the effects of the iron of the hull. Despite the fascination of the ship, it is surprising that Thomas managed to find enough local customers, as the slump in England was acute. At one stage at least one-third of Leicester's population was out of work, and the Union Workhouse in Sparkenhoe Street was full, but even so demand for Thomas's trip outstripped the available places.

Then, in February 1848, came the electrifying news of the *coup d'état* in France. While the deposed Louis-Philippe and his Queen, disguised as Mr and Mrs Smith, crossed the Channel to Dover, another political adventurer, Louis Napoleon, beaky nosed and moustached, left his apartment in Carlton Gardens, London, and crossed the Channel the other way. Louis-Philippe retired to Claremont in Surrey,[7] the former home of George IV's son-in-law Prince Leopold of Saxe-Coburg, king of the Belgians, whose wife was Louis-Philippe's daughter. The Elysée Palace was not empty for long.

By the end of the year Louis Napoleon was president and assuming the grandeur, but not yet the imperial title, of his late uncle Napoleon Bonaparte. During his twenty-two years in power, he would make investments in Egypt which would impact on Thomas's business.

On 21 September 1848, Thomas was again organising a Temperance train outing. To mark the twelfth anniversary of the Leicester Temperance Society, a 'Rural Festival' was held at Cossington. The *Leicester Chronicle* of 23 September reported that there were around 1,500 members and friends. Tea was served in the grounds of the rectory at the invitation of the Revd John Babington, the Church of England rector, then president of the society, 'on the gravel walk, beneath an extensive grove, adjoining the rectory, upon a table 126 yards long'.[8] This trip marked Thomas's return to the railways. By the end of 1850 he once again had 'arrangements' with almost all the railway companies of the Midlands, the North of England, the North West, the Eastern Counties and some southern lines.

On Wednesday 6 November, at 10.15a.m., a train departed from Leicester to Cambridge carrying about 800 passengers who had come from as far as Birmingham, Sheffield, Derby and other places to present Thomas with a gold watch and chain ('value about £25') inscribed, 'Presented to Mr. Thomas Cook by subscription, in approval of his able arrangements of special trips. Leicester, November 6th, 1850.' A group of loyal local passengers had formed a committee for 'his having for nine years zealously and satisfactorily served the public as a projector and manager of Cheap Excursions'. According to his calculations, he had escorted a total of 15,246 passengers over 7,525 miles with fares of £5,090 9s 9d.

Just as Thomas was now on the brink of take-off, Lord Melbourne died at the age of sixty-nine. As the family stood beside his deathbed, his sister Emily, Lady Palmerston, was sure that he had gone to Heaven. Her son-in-law, Lord Ashley, had his doubts.[9]

SEVENTEEN

The Great Exhibition

The unplanned development of rail travel in the nineteenth century produced far-reaching and much criticised upheavals. By 1850, 6,000 miles of railway track had been laid, altering forever Britain's townscapes and landscapes. The road system, in decline since the departure of the Romans, had begun to improve in the eighteenth century, when the turnpike movement produced roads with surfaces fit for the 'flying coaches'.[1] Further improvements in transport occurred with the construction of canals, as a fundamental element in the industrial revolution. Now, both roads and canals were losing passengers and freight to the new rail network.

Thomas, anxious to pre-empt the mounting number of competitors who were also utilising trains, set up tours to new destinations. His survival depended on creativity, stamina and an ability to keep just a little ahead of the competition. He let his old ambition surface and began seriously to 'give his attention to Eastern routes', knowing that many would clamour to make such a journey. Indeed, the advantages of trips to 'the Eastern Lands of the Bible' were acknowledged by many clergymen. The stories of David and Jesus made Jerusalem a unique and sought after destination.

There was an enormous desire for many Protestants to return to the roots of their faith, and to see the places mentioned in the Bible. For some Nonconformists, the motivation for visiting the Holy Land was to return to the very beginnings of the Church, to pre-Roman Christianity, before it had become an institution and before Jesus' teachings had been embellished and altered by the disciples and the popes. The historic evidence of Christianity and continuity back to the times of Abraham and Sarah was now being scrutinised by archaeologists and scholars.

105

In the nineteenth century one of the first well-known English writers to make a trip was the tall, stooped, bespectacled master of satire, William Makepeace Thackeray. P. & O. Line, which had regular ships to Alexandria, was promoting Mediterranean 'cruises' with round tickets, including shore excursions. Thackeray was given a free passage in exchange for writing up his experiences.[2] Far from producing an uncritical and laudatory book[3] about his excursions, he painted a vivid picture showing the difficulties of travelling, stressing that in the Holy Land he had had to travel in a party 'well mounted and well armed'.

When in London again Thomas discussed Holy Land tours with Silk Buckingham, who compared North America's 8,000 miles of rail tracks with Palestine where there were none. And it was expensive. There were taxes on departing from Jaffa, on arrival in Jerusalem and on accommodation. Few of the roads were passable and in many places the old Roman highways were hardly more than mule tracks. Tourists had to move around on donkeys, mules, camels or horses, generally, as Thackeray had pointed out, in convoys. Armed escorts were the norm, but most tourists had to pay what was jokingly called the 'Sultan's tax', a kind of protection money given to local chieftains, plus *baksheesh* for obtaining reductions in some of the regular taxes.[4] Many local costs were unpredictable and difficult to calculate in advance. On top of this there were also sandstorms, fleas, mosquitoes and the odd raiders on horseback.[5]

For those intrepid enough to persevere, the journey from Jaffa to Jerusalem took about fourteen hours, made up of two or three to Ramleh and then about eleven to Jerusalem. The hills to Jerusalem were so steep that it took two hours more going up than it did coming down. In an effort to beat the winter winds and storms which brought havoc to the Mediterranean, Christian pilgrims generally arrived in November and stayed most of the winter.[6] When Princess Caroline, George IV's estranged wife, had visited in 1817, her sailing boat had been chased by pirates and nearly shipwrecked in a storm. Then, when finally anchored in Jaffa, the royal party had been barred from landing because they had insufficient permit paperwork, forcing them to sail to Acre.

Buckingham sympathised with Thomas's idea of 'bringing together people of various nationalities and social distinctions' to the Holy Land, but argued that, despite the rough crossing of the Atlantic, the United States was a better bet. Before Christmas, Thomas was on his way, ready to make arrangements for breakthrough tours to New York and beyond. But the destination was changed at the last minute.

Just as Thomas had escorted his first commercial trip to Liverpool in 1845, in 1850 he again chose it to initiate a new phase in tourism: tours to America. After visiting shipping companies about reduced fares for packages, he took a train home, via Derby Station. Here he met his good acquaintance Ellis and his fellow director Paxton, who, by chance, was the architect of the forthcoming Great Exhibition in London. Paxton casually made a daunting proposal which would change Thomas's whole life.

A year earlier, in 1849, Prince Albert had started preparations for the biggest and most diverse exhibition ever held in Europe. This 'Great Exhibition of the Works of Industry of All Nations' would show everything from railway carriages and textiles to butter churns and Bovril, and confirm London as an exemplary modern metropolis, a major player on the world stage. In contrast to previous exhibitions on the continent, London would invite contributions from every corner of the earth.

Albert and the other organisers, including Paxton, feared that not enough people would come to the exhibition. The expertise of Thomas and his competitors was needed to tempt and move large numbers of visitors from all over Britain. Each operator could have the exclusive rights on certain lines coming into London. Thomas's territory was to be the southern part of the Midland Line. He would receive a fee for every excursion passenger who purchased a fifteen-shilling ticket. Thomas jumped at the idea, especially as he knew he could have the assistance of John Mason, who was just seventeen and had recently finished his printer's apprenticeship.

When Paxton[7] met Thomas in Derby, the nine-acre site in Hyde Park, near Knightsbridge barracks, was waiting for the 2,000 tradesmen to start erecting the massive prefabricated building. Paxton's showplace palace of iron and glass, an overpowering example of the new mass-manufacturing processes, would turn out to be the star of the exhibition, based on designs similar to the giant greenhouses he had already built for the Duke of Devonshire. It relied on wrought-iron sash bars invented by John Loudon in 1816, which could be bent in any direction and still maintain their strength.[8] Loudon had died in 1843, so Paxton received the credit.

Albert's plans to stage a large industrial exhibition in London had earlier been met with scepticism by many members of the upper classes, who were aghast at royalty thrusting itself into trade and modernity. Albert, who had been a keen visitor to the Frankfurt fairs in his youth, persisted, and thought England could easily compete with the continental fairs. The idea had initially come to him from Henry Cole, then Assistant Keeper of the Public Records and a member of the Royal Society of Arts of which Albert was president. Cole, who had earlier published the first Christmas card in England and helped launch the new postal service, had returned from France in 1849, bubbling over with enthusiasm for the Paris *Exposition.*

Unlike the fairs that exhibited the latest styles in expensive and fashionable items, such as fine silks, velvets and Empire-style chairs, the Great Exhibition was to assert Britain's domination in arts, sciences, industry, commerce, armaments and medicine. It would stimulate trade and create jobs by obtaining orders for both the products and the machines which made them.[9] Albert, keen that the exhibition should be self-financing, asked his banker, Lionel Rothschild, to underwrite £50,000 of the £200,000 initially required. (It actually made a large profit.)

The first of the 1,060 iron columns went up in the autumn of 1850, followed by 300,000 panes of glass which were fixed with over 200 miles of sash bars – a celebration of the end of that old enemy of light and air, the outdated window tax. Being prefabricated, it took 2,000 men only eight months to finish and cost just £79,800. As glazing was moved on special trolleys, one man alone could fix 108 panes in a day.

Fears that the structure would collapse in the first high wind were soon dispelled. As autumn progressed into winter, the light which poured through its glass was so dazzling that *Punch* magazine christened the pavilion a 'Crystal Palace'. In less than twelve months, this pavilion, which was waterproof and more than a third of a mile long and 408 feet in width, would be complete – and, at 108 feet high, tall enough to enclose the lofty elm trees on its site. The splendid gala opening was planned to take place just eighteen months after the day that Albert had agreed to Cole's idea. Paxton's impact would go far beyond Hyde Park, soon becoming the prototype of all the classic glass-and-iron functional buildings of Victorian England. Its influence would be seen in the glass dome in the British Library reading room and the stately glass roofs of new railway stations, everywhere from King's Cross to Sydney.

As well as transporting thousands of travellers to the exhibition, Thomas decided to provide accommodation. Before the exhibition he tramped the streets of London looking for cheap, clean beds. Most boarding house owners declined to register with him at fixed prices, as they were sure prices would surge when the Great Exhibition finally opened. In the end Thomas gambled and took out a few leases to create lodging houses for the summer. 'The Ranelagh Club Mechanics Home', rented from a Mr Thomas Harison in Ranelagh Road, Pimlico, near Vauxhall Bridge, could accommodate a thousand people a night. Here, for 1s 3d a night, each male guest would have a partitioned-off area in a dormitory that contained a bedstead with sacking and a good hair mattress, blankets, coverlid (bedcover), soap, towel, 'every convenience for ablution' and a key to his unit. The partitions between areas were seven-feet-high boards. Boots and shoes could be cleaned for a penny a pair. Thomas thought of everything, even the warning, 'Should parties get into that state where they could not look after themselves at night, there would be a policeman in attendance to take care of them that they should not annoy other people.' To help people pay for their trips, Thomas started 'travel clubs' and 'Exhibition Clubs' which helped workers save part of their wages. Since the end of the previous century, the numbers of friendly societies that took subscriptions from members and insured them against death, illness and burial expenses had been increasing.[10] People could now put sixpence each week into 'travel clubs', which would later develop into people paying for their holidays in advance instalments, which was useful in days when there where were no high street banks in small towns and the average weekly wages for men on farms was just under ten shillings.[11]

A new monthly magazine *Cook's Exhibition Herald and Excursion Advertiser*, issued to promote his trips to London for the exhibition, helped generate enthusiasm about forthcoming trips. Thomas's pen was seldom still. This magazine continued as the *Excursionist* until the Second World War. It provided page after page of itineraries, fares, lists of hotels, testimonial letters, articles about tours, advertisements and editorial comment.[12] In an early issue the question was posed, 'How are working men, their wives and children to get to the Exhibition?' The answer was in the first paragraph – with Thomas Cook.

Excursions to Scotland were suspended, as six months were needed to make arrangements and obtain bookings. Thomas explained, 'the whole of the southern division of the line was exclusively offered to me, whilst north of Sheffield I had the chief obligations, two occasional Yorkshire agents being appointed to work with me'.

At last, with the blare of trumpets and all the tradition, glitter and pomp that 32-year-old Albert could muster, the exhibition was opened on May Day, 1 May 1851. The magnificent ceremony was heightened by the excitement of the awed crowds and the presence of the eldest two of their seven children, who stood clutching posies.

Victoria stood erect and stately on a dais encircled by palm trees and people, as the Archbishop of Canterbury said a short prayer and the massive choir and orchestra performed the Hallelujah Chorus from *Messiah*. As always, Victoria was surrounded by a curious, indefinable awe, having raised the popularity of monarchy to a pitch it had not enjoyed before under the Hanoverian dynasty. Plumed hats came off and ceremonial swords out as rope pulleys hauled the Union Jack to the top of the towering flagpole, while the military band struck up the national anthem. Speeches stressed crown and empire and the wonders of being British. Thomas, who managed to be one of the audience of 20,000, described this celebration of British imperial and industrial might as a 'galaxy of splendour which has burst upon the world'.

EIGHTEEN

Paxton, Prince Albert and the Great Exhibition

We must have RAILWAYS FOR THE MILLION
                                        Thomas Cook, 1843

After the formal opening of the exhibition, Thomas found he was in the centre of 'one of the hottest contests ever inspired by railway competition'. Cuttle and Calverly, of Wakefield, had been appointed to cooperate with him in Yorkshire, but 'the Midland and London & North-Western on one side, and the Great Northern on the other' were in fierce competition with him. Thomas became desperate when the Great Northern Line reduced its tickets to five shillings, a third of the price of Thomas's fifteen-shilling fare on the Midland Railways.

Unable to persuade the Midland to reduce its fares, Thomas tore up his contract, but at nine o'clock the fare was down to five shillings from Bradford, Leeds, Sheffield, and other competing points, and it stood at that rate to the close of the Exhibition. Thomas recalled that it 'was a time of intense excitement, and all the trains on the line, except for the day Express, were made available for excursion tickets. Frequently the night mail would be run in from two to six divisions.'

'Five shillings to London and back' was Thomas's war cry as he threw himself into the race by travelling to Leeds, Bradford, Sheffield and Derby with notices on street corners, on factory gates and on a van followed by a brass band. Both he and John Mason laboured well into each night for over three months selling tickets and ferrying the parties to and fro. Thomas later related his sales methods: 'At the call of a band of music, I saw workpeople come out of factories in

112

Bradford, pay five shillings for a ticket, and with a very few shillings in their pockets start off on Saturday night to spend Sunday and Monday in London, returning to work on Tuesday morning. The people of Yorkshire were thus educated to travel . . .'

The exhibition broke all records. Never before had London had to deal with such huge crowds or had so many people attended one single event. The carnival atmosphere inside the Crystal Palace extended on to grass plots with stalls, sideshows and kiosks selling souvenirs and lemonade. However, its aim to bring all sectors of British society to mingle together under one roof was initially countered by the entrance ticket price of five shillings, limiting it to what *The Times* called 'the wealthy and the gentility and nobly born'. At the end of May the price was dropped to a shilling.

The Queen applauded Albert's exhibition by visiting it no less than forty times during the six months it was open.[1]

Thomas, it seems, visited it even more than the Queen. For six months he devoted himself to nothing but the exhibition, rarely sleeping a night at home. As he said, his 'well-aired bed' was often the floor of a railway carriage, because many of his exhibition trains to and from London ran through the night. John Mason travelled three or four times a week in each direction between Leeds, Bradford, Sheffield and Derby.

Only non-alcoholic beverages were being served at the exhibition – a sensational step forward for Thomas and other Temperance men (there were then around 11,000 spirit shops in London, as against 4,000 butchers and bakers).[2] The limitation was criticised by many visitors and *Punch* complained about 'only ginger-beer' being served. The phrase 'spending a penny' dates from the exhibition, as George Jennings installed something that was then just growing in use, public water-closets, and charged 827,000 users each a penny. These facilities, though, were not backed up with an adequate drainage or sewerage pipes, so cesspools near the Thames overflowed with the massive volume of water. But most consequences of the exhibition, especially for Thomas, were positive.

Seen as a feat of peace and internationalism, a way to combine art, industry and social progress, the exhibition stimulated industrial design and showed the virtues of joining art and science. Exhibits with innovations for manufacturing were a priority. Passionate about science, Albert ruled that objects defined as 'fine art' were to be disqualified unless they included some technical expertise. Nevertheless, the exhibits included Augustus Pugin's 'medieval court' of neo-Gothic carpets and tiles, a display by the Religious Tract Society and Novello's cheap editions of oratorios. Three of the most admired objects were the gas cooker, the sewing machine from America and, as domestic canning was still in its infancy, tinned mutton from Australia.

Thomas, who transported 165,000 people from the Midlands to the exhibition, did not forget the young. Anxious that children should see this 'unprecedented and never-to-be-rivalled' show, he escorted 3,000 children and their teachers from the Sunday and day schools of Leicester, Nottingham, and Derby. His new paper the *Excursionist*, the first travel newspaper in the world, allowed him now to be a published author and also to promote his ideas: 'The Great Exhibition is mainly indebted for its astonishing interest to the skill and industry of mechanics, artisans and other operative classes. And in many instances the honour of invention and execution which properly belongs to those classes is monopolized by the principles of manufacturers (who may be mere noodles) or the wealthy millionaire, whose gold had made him representative of the products of better men's brains and hands.'

With 112,000 exhibits from 7,381 British and 6,556 foreign exhibitors, the exhibition proved that British factories could cope well with competition. Britain had become the powerhouse of Europe, a kingdom of traders, importers, exporters and factories churning out everything from stockings to machines, all which would be exported to every corner of the earth. Since the abolition of the Corn Laws and the ending of import tariffs on raw materials and foodstuffs, Britain had set out to conquer overseas markets by means of well-made, cheaply produced products. The old Free Trade campaigners saw the exhibition as a triumph, the result of their long struggle. Entrepreneurial skills had turned the British Isles from an agricultural country into an industrial giant.

There were many spin-offs from this, the biggest event of any sort ever held in Britain. One historian suggested that it resulted in 'the largest movement of population ever to have taken place in Britain'.[3] A landmark in international exhibitions, it set the standard for all future similar events throughout Europe, and it also became a milestone in transport. In a way, the exhibition was following the lead of Napoleon Bonaparte, who had been one of the first political leaders to be aware of the unifying effect of pomp and ritual.

In England, the exhibition was a precedent for attracting 'the public' to gigantic gatherings[4] and in bringing people from the provinces to see the wonders of London. During its four months of existence the exhibition was open for 140 days (closed on Sundays) and dazzled six million visitors – a fifth of the population of Great Britain. But many foreigners visited and many people returned more than once. Numbers increased as the show went on, with over 100,000 a day. It was also a milestone in the history of many new inventions, even institutions, such as the Young Men's Christian Association (YMCA). Thousands of leaflets were distributed telling workers to visit the YMCA. Alarmed at the temptations luring young men in London, George Williams, who was later knighted, set up clubs in an attempt to stop them being pulled into the growing underclass of London. Each club had reading rooms, refreshment areas, accommodation and places to meet and make new friends.

The year marked the third triumph for Nonconformists in twenty-three years. Results of the first religious census in England and Wales shook the complacency of the Church of England, as they showed that it had the allegiance of only about half of all practising believers. About one in two of the population had attended a chapel[5] on 'Census Sunday', 30 March 1851, with Nonconformists outnumbering Anglicans by two to one in places like Manchester. Figures showed attendances that day as Church of England 5,292,551, Roman Catholics 383,630 and the main Protestant dissenting churches (Presbyterian, Methodist, Congregationalist, Baptist) 4,536,264. As the total population was 17,927,609, the census also revealed that large numbers were staying away from church. Figures for Wales fuelled the fight for disestablishment. Here only one in five attended an Anglican church.

And so the first decade of Thomas Cook, Baptist, Temperance campaigner, printer and travel agent, ended on a high note. He could also see the results of his own efforts, but the risks he was taking were the sort that would hasten heart attacks in many men. Would he in the next ten years overreach himself and end up again in the bankruptcy courts?

NINETEEN

Building Houses

Down came fifty ramshackle lodging houses, known as 'rookeries', in Granby Street, Leicester. Homes crammed in narrow spaces, jammed tightly between bigger buildings, were demolished almost overnight to make two new construction sites. Enormous blocks of granite, bricks and mortar were hauled in wide carts along Granby Street ready for a Corinthian-pillared building which would look like a foreign bank in the colonies.

When the foundation stone of the Temperance Hall was laid on 2 June 1852, Thomas was out in front, looking like a gentleman. The whiteness of the gleaming stiff front to his shirt matched his stiff white shining cuffs and collar. Here he was, director of the Temperance Hall Company and 'Corresponding Secretary of the Leicester Temperance Society',[1] greeting the local luminaries – the Leicester Temperance Hall Company had raised £2,000 from a local building society loan[2] and £10,000 from selling 844 shares. He handed a silver trowel to the president, the Revd Babington, who was ready to cement in a stone. Winks's younger brother Fred, who met his death three years later falling off a ladder, was soon to start work on the building as one of the decorators.

Thomas was changing gear and combining piety with progress. Materialism was, just a little, tingeing his idealism. As well as organising the Temperance Hall,[3] Thomas was about to build a palatial home (albeit also a hotel) next door at 63 Granby Street. Three days after the laying of the stone, an advertisement in the *Leicester Chronicle* invited tenders to build a Temperance hotel there for Mr Thomas Cook.[4] The same architect, James Medland of Gloucestershire, was supervising this smaller building, which was also to be a tour office and print works. Where had the security for the loan for Thomas's share in the Temperance Hall and the money in the Thomas Cook hotel come from? It was a huge gamble to put on such an impressive front, but his track record at the Great Exhibition had left him in no doubt about profiting from fine margins. His compromise was shown by the inclusion of a smoking room, and his new confidence was seen by the site of the hotel and Temperance Hall. Departing guests would be confronted with the noisy Nag's Head, a busy pub on the right, or, adjoining the Temperance Hall, the equally noisy Waggon and Horses.

No expense was spared. Both buildings were the first premises in Leicester to have piped water, which came from the new reservoir at Thornton, a village to the north-west, but plumbing and drainage were still in their infancy. Hot water had to be carried in jugs up three or four flights of stairs by maids to washstands – as did a yellow tin bath. All these refinements, as well as the building costs and land, totalled between £3,500 and £5,000. The large house would be modern and easy to clean. Good ventilation and an up-to-date kitchen and laundry meant that the smells of drying clothes, hot bread or cabbage would not float through the upper rooms.

Everything was growing, but there was one element missing which had contributed to Thomas's success with the exhibition traffic: John Mason. This absence though was more to do with a personality clash than an inability for Thomas to pay a wage. But the end of the year saw even bigger issues of the *Excursionist* being circulated. Its readers were offered at least twelve tours, some of which were escorted, and circular train and boat tickets to Ireland and a new handbook. But the 'Emerald Isle', with its lack of prosperity, fierce religious conflict and political troubles, never found the place in Thomas's heart that Scotland had. For Thomas, Scotland had the advantages of a booming printing trade, ancient and new Protestant kirks bursting with evangelical fervour linked to worldwide missionary activity[5] – and trips did not involve a rough night crossing over the Irish Sea with the boat heaving sickeningly and the passengers thrown off balance. Thomas, though, did his best to promote Ireland. Many of his advertisements, at this stage, were more than a little flowery: 'From Derby to Dublin and back for 13s!

is an astounding announcement; and the artisan and mechanic classes may now regale their spirits with the pleasure libations of travel.' In another article he cautioned readers about the impositions of 'Irish car-drivers . . . as jovial a set of Jehus as ever took a whip in hand'.[6]

Dublin, with its well-proportioned Georgian terraces, still had the appearance of a late eighteenth-century city, but Ireland, the first country where potatoes had become a major food source, was in a pitiful state following the Potato Famine. The potato crop had first failed in 1845 because of blight, the fungus *Phytophthora infestans*, then again in 1846 and in 1848, the year in which Thomas had started tours to Ireland. People in western Ireland literally had nothing to eat, some surviving on weeds and grass. Out of a population of eight million, over a million died of starvation, while others perished in the dirty and overcrowded sailing ships which took a million survivors to America and Australia.

General interest in horticulture increased so much that Thomas continued to promote tickets for trains to annual harvest home and Michaelmas fairs, such as the Great Onion Fair at Birmingham on 30 September 1852, an ancient annual fair comparable to Nottingham's Goose Fair. In the old Bull Ring area,[7] onions of every description and size were displayed near theatrical booths, funfairs and menageries. Frivolity was such that the fairs were later moved from the centre of town because of 'shouting hobbledehoys, screaming girls, drunken men and shouting women, swarming in their hundreds . . . the public houses packed and customers having to fight their way in and out, the floors swimming in spilt beer; the general proceedings offering a spectacle of debauchery, drunkenness noise and blaspheming!'[8]

Thomas maintained this riotous event in his annual schedule – as is seen by colourful posters.[9] The fact that he was now including such destinations shows that he had relaxed some of his straight-laced attitudes even more. One reason for finding a middle ground was the need to pay his mortgage, another was the realisation that if he let personal scruples interfere, his lead in the travel business would be overtaken. Competition was appearing from all directions, so it was always reassuring when his position was recognised by some of the highest in the land. After the death of the 83-year-old Duke of Wellington on 14 September 1852 at Walmer Castle, Thomas was asked by some railway companies to bring crowds for his lying-in-state and the funeral procession.[10] The Iron Duke was to have one of the great pageants of the century – Britain's first public-event funeral. Careful embalming and the use of formaldehyde gave the organisers two months in which to stage-manage every detail. Just as it had broken all records with the biggest exhibition in history the previous year, the government would put on the grandest funeral ever held in the British Isles. Previously, the most expensive funeral London had ever witnessed had been on 23 November 1658 – Oliver Cromwell's seven-hour funeral procession, to Westminster Abbey, modelled on that of the King of Spain.

Now, nearly two centuries later, on 18 November 1852, over half a million men and women came to see another procession of 'unexampled magnificence'. Twelve black horses with black plumes pulled the black-draped hearse, following Wellington's empty-saddled horse with Wellington's black boots turned in the stirrups, in the traditional manner of funeral parades. The bells of St Paul's started their sonorous tolling; the streets were sombre. Black crepe even covered the muffled drums of the military bands which accompanied the solemn procession on its way from Chelsea Hospital to St Paul's Cathedral where the duke was interred beside Napoleon's other foe, Nelson. It augured well that Thomas was involved in what turned out to be a dress rehearsal for royal spectaculars.

In Leicester, come rain or shine, the building of Thomas's hotel and Temperance Hall went on at a frenzied pace. The hotel was the first of the two buildings to be finished. With much excitement the Cook family moved into the house that would remain the nucleus of their peripatetic family life for the next ten years. John Mason frequently spent long periods in Derby with his grandmother, who set such an example of hard work. Annie, with dark eyes as brown and as lively as Thomas's, was now nearly seven. With her eagerness to learn and her mischievous laughter, from the time she was a toddler Annie was Thomas's favourite. When he returned home at night the mood of the house lifted. But, like the household accounts, which were written up every night with each penny scrupulously accounted for, her childhood was ordered and predictable. She could never roam in the nearby country lanes and fields with other children, climb fences and trees or run wild. Instead, she was expected to help her mother in running the hotel and to spend many hours practising the piano or speaking French. She was adored and cosseted by her parents, but, compared with the rough and tumble school days of her brother, who had frequently laboured through the night, her life was easy but dull. Despite the drudgery of checking that the bedrooms had been properly cleaned, the never-ending laundry and the counting of the sheets and assorted linen, her days were a little too protected and organised. Sheltered by her parents, young Annie passed into her teens. She also fulfilled the role of buffer, as Thomas and Marianne both focused on her, and were seldom really alone together.

On 7 May 1853, advertisements for 'The New Temperance Hotel, Granby Street'[11] were followed by notices offering tickets for two shillings each for a public breakfast in the Temperance Hall. No other building in Leicester then had such facilities: a library, a lecture room, a hundred-foot-long hall, a gallery which seated 1,700 people with space for a magnificent orchestra above the stage, a committee room plus various other rooms. Here people could have everything – except a glass of wine.

Among those who inaugurated this temple of Temperance were shopkeepers and craftsmen, factory owners and factory workers, farmers and agricultural labourers, Catholics and Quakers, Baptists and Anglicans. Temperance followers, like the members of YMCA clubs, crossed the rigid lines that separated churches and social classes and widened the limited spheres of many different cross-sections of society. Rain on the opening day did not deter the curious crowds, many of whom had arrived in special trains. Thomas was praised in the many speeches. Another guest was Henry Lankester, the Cook family doctor and surgeon to the

Midland Railway Company, sixteen years younger than Thomas, who had moved from Poole and built up a large practice in the town. Like many of Thomas's friends he was a Nonconformist, a Liberal and an anti-drink campaigner.

Thomas advertised his hotel, saying, 'This new and beautiful edifice . . . with adaptation to the special character of hotel business . . . comprises commercial-room, dining-room, coffee-room, sitting-rooms, and numerous bedrooms, all newly furnished in style corresponding with the general appearance of the house . . .' Just how much he had gained by compromising and finding the middle ground is seen in his arrangements for 'those to whom tobacco-smoking may be offensive are free from the annoyance, a Room being appropriated to the use of smokers'.

'Mine host' was more and more absent, leaving the running of the hotel in the capable hands of Marianne. Each spring and summer Thomas was now spending at least two months in Scotland, shepherding nearly 5,000 visitors, alternating the east and west routes with four large train parties, each covering in all up to 2,000 miles by sea, rail and road. A pattern had begun in 1848 and, except for the year of the Great Exhibition, would go on until 1863. This was not just because Scotland was a popular tourist destination. Thomas had great affection for the country and made over sixty visits. His lifelong fascination with all aspects of printing and publishing added an extra dimension, and he enjoyed friendships with many Scottish printers and publishers, such as William Collins, who specialised in church history and pioneered school textbooks, and William Chambers, who was so impressed with the way Thomas escorted his troops of tourists that he called him 'the Field Marshal'. Scotland had always been in advance of England in literacy, education, printing and publishing so was a place of particular appeal to anyone with a passion for printing, like Thomas. A survey in 1795 had shown that out of a total population of 1.5 million, nearly 20,000 Scots had jobs connected with writing and publishing – and 10,500 with teaching.[12]

Scotland had the best state education in Europe. It shamed England, which, except for charity and religious schools, still had neither free nor compulsory schools. Before the Act of Union, throughout the seventeenth century, Scotland's parliament had passed various acts[13] to ensure that there would be schools and paid teachers in every parish. Education had progressed because of John Knox's insistence that everyone should be able to read both the Bible and his *Book of Discipline* of 1560, issued the same year that the Presbyterian religion became the official religion of Scotland. Apart from providing primary education, Scotland, in contrast to England's two universities, had four,[14] all open to a wide range of students[15] and all with lower tuition fees.

The year 1853 also included plans for Thomas to take shiploads of visitors to the Dublin Exhibition, organised to boost the ailing Irish economy after the Famine. He wrote that 'early in that year the late Sir C.P. Roney sent for me to Ireland, to confer and to cooperate with him in arranging for and working out a double system of excursion and tourist arrangements':

> Cheap excursions were to be worked by special trains, and a fortnight was to be allowed on the tickets; the tourist tickets were to be good for all trains, and valid for a month, at rates really double those of the excursions. I was to undertake the excursion department, whilst the various railway companies of England would take charge of the issue of tourist tickets with the view of encouraging travel in Ireland. I was to be able to give my travellers tickets for Cork, the Lakes of Killarney, Connemara, etc., at greatly reduced prices . . .

Thus was inaugurated the tourist system of Ireland, which, with certain modifications and extensions, has continued to this day.

Rival English agents were bringing tourists to the Dublin Exhibition, but Thomas organised both weekly and fortnightly excursions. At this stage he defined the difference between his excursion tickets and tour tickets: 'The term EXCURSION is generally used to designate a special trip, or trips, at very reduced prices, and under extraordinary arrangements . . . whilst the word TOUR takes a wider and more circuitous range, and provides the means of travelling at special rates, and by a more organized system, but taking the regular modes of conveyance.'[16]

There was also a major change in Melbourne. For the third time in five years Melbourne Hall had a new owner. When Lord Melbourne had died childless in 1848, his brother, Frederic, had become the 3rd Lord Melbourne, but he died five years later leaving no heirs. The title became extinct, but the property passed to their sister, Emily, who had married a second time, becoming the wife of Lord Palmerston, the most colourful and best-known foreign secretary in the nineteenth century. When in the government of his brother-in-law, Lord Melbourne, he had been responsible for setting up the first British consulate in Jerusalem and managed to bypass Turkish prohibition on building a Protestant church there by calling it 'the Consul's private chapel'. Emily's son-in-law, who had now inherited the title of Lord Shaftesbury, had been the moving force behind the promotion of British links with Jerusalem and also went to extraordinary lengths to protect and promote the Jews in Palestine.

TWENTY

Crimea

In February 1854, Thomas's grief had been acute when his mother Elizabeth Tivey, at the age of sixty-four, lay on her deathbed. Apart from his wife and Annie, it had been from her that Thomas had received physical affection. She had been the mainstay of the family. It had been through her strength that Thomas and his brothers had survived in those pre-railway days, cocooned in the little cottage with no money, few prospects and few possessions. Her instinctive reactions to events had kept them afloat and she had saved him from going down the mines. So great had been the bond between mother and son that Thomas had almost taken on the role of husband after her second widowhood. It was in him that she had confided, and they had often sat up at night talking, or she would listen while he read the Bible aloud. In stark contrast, John Mason's relationship with his own parents was cold and his feelings hesitant and ambivalent, but he became close to Elizabeth and again lived with her in Derby for a few years, when he had a job as a compositor. Her death left the two men and Simeon quite desolate. Simeon's Temperance Hotel in Corn Market was already being absorbed into her boarding house, which would become Simeon Smithard's Private Temperance Boarding House.

Elizabeth had wanted to be buried beside John Cook in the little graveyard behind the Baptist chapel in Melbourne. But the train did not yet go there from Derby, so a hired hearse-carriage, with Thomas guarding the black-draped coffin, made its way in the dull winter light over the hills to the village of her birth. John Mason and Simeon, who had seen much more of her in the past ten years, sat in front of the draped coffin.

This was the first occasion on which Thomas had returned since Lord and Lady Palmerston had inherited Melbourne Hall, but they were then in London, as Palmerston was attempting to limit Britain's spiralling involvement in the Crimean War. Within days of Elizabeth's funeral, in an effort to prop up the Turks and prevent the Russians holding Constantinople and the Straits, the first of many British troops set out for the East.

Fighting began on 14 September 1854 when the Russians crossed the Danube and the British and French laid siege to the port of Sebastopol, the great naval port of the Russian Empire in the Black Sea. The initial cause of the war was a long dispute over the holy places in Jerusalem and Bethlehem and resulted in a spiralling quarrel between the French emperor, the Russian tsar and the Turkish sultan over the right to hold the custody of the churches and holy places. Quarrels were heightened by the loss of the star over the grotto in Bethlehem and a tug of war over the keys for the Church of the Holy Sepulchre.

Napoleon III had insisted on confirmation of his role as the patron and defender of Roman Catholics in the Holy Land, and had sent an envoy to Sultan Abdul Medjid in Constantinople. Tsar Nicholas I also sent a series of demands, including the right to protect all Orthodox Christians throughout the Ottoman Empire, a right which had been held for centuries by the Greek Orthodox Church. Jerusalem's priorities were fought out in a war which soon embraced other issues. For nearly two centuries, the Russians had kept covetous eyes turned towards the Mediterranean, but France and Britain had blocked them.

When Britain had declared war on Russia in March, Britain had to turn to the bond market for finance. Gladstone went to Lionel Rothschild and arranged loans of undisclosed millions over two years. The whole country had been in such a state of patriotic fervour that in some places the Russian Emperor, Nicholas I, was burned in effigy. However, in Leicester, William Biggs, like other Liberals, was an opponent of England's involvement in the Crimean War and wrote a pamphlet entitled *Never Go to War for Turkey*. He, like John Bright, Richard Cobden and thousands of other Anti-Corn Law campaigners, joined the Peace Society and energetically denounced the war as un-Christian, against the principles of Free Trade and harmful to British interests. Bright said that 'the Angel of Death has been abroad throughout the land; you may almost hear the beating of his wings'. He blamed Palmerston and the aristocracy for deluding the people.

Ignoring the huge backing given to the Peace Society by many of his friends, Temperance supporters and Corn Leaguers, Symington in Market Harborough was pleased to provide the British troops in Crimea with pea flour to make soup.[1] This was used by Alexis Soyer, the chef at the Reform Club in London, who heroically went to Scutari and devised both a field kitchen and new methods of army cooking. Crimea was also the first war to use railways and telegraphs. Railway manufacturers in England sent track, locomotives and carts to build thirty-nine miles of tracks, the first railway ever used in battle. Seventeen engines pulled urgently needed supplies to the front.

Another innovation from the Crimean war were daily battle bulletins sent by the newly installed telegraph. From the shores of the Black Sea, each day the legendary Irish-born war correspondent, William Howard Russell, sent reports to *The Times*. The graphic and horrific tales of bungling, incompetence and the army's mismanagement had far-reaching consequences. His reports of the unnecessary deaths and extreme suffering, plus the photographs taken by one of the pioneer war photographers, Robert Fenton, made Crimea the first media war. It also helped bring Lord Aberdeen's government crashing down, and brought (much to the delight of the villagers in Melbourne) Palmerston in as prime minister. Most importantly, Russell's articles inspired Florence Nightingale, 'the lady with the lamp', a trained nurse whose family came from Nonconformist stock in Derbyshire. Russell also brought to the world press the gory descriptions of the gallant charge of the Light Brigade of Lord Cardigan, in which 673 cavalrymen rode down a valley of death and became immortalised by Alfred Tennyson with the lines, '"Forward the Light Brigade! | Charge for the guns!" he said. | Into the valley of Death, | Rode the six hundred.' A journalist as powerful as Russell had never held such sway before. He would soon cover the Indian Mutiny and the American Civil War, with his story of 'The Battle of Bull Run', and in fourteen years' time he would use the same ferocious passion to mock Thomas and his tourists in Egypt.

Soon after the emotional blow of his mother's death, Thomas took a brave step. He gave up his printing business so he could become a full-time tourist operator, having already been in travel commercially for ten years. Liverpool and Wales were augmented by more destinations and more trips to seaside resorts like Scarborough, with its steamboat trips, the town near Melbourne, Ashby-de-la-Zouch, with its baths, castle and pleasure grounds, the Lake District, the Isle of Man and Ireland.

Next, in 1855, with some trepidation Thomas decided to extend his business to non-English-speaking countries and he went off to France and Belgium to make advance preliminary arrangements. The highlight of the trip was to take visitors to the Universal Exhibition in the Champs Elysées. Napoleon III, not to be outdone by the English, was putting on an equivalent show to the great exhibition on a site of twenty-four acres with 20,000 exhibitors. Much to the surprise of many critics, Victoria and Albert accepted the invitation from the self-styled emperor and would make the first visit of a British monarch to France since 1431. This contrasted with the government of Victoria's grandfather, George III, who had ignored post-revolutionary French titles, and referred to the emperor as 'General Bonaparte'. So, as with his second Scottish trip, Thomas yet again followed the route of the Queen.

The *Excursionist* carried a proposal that 'on or about 7 August we will start an excursion to the Continent for a fortnight, on condition that we have guaranteed by a deposit of 20s each person before the 9th of July, not less than 50 passengers'. Thomas was again in an only too familiar role, fighting reluctant companies for group concessions. This time his struggle was with the controllers of the cross-Channel traffic. Eventually, unable to make bookings on direct trains from England, he planned a circuitous route on the Great Eastern Railway.

His first party set off on 4 July with much gaiety and expectation, not on the Calais to Dover route, but via Antwerp, Brussels, Aix-la-

Chapelle, Cologne, up the Rhine to Mayence, Mannheim, Frankfurt, Heidelberg, Baden-Baden, Strasbourg, Paris, Le Havre, Southampton, London and back to the Midland district. Apart from education and enjoyment, one of the aims of the trip was to cement a new era of peace. Travel, said Thomas, made people more tolerant of foreigners, and reduced the hatred and narrow-minded attitudes that led to wars.

Unfamiliar with either the languages or customs, he wrote:

> the difficulties . . . were neither few nor small. In making arrangements we had a hard fight with Continental Companies; and it required unceasing vigilance to keep on the good side of hotel keepers, money changers, booking clerks, and others with whom we had pecuniary transactions. The fluctuating rates of currencies; the wretched and uneven appearance of coins and notes; the conglomeration of francs, centimes, thalers, gold and silver groschen, pfennigs, florin and kreutzers; the loss inevitable on every transaction; and the still more vexatious loss occasioned by the advantage taken of John Bull's ignorance of the amounts and comparative value of 'small change;' – all these monetary perplexities caused continued annoyance to most of the Parties. . . .

Thomas warned his men of the temptations of Paris: 'The can-can is danced by paid performers, and is altogether an unnatural and forced abandon.' The women in the party were cautioned not to 'enter the cafes on the north side of the Boulevards, between the Grand Opera and the Rue St. Denis'. Meanwhile the French came from far and wide to welcome Queen Victoria, who caused a stir by going to Napoleon's marble tomb.[2]

After doing everything from exploring the Louvre to floating on a barge down the Seine, for two days Thomas's tourists became part of the excited throng jostling the exhibition hall in Paris to see the latest in inventions, design and art – even a collection of watercolours by the Scottish artist David Roberts, who had visited Egypt, Syria and Palestine in February 1839. With some new friends Roberts had trudged across the Sinai to the legendary ruins of Petra, arriving in

Jerusalem for Easter. On his return, a publisher had paid him 3,000 pounds sterling[3] for the lithographs, which became the three volumes of *The Holy Land, Syria, Idumea, Egypt, Nubia*, published in 1842 and 1849 and did much to stimulate interest in the Holy Land.

The next destination on Thomas's itinerary, Waterloo, was unexpected. Like many Baptists and followers of the Anti-Corn Law movement, he promoted pacifism and opposed the annual celebrations of the anniversary of Wellington's victory. But he could not hide his fascination for battles and battlefields. By charging tourists a supplement to accompany him to Waterloo, he again showed that he was compromising. It was already a place of pilgrimage. The frequently described relics of the battlefield – the bones of horses, hats, rags and scraps of leather and uniforms, account books, prayer books and papers – had long gone, but tourists were given graphic re-enactments. Sir Walter Scott had been followed by Victor Hugo, who also came there, immortalising the place in *Les Misérables*.

Already a competitor, Henry Gaze, who had escorted tours to Boulogne and Paris seven years before Thomas, had beaten Thomas to Waterloo. Gaze never conducted such large numbers as Thomas, but he accused him of copying his ideas and produced a pamphlet claiming that certain companies were apt to monopolise powers which are the property of all tourist agents. Rivalry between them persisted until the end of the century when Gaze and his business vanished.

Thomas's second party to Paris which set off on 16 August was easier to organise. 'In the former trip we had to keep re-booking the passengers at every stopping place but we have now provided a ticket which will take the tourist upwards of 1,000 miles without further trouble.' He added that by the close of the second excursion 'we had gained a pretty ready acquaintance with these varieties in currencies, coins, prices, &c; and this knowledge, though dearly purchased, we felt to be very essential'. The second trip also had the option of a trip which included Aix-la-Chapelle, Cologne, where they sailed on the Rhine to Coblenz, Mayence, Frankfurt and Heidelberg.[4]

Although these trips were a financial loss, Thomas stored up knowledge from them for later years, when he would send clients abroad with bilingual nanny-like tour leaders. Reluctantly he admitted that these 'were charming Tours, but denuded of much of their enjoyment by pecuniary losses'. A third trip failed to materialise, as did any further excursions to the continent for the following year. With resignation he wrote that 'we have abandoned all thoughts of invading France on a Tourist Campaign'.

Other parts of England were determined not to be outdone by the Great Exhibition. On 5 May 1856, the Exhibition of Art Treasures at Manchester was opened by the Prince Consort. Everything was ready except the crowds. When the desperate organisers heard that Thomas was in Oban escorting a tour to Scotland they sent 'Mr. Deane, as Chief Commissioner of the Manchester Fine Arts Exhibition, especially to ask my assistance in promoting excursions to that exhibition . . . I completed arrangements with the Scottish Companies for a number of trains on their lines . . .' The more he was told by pessimistic railway managers that all efforts to move Scottish people would be futile, the more determined he became and, as Thomas said, 'to the astonishment of those gentlemen, the trains were thoroughly successful, and were patronized by many of the most influential citizens of the chief places in the country'. In a few days he set up tours from all parts of Scotland, from the Lancaster and Carlisle District, Maryport, Newhaven, Broughton, Furness and Ulverston.

Later, he wrote:

I instantly went to work, submitted my plans to the Scotch companies, to the Lancaster and Carlisle, and to the North-Eastern. The canny Scot who commanded the chief route told me it was all in vain. I could not move the Scotch people, as it was evident they cared but little about the Manchester Exhibition. They . . . only got thirty passengers for a special train. I pleaded hard for a few concessions in fares and travelling arrangements, but they were only granted on condition that I gave a guarantee of

£250 per train. That condition I accepted for each of four weekly excursions, the first of which yielded an aggregate of £500, and for each of the other three I covered my guarantee, exclusive of large additions from other contributory lines, such as the Glasgow and South-Western, the Lancaster and Carlisle, the Maryport and Carlisle, the Furness, and other lines of the Lake district.

In six weeks Thomas took 26,000 visitors to the exhibition. As he said, 'it was a singular coincidence that the last 26,000 shillings saved the exhibition from loss'. When the exhibition closed on 5 October, it had clocked up 1,335,000 visitors and taken £100,000 at the gate. The organisers, recognising that Thomas had saved the exhibition 'from pecuniary loss', presented him with a silver snuffbox. Little did they know of his horror of smoking. It was kept and remained 'as bright and unpolluted to-day as it was twenty-one years ago'.

Faced with the problem of finding comfortable accommodation for the 'uncertain number of passengers who crowded upon us at the departure of the Train' he set up 'Moonlight Trips', designed for workers who would sacrifice two nights' sleep in a bed to ensure a day at the exhibition: 'The moon was approaching the full, and I was moonstricken, and advertised a "moonlight trip to the Manchester Exhibition". The neighbourhood of Newcastle caught the infection, and by the light of the moon we filled eighty large carriages on the first night and had to follow up the trip . . . By the next moon we tried Scarborough, Malton, and other distant places', and on the first night there were so many passengers that they needed from ninety to nearly one hundred carriages.

TWENTY-ONE

The Second and Third Decades

Railway travelling is travelling for the Million: the humble may travel, the rich may travel. Taste and Genius may look out of third-class windows, meekly rebuking Vice and Ignorance, directly opposite them.

Thomas Cook, *Excursionist*, July 1854

Thousands in Leicester were in dire need during the terrible period of winter of 1855/6. Again Thomas showed that he was loyal to his goal to hearten the poor and help them to strive to improve their lot. With £500 raised by public subscription, he purchased vegetables and meat, and supervised a make-shift kitchen. Night after night, as merchant and chief cook, he produced around 15,000 gallons of 'very superior soup' to be carted through the town three mornings a week. Ever since the Society for the Poor and Wilberforce had set up soup kitchens in London in the late 1790s, at times of hardship country parsons doled out nourishing meat broth.

Soup kitchens are just one example of Thomas's philanthropy. During one of his many regular steamer trips to Iona, he had collected more than £50 from the passengers for the Ionians to 'replenish their Library and to stock them with Fishing Boats, Lines, Nets, etc.'. This led the *Daily Bulletin* of Glasgow to praise Thomas's gesture, saying that 'to these islanders Mr. Cook and his friends may be more useful than many Dukes'.[1] The names of two of the boats purchased showed the appreciation of the islanders: *Brotherly Love* and *Thomas Cook*.

Frenetically busy with home arrangements, taking parties to Land's End and the new romantic destination of the Scilly Islands, Thomas still did not neglect tours close to Leicester. Perhaps he was prompted by his tours to Land's End passing through Exeter in Devon, but whatever the reason, soon the Earl of Exeter's magnificent Burghley House, between Leicester and Peterborough, the largest palace of the Elizabethan Age, was on his itinerary. Lord Exeter, a train-hater, keenly welcomed all horse-drawn coaches. Thomas's tickets for outings to grand houses were still selling well but nothing stopped petty mocking. To counter critics Thomas copied an article from a local newspaper, praising his tourists after a visit to Burghley House. The housekeeper had 'not witnessed nor heard of a single act of rudeness or indiscretion; and on examining the rooms she could not perceive a trace of dirt, or disarrangement of any article'. Never immune to exploiting the kudos of rubbing shoulders with the aristocracy, Thomas added that, in his special meeting with the Marquess and Marchioness of Exeter, they had invited him to return, 'so admirably did the visitors behave'.

In July, remembering his own deprived childhood, Thomas arranged Juvenile Excursions to Scotland with two packed trains from Newcastle, Sunderland and South Shields doing the return trip to Edinburgh in just one long day. He wanted young people to be introduced to

the scenes with which many of the more intelligent and well-read have been familiarized by history, tale, and song . . . Seven years ago we proposed to take down from the Midland towns a Special Train of youths for the modest sum of 5s from Leicester, Derby and Nottingham to Edinburgh and back. Hoping to meet with a ready response, we canvassed every hotel and lodging-house in Edinburgh for accommodation, and arranged for terms exceedingly moderate – generally fourpence to sixpence per head for sleeping accommodation, and about the same sums for breakfast . . . We found bed room[s] in Edinburgh alone for 1000 upon those terms. But all our enthusiastic dreams were exploded by a flat denial by one of the Companies.

As Thomas recounted, 'The day was a glorious one for the Northern youths who made the trip, only marred by the Tea provided in the

Corn Exchange by a person of Edinburgh, which was a dead failure and has left us two years of annoyance and litigation.'

Severe ups and downs in the economy for much of Victoria's reign made the demands for Thomas's business unpredictable. Even before the general recession of 1857, many trades were hurt by the high interest rates of the previous three years; for instance, by the winter of 1856–7 about 25,000 building workers in London alone were unemployed.[2]

The year 1859 saw a book shaking the very foundations of science and religion. Charles Darwin published his *On the Origin of Species*, explaining evolution by natural selection, the theory that all life on earth had evolved slowly over millions of years 'at hazard and at rare intervals'. The book, the most controversial publication of the nineteenth century, provoked Disraeli to shout the much-repeated question, 'Is man an ape or angel? Sir I am on the side of the angels.' One clergyman called Darwin the most dangerous man in England. Darwin's theory was the second blow to the roots of Christianity. Geologists' proof that the earth could not have been made in six days, or created in the year 4004 BC, showed that parts of the Bible were mere legends. This threat to the established order alarmed men like Thomas, and, odd though it seems, General Charles Gordon. Both were soon to see for themselves the historic proof of biblical events in the Holy Land.

By 1861 Paxton was again luring Thomas into a new scheme: a six-day excursion over Whitsuntide to Paris with the London Committee of Working Men, of which Paxton was the president. The idea, as described by Thomas, was for workers to 'shake hands with the Parisian *ouvriers*' and assure them of their feelings of good will and that 'the British people have an earnest desire to live on terms of amity with neighbouring states'. Securing over a thousand cheap and clean beds was fraught with obstacles. Thomas had gone to Paris to organise accommodation:

I paid a visit to that city, with the view of facilitating the visits of English Excursionists, by providing for them cheap railway

135

arrangements and suitable homes in Paris. I also travelled, in anticipation, from Paris to Brussels, Antwerp, &c., with the desire of combining Continental Tours with a series of Trips to the Exhibition. But in these projects I only met with very partial encouragement from the Railway Administrations of France and Belgium; and the English Companies had agreed upon unalterable terms betwixt London and Paris. Nevertheless, I was encouraged by the public spirit of Mr Church, Superintendent at that time of the Eastern Counties Railway, and of the Steamboats plying between Harwich and Antwerp; and with the hearty and liberal co-operation of that gentleman, I announced two Excursions from all parts of the Eastern Counties Railway to Belgium, the Rhine, Germany, and France.

On 17 May, six years after his last loss-making French trip, he set off again with 1,673 tourists, many of whom had never been out of their own counties. They were all attracted by a London to Paris return fare of just £1 and the sense of adventure promised in Thomas's posters and pamphlets for 'The Great International Excursion to Paris'. Among the pioneer tourists were assorted groups from every walk of life, including 200 men from Titus Salt's cotton works in Bradford,[3] plus a group of rumbustious high-spirited Cockneys, and a journalist and a photographer from the *Illustrated London News*.

Just as 1841 had been a milestone in tourism in England, 1861 was a milestone in popular tourism abroad. Nothing before competed with it in size. Thomas was widening the frontiers of people who otherwise would have had limited horizons, who might not have left the safety of their own town and who were now enjoying climbing into boats and crossing the Channel. It was not just the poor whose families for generations had seldom ventured from their inland parish. Even in the eighteenth century Horace Walpole said that George III had not seen the sea until the age of thirty-four, and in the 1830s there were many boys in the sixth form at Rugby who had never seen the seaside.[4]

Everyone had a great time, and the steamer returning to England was 'a scene of enthusiastic excitement, expressed in song, speech, and hearty cheers'. It was a new epoch, a new dawn, but Thomas was left with a bill for £120 for advertising and again lost money. The whole trip was written off as a 'labour of love minus profit'.

Thomas returned to London to a different sort of trouble. On 6 October *The Times* printed a leader denouncing 'excursion mania', and further, under the heading 'Eagle Murder', reported the shooting of an eagle in Iona for which Thomas was responsible. He managed to respond well to the criticism about excursions, saying that 'every watering place on the English coast has been glutted with gossiping [*sic*], flirting, listless indolence . . . Bosh! Such thunder will never terrify anyone who understands what it is to travel in the Highlands.'[5]

It was easier to defend tourists rushing off on their rambles than to explain away the death of the powerful eagle. Thomas's explanation that the bird was 'to form the centre of a case of ornithological specimens from Iona for visitors to see if a hotel was built on the island' proved unconvincing and did not lessen the consternation among ornithologists. Thomas had not shot the bird himself, but the unfortunate incident was a bad omen for him. Future tours to Scotland were looking less promising.

Then the whole country went into mourning. Victoria's 21-year marriage, one of the happiest in the history of royal marriages, was over. On 14 December 1861, Albert, aged forty-two, died at Windsor Castle. His death was attributed to typhoid fever, but it may have been a worsening stomach complaint. Devastated, Victoria sought seclusion as a grieving widow, but ensuring that Albert's name was to be commemorated in many ways. The most elaborate and expensive monument ever created in England was planned on the site of the Crystal Palace itself,[6] opposite the new Albert Hall. Designed by Sir Gilbert Scott,[7] the 175-foot-high memorial, with the winged angels holding gilt trumpets, had twelve heads representing the arts and sciences: Michaelangelo, Wren, Inigo Jones, Raphael, Beethoven, Mendelssohn, Goethe, Schiller, Milton, Shakespeare, Tasso and Dante.[8]

That grim December of 1861, the month of Albert's death and the official mourning period, coincided with John Mason's wedding.

Described then as a very dapper little man, thickset, with a small beard, he could well have remained a bachelor, as many people were cautious of being close to him. At the age of twenty-eight, his presence was formidable and, if provoked, he had a fearful temper, but the bride-to-be, Emma Hodges – the eldest daughter of a Unitarian and a prosperous elastic web manufacturer, who lived in a sizeable house in Mayfield Road, Stoneygate – was radiantly happy.[9] The extended Hodges family had earlier enjoyed an illustrious association with another Cook connected with travel and adventure. In the eighteenth century William Hodges (1744–97) had been the artist on board the *Resolution* on Captain James Cook's second voyage to the South Pacific and Antarctic. As the banns for John Mason's wedding had already been posted, despite Albert's death, the marriage took place on the day after Boxing Day in the 'Great Meeting' chapel. Like her mother-in-law, Emma conceived almost immediately and the first of their five children, three sons and two daughters, was born in September 1862.

On the wedding certificate John Mason's occupation was listed not as a printer or travel agent, but as 'corn dealer'. Five years before the wedding, he had showed that he had his *own* methods of business. No longer dominated by the strong personality of his father, he took a job with the Midland Railways as superintendent of their excursion traffic on a salary of £75 per annum, a position he held for three years. Although in competition with his father, he was also in a good position to give him business.

In the early 1850s, Thomas's second decade as a travel agent business had started on a high note with the construction of the Temperance Hotel and Temperance Hall, but he began his third decade in 1861 with less optimism. His religion, which had empowered him through boom and bust and widened his horizons, now scarcely lifted him from the despair caused by the Scottish railway companies dispensing with his services. Sadly, he wrote that 'a thick Scotch mist overshadowed our Northern prospects; in England it was doubtful if there would be sufficient local traffic to justify the running of provincial Excursions; the Railway companies we usually served resolved to keep the London Trains under their own management, and not to employ agency'.[10]

To counter this, in London he again leased premises as temporary hotels for the International Exhibition at South Kensington. The new pavilion, covering 23 acres between Cromwell Road and Exhibition Road, lacked both the elegance of Paxton's Crystal Palace and the energy of Prince Albert but continued the theme of uniting art, science and manufacturing. The land was the site for the Natural History Museum, the Science Museum and the Victoria & Albert Museum, to be built with profits from the Great Exhibition.

Yet again Thomas had to compromise. When he was not offered rail excursion concessions to take passengers to the exhibition, he leased large properties and set up boarding houses which would accommodate all classes of assorted visitors, including 200 rooms in two newly built red-brick tenements in the Fulham Road on the border of Chelsea and South Kensington, across the road from Pelham Crescent – 'convenient for Exhibition Clubs, Family parties and for Visitors of both Sexes . . . Relations or Friends, in Parties of two or six persons, may have a Tenement to themselves . . . There are large cupboards . . . for storing Carpet Bags, etc.' He spent £1,000 on furniture and each room accommodated between two and six people. As each room 'had not yet been occupied', each was 'perfectly clean',[11] and he added that they were 'free of bugs'.[12] Bed and a 'plain substantial breakfast' cost two shillings, and a smoking room was provided for those 'who fancied they could not exist without a little smoke'.[13] Nothing was forgotten – even a raised stage in the courtyard for open-air meetings. Customers wanting superior services could pay six shillings a day for bed, breakfast and tea, both 'substantial Meals with Meats' and go to a 'Select Boarding and Lodging House at No. 23 Ovington-square', completed only ten years earlier, not far from the Albert Hall.

The gala on the first day of his new enterprise on 30 April 1862 had two strands: one was a Temperance meeting, complete with a minister, ritual, speeches and music; the other was enlivened with the Chelsea Drum and Fife Band playing under a giant flag bearing the words 'Exhibition Visitors' Home'. So great was the demand that each night the refreshment hall was converted into a temporary dormitory with a hundred beds. By the end of the summer Thomas could boast that more than 20,000 visitors had stayed in this boarding house, many more than one night.[14] Guests had included parties from Fry & Sons, the chocolate manufacturers, coal miners from West Retford collieries, hands from Allbright & Wilson's chemical factory near Birmingham, plus forty Italians from Turin who stayed for six weeks, sixty-five Germans from Mecklenburgh for a fortnight and visitors from Paris, Toulouse and other places abroad. Some also came to attend the International Temperance Convention, which was held there – mostly in the open air on 2 September.

Ovington Square, too, was booked out. The initial accommodation was enlarged with five more 'First Class Houses', in Pelham Place, Pelham Crescent and Sydney Place. All these, according to the *Excursionist*, were 'conducted under the immediate direction and control of Mrs. and Miss Cook'. Thomas now opened himself up to more competition. As the circulation of the *Excursionist* was increasing, he decided to accept outside advertisements as an extra source of revenue.

At the same time as Marianne and Annie were looking after the boarding houses, Thomas was exercising all his theatrical skills and salesmanship at his stall, the Scotch Court, outside the exhibition hall, among the cluster of booths and stalls of the Exhibition Bazaar, which bypassed the ban on sales inside the main hall itself. Thomas's stall still captured the resurgent interest in Scotland's history, particularly in its Celtic past, with everything from Celtic jewellery to fabrics and mementoes of its history, music, culture, cuisine and printing. Lithographs of Scottish and other celebrities included the greatest historian of the age, Lord Macaulay, and Prince Albert. Visitors could buy 'The Excursionist' Tweed Suit at forty-five shillings, eat Edinburgh rock, Scottish shortbread or Edinburgh toffees, purchase books and maps to study, and shawls and kilts. Tartans, of course, were prominently displayed. There was also 'An

Office for the Issue of Scottish Tourist Tickets – all by Commission . . . from his long and familiar acquaintance with most parts of Scotland.'[15] Thomas showed his determination. He may have been stopped from escorting groups to Scotland, but he could still sell hundreds, indeed thousands, of return tickets.

TWENTY-TWO

A Leap in the Dark

Ten years after Thomas had moved Marianne and Annie into his imposing hotel in Leicester, he shifted them, along with his headquarters, into 59 Great Russell Street,[1] part of the Duke of Bedford's estate in fashionable Bloomsbury in the heart of London. Owning a lease on this charming Georgian townhouse delighted Thomas in many ways. For instance, gas had not been widely used in London until about 1860, but the Bedford estate had designed an innovative method to distinguish the houses at night, as each fanlight above the main front doors was distinctly different from its neighbours.

No. 59 was typical of the tall houses of London's middle-class families. Here the occupants and rooms were kept clean by servants who slept in attics and ate and lived in the kitchen basements, who had to trudge up and down four flights of stairs with water from a pump in the basement. Thomas's hotels in Leicester and in London, perpetual struggle though they were, brought in a steady income. They were run as one enterprise, as shown on a surviving printed invoice headed 'London, Cook's British Museum Boarding House, 59 Great Russell St., Bloomsbury, Leicester, Cook's Commercial & Family Temperance Hotel, 63 Granby-Street', which shows a total of £1 4s for three days. Thomas, Marianne and Annie would now centre their lives in London for the next thirteen years.

Not only was Thomas stretched between Leicester and London, but his feet were in two camps. Although always aware of working-class sentiments and traditions, he constantly readapted his principles and inclinations. Compromise as he did, he still refused to go to theatres or to advertise them in his newspaper. He continued, like all strict Baptists, to look askance at the immoderation of

142

modern entertainment, especially playhouses, music halls, dice, cards, gambling, church raffles and theatres. Plays were dismissed for their sexual and bawdy content.[2] In his forty years of setting up package holidays Thomas avoided anything that he considered was hedonistic or *louche*. Even when Sir Arthur Sullivan's light operas with lyrics by Sir William S. Gilbert were the rage and *Trial by Jury*, *HMS Pinafore*, and *The Pirates of Penzance* took London by storm, Thomas would not attend.

The year 1862, though, saw Thomas's transformation from 'provincial gentleman' to 'London gent' with a black bowler hat, folded umbrella and frock coat. This was a classic case of putting a good face on things, a way of lessening the uncertainties of his status. His awareness that clothes were also a way of adding style and glamour to travelling resulted in the frock-coats which later became a uniform for his tour guides. But sartorial elegance escaped Thomas – a photograph of him sitting on the ground reveals loose socks that had slipped down to his ankles.

In Great Russell Street, limits on advertising and business announcements meant that Thomas could only have a discreet brass plate near the front door indicating either the boarding house or his travel business. As the Leicester office was also kept going, Thomas managed to squeeze his London office staff into a conservatory at the back of the building where, as he explained later in his memoir, *Travelling Experiences*, his tourist business 'took root and flourished, though frequently assailed by the pelting missiles of a portion of the Metropolitan press. But there the late Charles Dickens found me out and sent one of his subalterns to collect notes for a commendatory article in "All the Year Round". The same representative of Mr Dickens afterwards travelled with one of my Italian parties and gave a graphic description of the tour in "Temple Bar".'

Ties with Leicester were easy to maintain as there were daily trains from King's Cross[3] to the Midlands. If the pavements were not crowded, and it was not foggy or icy, the distance to King's Cross from Great Russell Street could be covered in about twenty minutes. The route took Thomas past squares, shops, offices, grand terraces, shabby houses and slums similar to those in Dickens's *Oliver Twist* where some of London's prostitutes plied for business.[4] Many places were in easy walking distance from Great Russell Street. A five-minute stroll through crowds of people jostling one another's umbrellas took him to Oxford Street, at that time well on the way to becoming London's premier shopping destination. The new Cook home was also just around the corner from London University, the first university in England to open its doors to Nonconformists and Jews.[5]

In the centre of the terrace, each front window of 59 Great Russell Street looked across a courtyard into the British Museum, repository of one of the world's greatest collections. Its acres of exhibits already included the Elgin Marbles and some of the legendary wonders of ancient Egypt, including the Rosetta Stone, mummies and relics dug up by funerary archaeologists. Shelley's best-known sonnet, 'Ozymandias', with its haunting lines, 'My name is Ozymandias, King of Kings', was inspired by his visits.[6] Dominating the galleries was the colossus of Ramses, the legendary Egyptian king who spoke with Moses at the time of the Hebrews' exodus from Egypt. Other ancient relics from the shores of the Nile displayed at the museum also acted as the muse for the windows, 'Adam, Flight into Egypt', executed by Edward Burne-Jones. The Shelleys had stayed in the street at No. 119 before they sailed for Italy in 1819, as had Keats, further along at No. 20.

Thousands flocked to see the staggering antiquities in Great Russell Street and nobody, let alone a seeker of knowledge like Thomas, could live there and not know the history of Egypt. The great domed reading room, inspired by Paxton,[7] had opened in 1857 with the largest library in the world. In the earlier building, Montague House, Dickens, attempting to supplement some of the shortcomings of his schooling, had been a frequent visitor. For an amateur historian like Thomas, Great Russell Street was more than a suitable place to live. The most famous of all the visitors to the street, though, was a 44-year-old German refugee, Karl Marx. When Thomas gazed through the net curtains he might have seen a short, plump, bearded man walking through the iron gates daily to spend his day inside writing, which would result in five years in his *magnum opus*, *Das Kapital*. In 1862, of course, Marx's name was not well known, nor was that of Thomas's new neighbour, the painter Edward Burne-Jones. Burne-Jones had moved there after his marriage to Georgiana in 1860 and would live there until he moved to Fulham in 1867. John Ruskin, a vocal critic of mass tourism, was a patron of Burne-Jones, and when Thomas moved in, Ruskin, Burne-Jones and Georgiana were touring near Rome. Illness marred long periods of Burne-Jones's career, but it was when Georgiana was deliriously ill after contacting scarlet fever and giving birth to a child prematurely that Ruskin paid to have a carpet of deep sawdust laid outside the Burne-Joneses house to soften the noise of the horses' hooves,[8] as the sound of metal-shod horses' hooves and iron-shod wheels was usually constant.

Streets were often so crowded with pedestrians that it was hard to manoeuvre past those dawdling in pairs. The proliferation of railways, the centralisation of commerce, and the transfer of the financial centre from Amsterdam to London all meant that the capital had grown from less than a million in 1801 to about two and a half million by 1850. Railways were making commuting easier. Daily trains brought office workers from new suburbs everywhere, from Surrey to Essex. When the Metropolitan, the world's first underground railway, opened in 1863, it did for London what rural railways had done for the country.

In the same year Thomas was suddenly confronted with tremendous change. When the Scottish railway managers broke off all their remaining engagements with him, he could no longer afford to maintain his issuing offices north of the border. Leicester to London routes with return tickets – covering transport, accommodation and meals, the first 'package' tours[9] – were not enough; he decided to risk another challenge. The pessimism that caused him to write that he would confine 'operations for a few years' to the West country'[10] was brief. His substitute for Scotland as a destination would be the snow-clad mountains of Switzerland. Again Paxton helped out. This time it did not take long to convince the London, Brighton and South Coast Railway to give discounted prices to Newhaven.

On 26 June 1863, with between 130 and 150 tourists, Thomas and his assistant, John Ripley, a former Temperance missionary in Leicester, arrived in Dieppe on the first leg of their journey to the Swiss Alps via Paris. In Paris they split up, with about sixty-two men and women going via Dijon to Geneva and then on to Chamonix to conquer the summits of the Swiss Alps. One member of the party, Miss Jemima Morrell, who kept a diary, wrote of a visit to Leukerbad and the Gemmi pass by way of a narrow zigzag path. Neither she nor another woman was inhibited by crinolines or corsets from climbing over precipices or indulging in a luncheon in Geneva of ten courses: soup, salmon with cream sauces, sliced roast beef with browned potatoes, boiled fowl served on rice, sweetbreads, roast fowl, salad, artichokes, plum pudding steeped in brandy and a choice of sweets.[11]

Crossing and recrossing the Alps, penetrating into the very heart of Switzerland, brought so many new clients that by the end of the first season alone more than 500 Cook tourists had climbed over the Swiss mountains. Some overcame Switzerland's lack of plentiful railways with a sledge and a coach drawn by thirteen mules. Tours covered almost every part of Switzerland so that the holiday-makers could travel independently, all the year round, using Interlaken and Lucerne as the main centres. Deals with innkeepers and hotel proprietors resulted in good rooms and meals at competitive prices. Swiss travellers were from the growing middle classes and expected better accommodation than many earlier customers.

The Swiss seized on this new trade to supplement their income from cheese-making and watch-making. As Thomas said, 'That which took *tens* of years in Scotland seems to have been acquired at a single bound in Switzerland, where "Cook's Tours" already rank among the Institutions of the Confederation.' Foreign languages he certainly lacked, but his friendships with hoteliers grew and enabled Thomas to put his Swiss accommodation arrangements on a solid basis. Ironically, it was easier for him to organise tours in Switzerland than it would be in America where there were no language difficulties.

Switzerland's imposing peaks, especially the Eiger, the Jungfrau and the Wetterhorn had recently been made even more enticing by the poetry of Byron, Shelley and other writers of the Romantic Movement. Earlier, they had been brought to the fore by English mountaineers, whose exploits thrilled all of Europe and in 1857 led to the establishment of the exclusive Alpine Club.[12] Until then climbing mountains was something the Swiss did only if they lost sheep or were hunting ibex, but they were pleased to guide adventurous visitors high into the cloudy heights if they were paid. Mass tourism, welcomed by the Swiss, was derided by the members of the exclusive Alpine Club, who included Matthew Arnold, John Ruskin and the Old Etonian Sir Leslie Stephen.[13] Having made mountain climbing an exclusive sport, they were now worried about their 'playground' being overrun. The idea that the Alps should be trampled on only by the aesthetic elite, and not by the philistine multitude, was taken up by Sir Leslie, whose first wife had been Thackeray's daughter, Minnie. A former Evangelical clergyman, a muscular Christian and passionate mountaineer and climber who had made several notable ascents of Swiss peaks, he was also the editorial mastermind behind the *Dictionary of National Biography*,[14] editor of the *Alpine Journal* and in 1882 to be the father of Virginia Woolf.

Later, in his book on Switzerland, *Playground of Europe*,[15] Stephen slated Thomas's 'Cockney travellers' and those who were just hill walkers and pressers of flowers, not mountaineers with rope, axe and alpenstock. With sarcasm he wrote of 'innumerable valleys which have not yet bowed the knee to Baal, in the shape of Mr. Cook and his tourists'. Stephen's argument was quoted by Ruskin in the *Cornhill Magazine* – that understanding art and natural beauty required much study, something not possible for people who spent all their time working.[16] Ruskin also complained that all his 'dear mountain grounds and treasure-cities . . . are long destroyed by the European populace'.[17]

For a few weeks in 1864, the swashbuckling Italian national patriot, Giuseppe Garibaldi, who, after years of uprisings and fighting,[18] had triumphantly led his 'red shirts' to victory in the War of Italian Unification, became London's hero. He radiated a romantic aura which many in the working class, seeking to achieve political rights themselves, found intoxicating. The new Italian government had glamour unlike any other, even boasting Giuseppe Verdi as a member in the first national parliament.[19] Wherever he went in London Garibaldi was overwhelmed by rapturous cheers. Crowds larger than those seen for years thronged the streets when he arrived for a state visit. Everyone from Lord Tennyson to trade unionists clambered to meet this champion of nationalism who had struck a blow for the freedom of his country. The Duchess of Sutherland threw a lavish reception for him at Stafford House.

Sixteen years earlier, in 1848–9, Giuseppe Mazzini and Garibaldi had led an assault on Rome which, after a few initial small victories, failed. Napoleon III had sent large numbers of French troops to reinforce the Pope's army of Zouaves and Swiss Guards. Eventually most of the Italian states united and Victor Emmanuel II was proclaimed king. But Garibaldi's vision of a totally united Italy was stopped by the Pope, who remained sovereign of the state of Rome, and by Venice, which was still controlled by the Austrians. As the Pope had excommunicated Garibaldi and his followers, he had a Protestant pastor for his troops, Alessandro Cavazzi, an Italian ex-priest who had gone from being a Roman Catholic to embracing Methodism.

The Liberals, who were then a bulwark against the Catholic Church in Britain, rejoiced in the victory of Italian nationalism and longed for the decline of the temporal power of the Pope.[20] Crowds surged forward to touch Garibaldi as he rode in a state procession and afterwards thousands of children lined the streets and chanted, 'We'll get a rope | And hang the Pope: | So up with Garibaldi!' One 'victory fighter' absent from the parade, though, was Giuseppe Mazzini who lived near the Fulham Road, an easy walk from the home of his friend Thomas Carlyle. He had distanced himself from Garibaldi's movement, disgusted at his monarchist tendencies and his need for royal ritual and splendour.

In July, only six months after Garibaldi's visit to London, Thomas crossed the Alps into Italy, anticipating expansion, as he put it, 'to this land of natural beauty, art and music'. Having managed a good reduction of fares on condition that there were not less than fifty in a party, he inaugurated a series of tourist tickets, which combined most of the railways, steamboats and diligences. 'These', Thomas said, 'were the first circular tickets issued in this country . . .' His party of more than ninety ended up going from the Coliseum in Rome, the catacombs and places connected with the romance of Keats, Shelley, Browning and Byron on to Naples, Pompeii and Mt Vesuvius. As Thomas wrote, 'In 1864 . . . I had the pleasure of conducting two Italian parties – one as far as Florence and Leghorn, and the other to Rome, Naples, &c. This arrangement was supplemental to my Swiss Tours, and the combined results of the trips to Switzerland and Italy gave a total of about 1100 tourists. My Swiss Tickets grew in favour with the public, and while the number of tickets issued was double that of the previous year, about half as many [again] as in 1863 availed themselves of my personal company on their travels.'

In each group there was usually someone who detested the Italian fare. Unable to eat such exotic dishes as octopus stewed in its own ink, let alone spaghetti, they longed for stodgy steak-and-kidney pie. Other irritations were also the inevitable mosquitoes and fleas, some of which responded to 'KEATING'S Persian Insect Destroying Powder' advertised in the *Excursionist* as 'unrivalled in destroying fleas, bugs, emmets, flies, cockroaches, beetles, gnats, mosquitoes, moths in furs, and every other species of insect in all stages of metamorphosis. A small quantity of it placed in the crevices of a bedstead will destroy bugs . . . It is indispensable to Travellers by rail or steamboat and visitors to the seaside . . .'

Even though, as Thomas said, for several years 'our way was through brigand-infested districts, when military escorts protected us', Italy was a source of warmth, health and sensuous inspiration for many English writers, and those who could afford to spend time there, including such writers as Robert Browning and his ailing wife, Elizabeth. The possessive attitude of the English towards Italy then is illustrated by Browning:

Italy, my Italy!
. . . Open my heart and you will see
Graved inside of it, 'Italy'.
Such lovers old are I and she
So it always was, so shall ever be![21]

There were now so many English people living on both the Mediterranean coast and the hinterland that the area had been given to the Bishop of Gibraltar as a new diocese in 1842, and Anglican churches were built everywhere from Nice, Monte Carlo and Cairns to San Remo. Some churches became such little pockets of England that they assumed the air of consulates.

Meanwhile, Thomas had changed the adversity of a closed door in Scotland into a thriving industry. His trips to Switzerland were altering the country's economy and the use of its snow-covered foothills and mountains. No longer were they just used as marginal agricultural land. Simple wooden homes expanded into guest chalets and hotels to accommodate not only Thomas's visitors but also the thousands of others who independently, or with other tour companies, followed his routes.

TWENTY-THREE

America at Last!

Taking large numbers of tourists overseas was full of problems, and germs. However, nothing obstructed Thomas's plans – not even the lack of amenities, such as public toilet facilities at destinations, let alone flush lavatories, running water, hot water, restaurants or quick communications. Railway carriages usually had no facilities such as restaurants or lavatories. Hygiene was often basic or nonexistent; the need to wash hands was not established until Joseph Lister proved his germ theory in 1867. Many places washed dishes in cold water,[1] and fleas, another source of disease, often accompanied passengers. Even primitive domestic refrigeration or ice-boxes were not common until the end of the century, so the freshness of food was a concern for travellers. With no telephones, reservations and messages had to be by letter. Weeks could pass waiting for confirmations. The electric telegraph, inaugurated in 1843 between Paddington and West Drayton, was not practical for another two years; the first underwater cable from England to France was not completed until 1851. Another decade passed before cables were laid across the Atlantic in 1866. Cables to Australia followed in 1872. Telegrams and cables were expensive and were used solely for special messages and events. Writing letters by hand was laborious, and typewriters were not in general use until the end of the 1870s. There was no commercial telephone service in London until 1879, nor long-distance calls to Paris until 1891. All this meant that Thomas's office work was time-consuming, as were his marketing and advertising to attract passengers.

Women were one of the mainstays of Thomas's overseas trips. Hordes of females lacking an escort – some spinsters, others widows – purchased his excursion tickets. As it was then socially unacceptable for any woman with aspirations to being 'a young lady' to travel without a chaperone, and walking in the streets alone was unwise, women outnumbered men on the majority of the earlier trips. His tours offered a safety umbrella to single women asserting their independence and exploring the world. Long journeys were said to be morally, physically and sexually dangerous. Thomas wrote:

> the oft-reiterated question: Is it safe and proper for ladies to join in Highland tours? . . . of the thousands of tourists who have travelled with us, the majority have been ladies. In family parties, the preponderance is generally on the feminine side; but there are also great numbers of ladies who start alone, and always meet with agreeable company and get through without any particular inconvenience or discomfort . . . As to their energy, bravery, and endurance of toil, as a rule they are fully equal to those of the opposite sex, whilst many of them frequently put to shame the 'masculine' effeminates.
>
> . . . The trappings of prevailing fashion may sometimes perplex them in climbing . . . and amongst rude blocks of granite and basalt; but there is a large class, who, defiant of fashion or customs . . . push their way through all difficulties . . .

Thomas was no 'ladies' man'. His mother, wife and daughter were the only women close to him, but his ability to listen and his extraordinary patience meant that, according to a journalist later writing in the *Daily News*:[2]

> Unprotected females confide in him . . . hypochondriacs tell him of their complaints; foolish travellers look to him to redeem their errors; stingy ones ask him how eighteen pence can be procured for a shilling; would-be dandies ask his opinion about dress; would-be connoisseurs show him the art treasures they have picked up; the cantankerous refer their quarrels to him, and the vacuous inflict on him their imbecility; but the great conductor never flinches.

This formal portrait taken of Thomas Cook at the age of fifty-five is one of the rare surviving images of this man who saw travelling as a way for workers to expand their horizons and to escape the drudgery of their lives. *(Thomas Cook Archives)*

Below: Thomas Cook's birthplace and childhood home, high on the hill at 9 Quick Close, Melbourne – now demolished. *(Thomas Cook Archives)*

When Joseph Winks arrived in the village of Melbourne as the Baptist minister, he changed the direction of Thomas Cook's life – after baptising him when he was sixteen, he taught him the art of printing, the skill that allowed him to promote his tours extensively. *(Max Wade-Matthews)*

Melbourne Hall, owned by the Melbourne family, dominated the ancient village of Melbourne in Derbyshire where Thomas Cook spent his youth. The village's famous namesake in Australia, now the capital of the state of Victoria, did not exist until Thomas Cook was nearly thirty. *(Howard Usher)*

The Cook-Mason wedding certificate on 2 March 1833. One of the witnesses at the wedding was Marianne's uncle, Henry Royce, whose grandson Frederick, an engineer, would later be the co-founder of Rolls Royce. *(Thomas Cook Archives)*

Thomas Cook met his wife, Marianne Mason, a Sunday school teacher, at the Baptist Chapel at Barrowden, near Peterborough, during his days as an itinerant lay preacher in Rutland and Derbyshire. *(Thomas Cook Archives)*

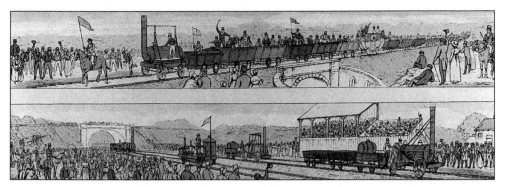

When the first British railway route was opened, between Stockton and Darlington, in 1825 Thomas was working as a carpenter. It would take another fifteen years before he escorted his first tour of excited passengers. This painting shows the race of locomotives at Rainhill near Liverpool. George Stephenson's *Rocket* won the race. *(Hulton/Getty Images)*

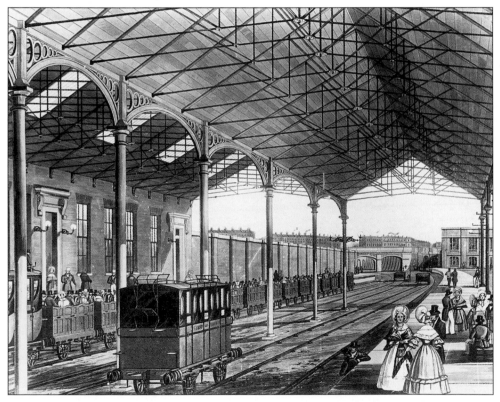

Carriages had not changed from these seen at Euston Station in 1837 to the day four years later when Thomas Cook escorted around 500 passengers in open tub carriages on a return train journey from Leicester to Loughborough to a Temperance meeting. Tickets cost one shilling. *(Hulton/Getty Images)*

John Ellis, a Temperance man, gave Thomas his first openings in major railway excursions. *(Andrew Moore)*

Joseph Paxton, a director of the Midland Railways and architect of the Crystal Palace. *(Hulton/Getty Images)*

Thomas Cook campaigned passionately against the Corn Laws. *(Hulton/Getty Images)*

Cook led the way with promotional material and marketing. *(Thomas Cook Archives)*

An enormous impetus to popular travel was given in 1851 by the Great Exhibition – a celebration of British imperial and industrial might held in Hyde Park in London in the specially constructed Crystal Palace. *(Hulton/Getty Images)*

Thomas Cook was one of the privileged guests present when Queen Victoria officially opened the Great Exhibition in 1851. Cook brought 165,000 visitors from the north to London to what turned out to be the largest public event in the history of England. *(Hulton/Getty Images)*

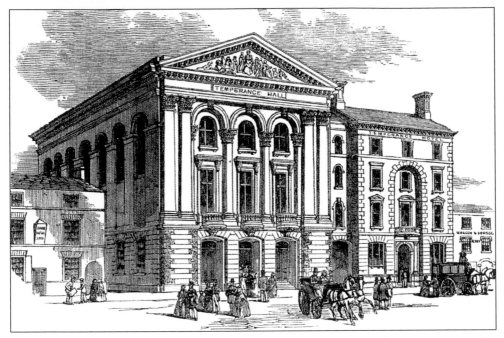

Cook was the driving force behind the building of the Temperance Hall in Leicester. 'Cook's Commercial & Family Temperance Hotel', which was built at the same time, is adjoining and became his family home. *(Thomas Cook Archives)*

Annie Cook's ability to speak French allowed her to help her father's tours abroad. *(Thomas Cook Archives)*

Cook set up 'The British Museum Boarding House' in 1862. *(Thomas Cook Archives)*

In 1861, at the suggestion of Joseph Paxton, Cook took 1700 working men to Paris for the Whitsun long weekend. The party was accompanied by a journalist from the *Illustrated London News*, which published these two illustrations. *Above:* Excursionists leaving the Gare du Nord in Paris. *Below:* The tourists in the Champs Elysées. *(Illustrated London News)*

While religion gave Thomas Cook his drive and purpose, after he had taken the Pledge at the age of twenty-four in 1833 Temperance was the catalyst. This photograph shows him aged fifty-six in 1864 at a Temperance meeting at Stratford. *(Thomas Cook Archives)*

The impact of the visit to England by the swashbuckling Italian national patriot, Giuseppe Garibaldi, in 1864 on Thomas Cook was enormous. Within months he was extending his trips from Switzerland to Italy. *(Hulton/Getty Images)*

According to *The Times* of 13 September 1870, Thomas Cook was in Paris when the Prussians surrounded the city. The Franco-Prussian War and its aftermath did not damage Cook's tours – indeed, the demand for combination, international tickets enabling travellers to reach the south of Europe without crossing the belligerent countries increased. This picture shows the Prussians' arrival in Paris on 1 January 1871. *(Hulton/Getty Images)*

On 20 September 1870, Italian troops took possession of Rome, the last phase in the Unification of Italy. After the reunification of Italy, Thomas Cook formed a committee and purchased land, once a garden, at 154 Via Urbana between the main railway station in Rome and the Coliseum for the first Baptist church for Italians. *(Hulton/Getty Images)*

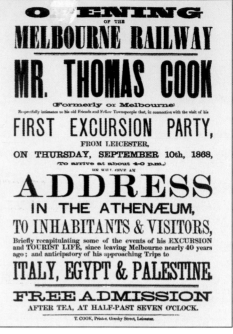

Ishmail Pasha, the Khedive of Egypt. Thomas Cook & Son were agents of the khedivial government for all passenger traffic on the Nile. *(Hulton/Getty Images)*

The occasion of a branch railway line to Melbourne in 1868 gave Thomas an excuse to advertise his first trip to Egypt and Palestine. *(Thomas Cook Archives)*

Amidst the long procession of decorated ships in the Canal for the opening was Thomas Cook himself on an Austrian Lloyd steamer, *America*. Egypt would grow to be the mainstay of the worldwide business of Thomas Cook & Son. *(Hulton/Getty Images)*

There was a twenty-eight year gap from Cook's first trip and the realisation of his goal to take tourists to the Holy Land. Because of him, thousands who had never sat on a horse took to the saddle to see 'the land of the Bible' – scenes that the Scriptures had made so familiar. *(Thomas Cook Archives)*

During Thomas Cook's famous eastern tours, his tourists travelled as a vast caravan – with around 65 horses, 87 pack mules, tents, beds and field kitchens. *(Thomas Cook Archives)*

Italy became a regular tour on Thomas Cook's itinerary. This group photograph of a tour group at Pompeii in 1868 shows Thomas Cook aged sixty sitting in the front of the group. His short socks, which have slipped to his ankles, show his practical attitude to dress. *(Thomas Cook Archives)*

Tewfik took over from his father in 1879 and continued the close association with Thomas Cook & Son, especially John Mason Cook. *(Hulton/Getty Images)*

Below: Two of Queen Victoria's grandsons, Prince Albert Edward and Prince George, visited Egypt and the Holy Land for six weeks in 1882, and were escorted by Thomas Cook's grandson Frank. They climbed the Pyramids, where, at the top, they found the initials 'A.E.' on the south-west corner, which had been carved there in 1868. The princes put their initials next to those of their father. *(Thomas Cook Archives)*

Below, right: A poster for the 1908 Palestine tours. *(Thomas Cook Archives)*

PROGRAMME OF TOURS
IN
Palestine
and . .
WITHOUT
CAMP. . . **Syria : :**
Under the Arrangements of
THOS. COOK & SON,
Chief Office:
LUDGATE CIRCUS, LONDON, E.C.

After his initial trip to the Middle East, Cook made Holy Land tours affordable. In the following thirteen years his firm brought 4,200 tourists to the Holy Land on a variety of pre-paid holidays. By the end of the nineteenth century the number, despite the Turkish–Russian war of 1877–8, had risen to 12,000. *(Christchurch, Jerusalem)*

Thomas Cook & Son were commissioned by the British government to convey 18,000 soldiers down the Nile to Khartoum to rescue General Gordon. But the expedition arrived two days too late. Gordon had been killed on 26 January 1885, murdered by the troops of the Mahdi on the palace steps. *(Hulton/Getty Images)*

Map of Palestine, 1892.

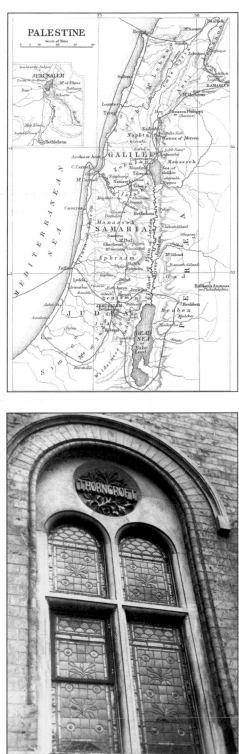

Above: This portrait of Thomas Cook in 1889 coincided with the year that Thomas Cook & Son acquired the exclusive right of carrying the mails, soldiers and officials of the Egyptian government along the Nile. Three years after this photograph was taken, he died. *(Thomas Cook Archives)*

One of the Arts and Crafts windows at Thorncroft, in London Road, Leicester, the red brick house that Thomas Cook built for his retirement and where he died in 1892. It later became the Red Cross Headquarters for Leicester. *(Thomas Cook Archives)*

At Thomas Cook's funeral in July 1892, the *Leicester Daily Post* of 20 July reported that Gladstone, prime minister for the fourth time, praised him: 'thousands and thousands of the inhabitants of these islands who never would for a moment have passed beyond its shores, have been able to go and return in safety and comfort, and with great enjoyment, great refreshment, and great improvement to themselves.' *(Thomas Cook Archives)*

Above: John Mason Cook died in 1899, after escorting the Kaiser to Jerusalem. The business was inherited by John Mason's three sons: Frank Henry, Ernest Edward and Thomas Albert. *(Thomas Cook Archives)*

This memorial statue of Thomas Cook outside Leicester Railway Station fails to capture the spirit of the man – a confirmed and proselytising teetotaller and passionate fighter for the rights of the working class. *(Thomas Cook Archives)*

This was just one portion of Thomas's growing business which was becoming too much for one man to run. The volume of people was burgeoning, so that in 1864, two years after Thomas had moved to London, he pleaded with John Mason, then working as a printer, to come into partnership. A realist, John Mason wrote that they had been unable to agree on matters in the past,[3] so why would their relationship improve? Thomas promised him more autonomy and, with his usual ebullience, talked him into being manager of a new London headquarters. The frustrations of the past would be forgotten; John Mason would control the new office.[4] Every penny that Thomas owned was put into purchasing 98 Fleet Street, on the corner of Bride Lane.

Thomas was now in Fleet Street, the mecca of the newspaper, publishing and literary world. As always, he liked mixing with other printers and publishers, but not in their usual meeting places, El Vino or the bar of the Olde Cheshire Cheese, famed for visitors in the past, such as Dickens, Samuel Johnson and Alexander Pope. Later, John Mason, a teetotaller from birth, appalled by habits in Fleet Street, started a teetotal club for pressmen in the upper part of the building. Despite the enthusiasm of its manager, a Yorkshire Quaker, it was sparsely attended and lost so much money that it was closed after a few years.[5] Thomas described John Mason's return to the fold with warm words:

An important event in 1864 was the adhesion of my son to the work which had been the study, the hobby, and the labour of a solo for twenty-three previous years. When very young, my son had worked with me in various ways; but he left me to go into the Midland Railway Office, and to take charge of the company's excursion business. He afterwards spent a number of years in mercantile operations of considerable magnitude. His return to my aid liberated me from details of office work, and enabled me to carry out foreign schemes of long projection, in both the Eastern and Western hemispheres.

The old fear of insolvency made Thomas turn part of the new offices into a travel shop. Customers could purchase baggage and items such as rugs, hats, telescopes, footwear, guide books, water purifiers, the old staple Keating's Persian Insect Destroying Powder and an adapted Gladstone bag with a rope and pulley inside which could be a fire escape in an emergency.[6] John Mason and his wife moved into rooms upstairs, part of which, as in the previous four Cook homes, became a Temperance boarding house/hotel. One sadness that year was the death of Paxton at his solid Victorian villa on Sydenham Hill, close to where his masterpiece, the Crystal Palace, had been re-erected. Six years previously Paxton's mentor, the Duke of Devonshire, had died, after having virtually moved in with the Paxtons.

During 1865, after he had widened his reputation by taking over 1,600 passengers to Switzerland, Thomas weighed up the advantages of going to either the Holy Land or America. Despite being fifty-seven, his energy was boundless. When the summer season was over, he took some tourists across the Alps and also escorted two trips to Rome and Naples. Then he suddenly decided to go to America, where the Civil War had just finished. So, sixteen years after his visit to Liverpool to arrange tours to the United States, on 29 November he boarded the small cramped *City of Boston*.

As Thomas was sailing across the Atlantic, the Palestine Exploration Fund was being set up in London. It was less than four years since Albert's death and although Victoria, a heartbroken widow, had gone into seclusion, she agreed to be its patron. On 12 May, in the 'Jerusalem Chamber' at Westminster Abbey, where Henry IV had died in 1413, the new committee made it known that the prestigious society would investigate the archaeology, geography, geology and natural history of Palestine and map the whole country, while verifying the sites in the Bible. This overlapped with the Royal Engineers' mapping expedition, for which the Turkish authorities offered protection, as the men investigated a stretch from Mount Lebanon, Nazareth and the Jezreel Valley to the hills of Samaria and Jerusalem.

Thomas, who was not a good sailor, stood on the deck of the steamer. Steamships were not yet stabilised and seasickness was common. Since 1838, when the first coal-powered paddle steamship, the *Sirius*, had made the journey, the sailing time between England and America had dropped to about fourteen or even twelve-and-a-half days,[7] but luxury had not yet arrived. Cats were a necessity, as mice abounded; hungry rats from the holds often ran down corridors. Cockroaches, too, scuttled into corners. Bedlinen was not changed during the voyage. But standards were improving. Thomas, who hoped to 'arrange Excursions to and from the United States and Canada', carried a letter from John Bright, written in Rochdale: 'from all I have heard of you, I feel the greatest confidence in your power to carry out your undertaking to the satisfaction of those who confide in you.'[8]

Abraham Lincoln, the leader of the northern states and sixteenth president of the United States, had been assassinated eight months earlier, his death adding to the bitterness of the four years of fighting. In a similar way to Thomas's tours to France, which had started after France's participation in the Crimean War, his tours to the United States began after the American Civil War. Over 600,000 people had been killed, but now there were peace and an upsurge in both Temperance and economic activity, including the building of more railways. The American Temperance Society[9] had been set up a few years before the first one in England, and by the 1850s thirteen states had forbidden the sale of liquor and there were moves to start a Prohibition Party. Passionate teetotalers, like John D. Rockefeller, a Baptist, sponsored anti-drink lecture tours.

Letters written home to Marianne during the tour show that Thomas's religious priorities were unwavering. From New York he emphasised a sermon at a Baptist chapel in Brooklyn. The letter also related how 'pained' he was by 'the Exposition of the 4th Commandment' in a new book, *Dale on the Ten Commandments*,[10] sent to him by the author, which promoted the advantages of extending public entertainment on Sundays.

Thomas, a Sabbath Observance man, stressed the importance of remembering 'the Sabbath day, to keep it holy. Six days shalt thou labour, and do all thy work: But the seventh day is the Sabbath of the LORD thy God: in it thou shalt not do any work . . .' (Exodus

20: 7–10). The growth of Sunday railway excursions was not something promoted by him.

In the depth of winter Thomas took trains across America, 'travelling over 4,000 miles of Railroads', enjoying the novelty of their corridors, lavatories, iced water dispensers and sleeping berths – facilities and comforts unheard of then on British or European trains. But they were slow. He visited Toronto and other parts of Canada, the Western States and the Central Districts of Pennsylvania, the District of Columbia, Niagara Falls, Chicago, Detroit, New York and Massachusetts. Just as he had diverted to Waterloo on a tour to Belgium, he visited the battlefields of the Civil War. Despite the long journey across America Thomas failed to make any firm plans, but within less than six months John Mason was escorting an exploratory group from New York to Washington, Niagara, Chicago, the Mammoth Caves of Kentucky and the deserted battlefields of Virginia with 'skulls, arms, and legs all bleaching in the sun'. Ignoring the difficulties, Thomas wrote 'and thus was inaugurated the first system of Tours to and through America'. He explained: 'In the following winter my son again crossed the Atlantic, with the view of promoting travel to the Paris Exhibition. He thought he had laid his plans securely, and several great companies promised their aid in giving effect to the arrangements; but our plans were again thwarted, after printing thousands of posters and tens of thousands of explanatory bills.'[11]

Back in England times were again troubled. In Hyde Park, in July, Reform Act agitators demonstrated. Railings were torn down and the old eighteenth-century fear of the mob revived. The government realised that reform was urgent. So, thirty-five years after the Great Reform Bill, the franchise was about to be extended.

TWENTY-FOUR

For 'All the People!'

In the eighteenth century, British tourists, whose ears were offended by the sound of lower-class and Cockney accents when abroad, had made condescending remarks about fellow countrymen travelling abroad being vulgar. Even in the twenty-first century, snide remarks are often levelled at either groups or classes, whether Americans, Germans, Japanese and the Dutch, or at 'ignorant masses' flocking to Majorca or the Costa del Sol, eating fish and chips, buying English newspapers and complaining about each other. The attacks, though, peaked when Thomas was making it possible for the mill-hand, the hairdresser's assistant, the labourer and the jobbing builder to save up and have holidays overseas.

Sophisticated tourists were noting that the highways of the world were becoming somewhat overtrodden. Growing groups of trippers to Italy, Switzerland and Scotland were seen as trespassers, spoiling the very ambience which made these destinations sought after. Many mourned the days when travel was the prerogative of the cultured and wealthy. As the horizons and numbers of British tourists broadened, so did criticism levied at 'common' tourists visiting Scotland and the Lake District. The Poet Laureate, William Wordsworth, in 1844, was most displeased about the groups of people delivered by railways to the Lake District. In his sonnet 'On the Projected Kendal and Windermere Railway', he queried,

> Is then no nook of English ground secure
> From rash assault?
>
> .   .   .   .   .
>
> Given to the pausing traveller's rapturous glance:
> Plead for thy peace, thou beautiful romance . . .[1]

Unmoved by the argument that large numbers of factory workers would be able to escape the horrors of their urban existence with trips to the Lake District, Wordsworth complained of the same intrusion described in his poem 'Steamboats, Viaducts, and Railways'. While George Cruickshank parodied Cockney tourists with good-natured humour in his cartoons, John Ruskin used venom, saying that the Lake District had become a 'steam merry-go-round' and that 'stupid herds of modern tourists' were dumped at Keswick and the shores of Windermere 'like coals from a sack'.[2] Later, Henry James deplored the 'cockneyfication' of romantic sites'.[3]

Thomas reacted to complaints about the rise of the lower-class tourist as if he was the spokesman for the entire class. One article in his *Excursionist* referred to those critics 'who affect to treat with disdain those who occupy a lower sphere than themselves, and then . . . think that places of rare interest should be excluded from the gaze of the common people, and be kept only for the interest of the "select" of society'.[4]

Anthony Trollope's mother, Fanny, the daughter of a provincial clergyman, who lived for many years in Florence and published thirty-two novels and six travel guides between 1832 and 1856, had also made a point of reproving the new tourists. Quoting Laurence Sterne[5] to the effect 'an English man does not travel to see English men', she censured the middle-class travellers who 'every year scramble abroad for a few weeks, instead of spending their money at Margate or Brighton',[6] most of whom, she despaired, seemed content to spend their time with their fellow countrymen.[7] Dickens too had criticised the middle- and upper-class travellers who went about Europe endlessly and aimlessly, absorbing nothing and 'worsening each other'.

Writing under the pseudonym of Cornelius O'Dowd in *Blackwood's Magazine* in February 1865, in an article titled 'Continental Excursionists' which was later reprinted in the *Pall Mall Gazette*,[8] Charles Lever[9] fulminated against Thomas Cook, his tourists and the rise of recreational travel. Eight years earlier, in 1857, Lever, an eminent Anglo-Irish novelist, had gone to live in

Florence and had seized the job as British Vice-Consul for La Spezia, a job he managed to carry out by and large from Florence, before he was promoted to be the British Consul in Trieste.

Lever's job as consul was to protect British visitors, not to abuse them, but he used his literary skills against the burgeoning mass tourist and Thomas, calling him 'that fussy little bald man whose name assuredly ought to be Barnum!' (P.T. Barnum ran a circus in America which toured Europe.) He added that Thomas was swamping Europe with 'everything that is low-bred, vulgar and ridiculous' and that Thomas's tourists were a 'new and growing evil' and that he had 'devised the project of conducting some forty or fifty persons, irrespective of age or sex, from London to Naples and back for a fixed sum . . . the cities of Italy deluged with droves of these creatures, for they never separate, and you see them forty in number pouring along a street with their director – now in front, now at the rear, circling round them like a sheepdog – and really the process is as like herding as may be. I have already met three flocks, and anything so uncouth I never saw before, the men, mostly elderly, drear, sad-looking; the women, somewhat younger, travel-tossed, but intensely lively, wide-awake, and facetious . . .'. In a century when even Balzac ate with his knife and blew his nose on his napkin, there was plenty for people like Lever to sneer at.

Then Lever regaled his Italian friends in jest, saying that Thomas was letting loose felons who were really convicts refused by the Australian colonies, 'and that they were sent to Italy by the English Government under arrangement with Mr. Thomas Cook, who was to drop a few in each Italian city'.[10] These soon became much-repeated rumours. Thomas lashed out against Lever, saying that a lack of schooling did not necessarily mean that tourists had no insight into either the people or the places they were visiting. Europe was no longer a vast playground for cultured English tourists exploring its architecture and galleries. A counter-attack, reprinted in the *Excursionist*, said, 'He, a British Consul, to whom in case of difficulty or emergency I may possibly have to appeal for that protection which is my right, deliberately asserts that he has spread

159

among the Italians of his acquaintance a report that I am engaged by the Government of this country to take gangs of convicts abroad, and by leaving three or four at each of the different cities I visit gradually distribute the sweepings of our prison-houses over Europe.'

The slanging match went on. There was a fear among many of tourism overwhelming unspoilt destinations in a similar way to the rising tide of mass production. Lever responded with another article in *Blackwood's* under the title 'A Light Business Requiring No Capital':

the Continental bear-leader, who conducts tribes of unlettered British over the cities of Europe, and amuses the foreigner with more of our national oddities than he would see in a residence of ten years amongst us . . . these Devil's dust tourists [who] have spread over Europe injuring our credit and damaging our character. Their gross ignorance is the very smallest of their sins. It is their over-bearing insolence, their purse-strong insistence, their absurd pretension to be a place abroad that they have never dreamed of aspiring to at home . . . Foreigners may say, 'We desire to be able to pray in our churches, to hear in our theatres, to dine in our restaurants, but your people will not permit it.' They come over, not in twos and threes, but in scores and hundreds, to stare and laugh at us. They deride our church ceremonies, they ridicule our cookery, they criticize our dress, they barbarize our language. How long are we to be patient under these endurances? Take my word for it, if these excursionists go on, nothing short of war, and another Wellington, will ever place us where we once were in the opinion of Europe.

Attacks on the working class to keep them in their place were again being taken up by the English press. Thomas retaliated and stressed that culture should not be confined to the elite; it could be diffused by education and travel. He avoided saying that his travel company, from opening up the narrow world of the poor workers, now also catered for the comfortable middle classes:

Let us ask why Mr. Lever's susceptibilities should be outraged, and his refinement trampled on, because thirty or forty Englishmen and Englishwomen find it convenient to travel in the same train, to coalesce for mutual benefit, and to sojourn for a like time in the same cities? Reference to a modern compilation shows me that this hypercritical gentleman started upon his career as a student of medicine in Dublin, and that he subsequently took a German degree, and that after practising for a short time he forsook his profession for novel-writing as being at once more profitable and less laborious. Apart, then, from his talent for producing fiction – of which I would speak with all possible respect – Mr. Lever is an Irish gentleman of the precise class to which the English clergymen, physicians, bankers, civil engineers and merchants, who honoured me by accepting my escort to Italy last year, indisputably belong. By what right, then, does he constitute himself their censor? By what right does he assume them incapable of properly enjoying and intelligently appreciating the wonders of nature, and the treasures of art, brought before them by travel? Drawn from the same sphere of society as himself, educated in a like way, and possessing doubtless many tastes and sympathies in common with him, the only social advantage he can claim is the doubtful one of having lived nearly all his life abroad. It is surely a moot point whether the surroundings and moral tone of the curious little colonies of English people scattered up and down the Continent are so vastly superior to those enforced by public opinion at home, as to entitle the self-expatriated Briton to look down upon us with contempt.

Seeing his tours threatened Thomas wrote to the foreign secretary, the Earl of Clarendon, a Whig who had backed the abolition of the Corn Laws. But Clarendon did nothing, saying that his consul was covered by writing under a pseudonym. Next Thomas published a shilling pamphlet which admonished Lever, saying, 'He would reserve statue and mountain, painting and lake, historical association and natural beauty, for the so-called upper classes, and for such Irish doctors with German degrees as choose to be their toadies and hangers-on. I see no sin in introducing natural and artistic wonders to all . . .' To ensure maximum coverage Thomas reprinted it in the *Excursionist* in April 1865, but by then he had conflicting emotions. While attracting the middle and upper classes, he remained loyal to the working class. Even though Thomas had a foot in each camp, in the next issue of the *Excursionist*, in May, he wrote about 'the odious and offensive stench of exclusiveness'.

The *Morning Star*, which described itself as an outpost of 'Manchester radicalism', took up the cudgel for Thomas and on 11 September, objected to the

lofty, lordly, genteel, and grumbling tone . . . The one theme perpetually harped on is the vulgarity and impertinence of people who presume to travel by excursion trains, or with cheap return tickets, or in companies, or in any way that is not grand, expensive and solitary. Every one (that is, everyone who writes) is indignant at the insolence of such people in daring to invade the sacred Continental haunt which, by virtue of a previous sojourn of a fortnight's duration, he has come to regard as his own exclusive possession. He cannot any longer enjoy the mountains or the castles, the picture-galleries or the glaciers, the cathedrals or the lakes, since these Cockney people or manufacturing people will persist in coming to look at them. You would fancy, to read his indignant sarcasms, that the Louvre was his private residence, that the Mer de Glace was his birthright, that the Cathedral of Milan was built by one of his noble ancestors, that Lago Maggiore was a pond in his own demesne.

These articles were timely, as the 'war of classes' was becoming heated with mounting agitation for parliamentary reform. Disraeli had earlier asserted the need for change and the Tories now agreed. He introduced resolutions which lowered the franchise qualifications and redistributed seats, thereby limiting the predominance of any one class. Gladstone, however, objected to what he called fancy franchises and dual voting while the extreme Liberals, known as 'the Tea-Room party', demanded the vote for the 'compound householder'. In July

1867 at last the Bill was passed which gave working men in cities and towns the vote. Now all adult male householders in boroughs who paid rates and male lodgers who paid £10 a year in rent could have their say – but in country areas property requirements remained a little higher. At the elections the following year the newly enfranchised urban householders brought the first unequivocally Liberal government into power and made Gladstone prime minister. It was a triumph for the Nonconformists – the first government ever underpinned by the forces of Nonconformist conviction. Gladstone intended to abolish compulsory church rates, launch national education, repeal the laws which blocked Nonconformists from teaching at English universities and, in recognition that it only ministered to a twelfth of the people in Ireland, disestablish the Church of Ireland. The new government cautiously started admitting the lower classes to the political nation. In just three years, legislation would be passed which allowed trade unions the right to exist as pressure groups. Seven years later 'peaceful picketing' would be legalised.[11] Attitudes, too, were changing.

A few years later the tables were turned on Sir Leslie Stephen and Lever. An article in the *Daily Telegraph* came out in defence of mass travel:

It is, or has been, the fashion among some empty-headed persons to sneer at 'Cook's Tourists'. Pretending to imagine that the pleasure of travel should be reserved for the upper classes, they protested against the beauties of Nature being examined by any but persons of the highest quality and seemed to think that the grey Highlands, the quaint Belgian cities, the castled Rhine crags, the glaciers, the mountains and waterfalls of Switzerland, the blue plains of Italy were exhibitions which should be open only to the holders of high priced stall tickets. What little mischief those notions occasioned was soon blown aside when, in the course of the last thirty years, a man has catered for the comfort of upward of three million persons – numbering among them Dukes, Archbishops and members of every class of respectable society – not merely to their satisfaction, but without the occurrence of a single accident throughout the whole period, he can well afford to disregard either spoken scoff or printed satire.

Since Paxton had opened the route for him to Newhaven, over five years 75,000 tourists had been on Cook's Tours on the Newhaven–Dieppe route to the continent alone.[12] In 1866, while John Mason was on his way to the United States, Thomas took a party of about fifty to Italy. When they arrived in Florence, they discovered that every hotel in Rome was booked for Holy Week. He was offered the Torlonia Palace – 'one of the most magnificent buildings in Rome' – near St Peter's, for ten days at a cost of £500. Members in his group agreed to chip in an extra £4 each and Thomas made up the difference. He let nothing drag down the general mood of enjoyment in travel. When the harmony of the party was disturbed by a few grumblers, he spoke out: 'We have no sympathy with individual expressions of discontent, by which it was attempted to destroy the harmony of the party. Those who travel to Italy must expect sometimes to have to sit on hard seats and place their feet on hard floors . . .'.[13]

The Seven Weeks War, otherwise known as the Prussian–Italian War, which began in June 1866, did not interfere much with Thomas's itinerary. Prussia, allied with Italy, attacked Austria, backed by the countries of Southern Germany and succeeded in pushing Austria out of Lombardy. France, anti-Prussian in sentiment, remained neutral. Thomas and his tourists arrived at the Italian lakes en route to Venice just as the Austrian troops were being evacuated, and stayed on to see the splendid arrival of King Victor Emmanuel II. Soon they were in Venice, where they visited the Accademia, the Arsenale and the Palazzo Mocenigo, once the home of Byron, the Bridge of Sighs and the Palace of the Doges.

While regular tours continued, another major exhibition was being planned in Paris, the Palais de l'Industrie of 1867. Beforehand, in Paris Thomas was gratified by a visit from a private secretary to Napoleon III, who offered assistance. Like the working-men's expedition, this trip would be another landmark in his career. He managed to provide transport for about 20,000 tourists from Britain and accommodate about half of them, as well as many Americans, in various leased buildings in the Rue de la Faisanderie. Once again Annie, now nearly twenty-two years old, helped arrange, supervise and act as interpreter. Arrangements were similar to those for the previous exhibition in London. As Thomas wrote: '. . . the second Paris Exhibition . . . was held in the Champ de Mars. In connection with this exhibition I opened extensive accommodation in the Rue de la Faisanderie; and in connection with several private houses we accommodated 12,000 persons, giving them good English fare for breakfast, tea, and bedroom, for five francs a day. This was a great success; but M. Chardon and myself jointly took another great house, for which we paid a rent of £100 a week, charged 20 francs a day and lost money by it.'

With 52,000 exhibits this was to be the fair to beat all fairs, but the small and weakening Napoleon III did not realise that the 1867 extravaganza would be his last international event before his disastrous fall. Over eighty sovereigns, rulers and politicians were invited to the opening of the fair, including the Tsar, the Sultan of Turkey, the Khedive of Egypt and the brother of the Mikado of Japan, but Victoria and the Pope were unable to attend. For the King of Prussia and Prussia's formidable chief minister, Prince Otto von Bismarck, though, the gaiety and music of the exhibition was the overture to war,[14] which would break out again in just three years.

In September 1868, a branch line opened from Derby making it easier to travel to Melbourne from Leicester. Thomas advertised its inauguration with a poster which included the words, 'Melbourne being the native place of the Agent for Midland Railway Excursions, he was anxious to have the privilege of arranging the First Excursion to that town.'

With hedges full of trailing brambles, canes heavy with ripe blackberries, and elder trees loaded with bunches of round black fruits, the journey through the early autumn countryside gave Thomas a feeling of nostalgia. After a few tunes from the brass band, local dignitaries and streamers welcomed the locomotive and Thomas took his sightseers on a tour of the gardens at Melbourne

Hall. As usual the owner, Lady Palmerston, was not in residence. Although Lord Palmerston had died three years earlier, she still did not find much time to visit Melbourne. Her three houses in the south, Broadlands, Brocket Hall and her mansion in Piccadilly, took up most of her time. But her voluminous correspondence shows she took an active interest in both local affairs and the garden at Melbourne Hall. After the tour of the gardens, Thomas laid flowers on his mother's grave at the Baptist chapel.

Though John Mason may have had cheerful memories of Melbourne from early holidays there with his grandmother, it is unlikely that he now had time to return. His diary entries over the autumn and winter of 1868–9 show that he travelled 20,000 miles, all over Europe, in his quest to further routes and traffic.[15]

TWENTY-FIVE

The Holy Land

Thomas's entrepreneurial mind again turned to the Middle East. James Silk Buckingham, whose advice on the Middle East had discouraged Thomas, had now died, and so he threw caution to the wind. The general belief was that once the Suez Canal was finished in 1869, nearby ports, such as Jaffa, would attract many tourists visiting the Canal to Jerusalem. Anticipating an increase in British ships sailing through the Mediterranean and bringing more visitors, the Turkish authorities had rebuilt the road from the coast to Jerusalem. The steamship services to Jaffa and Beirut operated by Austrian Lloyd and the French Messageries Maritimes now ran much more regularly than the sailing ships that had carried Thackeray twenty-five years previously.

Thomas was planning his first trip 'to the Levant, Egypt and Palestine, tours to which region I had long contemplated' at the end of 1868. His first trip to the Holy Land would be exploratory as this was the era of science, and a large number of intellectuals, following the trend of Voltaire and Gibbon, were confronting religion and questioning the authenticity of the virginal conception, the miraculous birth in Bethlehem, the Resurrection and how the universe came into being. Thomas believed that faith would be intensified and deepened by people visiting the source of their creed.

For the first tour thirty-two bookings were received for the Nile and Palestine, and thirty just for Palestine. After landing in Alexandria the tourists went by train to Cairo, one of the legendary cosmopolitan cities in the east. Despite the squalor and the clamour for 'baksheesh', Thomas fell in love with Egypt. Everything was exciting, bewildering – the noise, the smells of incense, cigarette smoke and opium, the beggars, the fortune tellers, the open display of sexuality, the mixture of Jews, Greeks, Arabs, Lebanese, black Sudanese, Turks, Europeans. The coins and notes were confusing and tourists often felt they were 'being had', when they were haggling to buy souvenirs to post home, but they could not resist the bazaars in the labyrinths of tiny streets crammed with veiled women, men with turbans or a fez on their heads, sitting cross-legged beside piles of carpets, sandalwood, brass pots, perfumes, silks, a snake in a cage or the latest copy of *The Times* from London. As always, Thomas emphasised the good things – the magnificent panoramas with ruins, the tranquillity, the Nile busy with feluccas, the palm trees, the minarets and the mosques. The tourists rode horses to the Great Pyramids one starry night to see the silhouette of the Sphinx against the dark sky.

Egypt, like the Holy Land, was also 'an alcohol free land',[1] where neither wine, whisky or beer were openly consumed by the population. The Koran bans the consumption of alcohol, although a thirsty Thackeray had found that a bottle of Bass beer or some local wine could be procured. Thomas, who had spent nearly thirty years fighting to suppress the use of alcoholic beverages, saw his convictions made real in Muslim countries.

The flamboyant Khedive, Ismail Pasha, grandson of Muhammad Ali and son of Ibrahim Pasha, was planning a grand celebration for the opening of the Suez Canal in November. Nine years since the first spadeful of sand had been turned – amidst conditions described by critics as slave labour – the engineers of the Compagnie Universelle du Canal Maritime de Suez were finishing the giant sluice gates. The canal, 101 miles long, would cut 4,000 miles off the sea journey to Britain from India: it would no longer be necessary to sail around the capes of Africa or South America. A trip from Australia to England, one of the longest passenger journeys in the world, would be reduced from eight to about five weeks.

The canal was the result of Napoleon Bonaparte's invasion of Egypt seventy years earlier in 1798. Scientists and artists from l'Institut de France, who had accompanied his army, had discovered the Ptolemaic ruins of the Suez Canal connecting the

Red Sea and the Mediterranean. Returning to Paris, Napoleon made a speech about plans to resurrect this waterway, which had started way back in about 1400 BC. Speeding up communication and cargo between the East and the West would bring outposts in France's empire closer.

Ferdinand de Lesseps persisted with Napoleon's plans. In 1854, he obtained a concession from the Khedive, Sa'id Pasha, in Egypt, but failed to raise the money in America, Britain and Russia. Finally, France and Egypt put up just enough – a year after Louis Napoleon, now Emperor, had married Eugenie, a cousin of none other than de Lesseps. An estimated 1.5 million Egyptians worked on the canal and 125,000 died, many from cholera.

Many British politicians believed a canal would bring an excess of French interests to Egypt, Syria and India. Hostility to the canal was widespread. British entrepreneurs had already set up a short cut overland. Passengers going to India often travelled overland to Brindisi, then by ship to Alexandria, by train to Cairo, and then to the Red Sea. Every year, thousands of people went from Alexandria by rail to Cairo – staying at the legendary Shepheard's Hotel – before going on to Port Said in the Red Sea to board a ship to India. Shepheard's, with marble columns, chandeliers, faded carpets and muted lighting, was one of the most famous old Middle Eastern hotels, catering both for travellers in transit to India, and the growing number of businessmen. Egyptian investment and trade with Britain had increased during the American Civil War when mills in Birmingham and Manchester, starved of American cotton, utilized the acres of cotton trees on the banks of the Nile. Such fine fibres were imported that British businessmen invested a great deal to increase its production.

Thomas promptly engaged two traditional Nile boats known as *dahabieh* on Gezirah Island, where the Prince and Princess of Wales, who were visiting Egypt well before the opening of the Suez Canal, were staying. The boats would take him to see the monuments associated with all that he had studied in Great

Russell Street. Indeed, it was the continuation of a journey which had started in the museum in London, just as in Shelley's sonnet 'To the Nile':

> O'er Egypt's land of memory floods are level,
> And they are thine, O Nile! and well thou knowest
> That soul-sustaining airs and blasts of evil,
> And fruits, and poisons spring where'er thou flowest.

The Khedive was said to be more than a little enamoured of the Empress Eugenie, and the most luxurious of the many new buildings going up were for her use – the Gezirah palace[2] in Cairo and a 'royal hunting lodge'[3] near the Pyramids. In France, the republican press was having a heyday criticising the expense of the Empress's trip and provocatively asking what impact her presence would have in a Muslim country where royal women were kept behind the lattice walls of the harem.

By chance (or was it?) Thomas's journey down the river coincided with the departure of a flotilla of boats carrying the royal party. The Khedive was lavishly entertaining the Prince of Wales[4] and had already presented him with a gaudy mummy (now in the British Museum), and for the five-week voyage down the Nile the royal party was said to be carrying 'a supply of 3,000 bottles of champagne, 20,000 bottles of soda-water, 4,000 bottles of claret . . . sherry . . . ale, and liqueurs of all sorts'.

Forgetting his old fights with the currents in the Trent, Thomas decided to dive into the Nile. When the boat arrived at Thebes, while 'bathing in shallows over the sands, I became instantaneously the sport of a rapid under-current, was carried beyond my depth, and the boatman had to reach out an oar to my rescue, whilst a group of Arabs on the shore called upon Allah to help me! – themselves, as I afterwards learnt, dreading to come to my rescue under the impression that a crocodile had seized me . . . This was my first and last attempt at bathing in the Nile.'

This was just one of the dramas on the cruise. Travelling with the royal party was William Howard Russell. Since Crimea his reports had brought down governments and altered the course of battles. Now his target was Thomas.

Russell accused Thomas's group of travelling far too close to the royal vessel and trying to gate-crash the royal party. The Nile is one of the longest rivers in the world, and for most of the trip Thomas's party in the *Beniswaif* and *Benha* was just behind the boats of the Prince and Princess of Wales. Russell wrote that 'a cloud of smoke rises from a steamer astern', referring to the vessel towing Thomas's two *dahabieh*, and added that 'Cook's tourists have arrived! Their steamers are just below us in the stream. The tourists are all over the place. Some are bathing off the beaches: others with eccentric head-dresses . . . Another day and the Prince and Princess would have been at their mercy!'

In a series of libellous and damaging reports about Thomas and his tourists, he made fun of the way that his boat hounded the royal party. According to Russell, the Egyptian monuments were of secondary importance to these people; their primary aim was to rub shoulders with their future king and queen.[5] In his book, *A Diary in the East during the Visit of the Prince and Princess of Wales*,[6] published later in the same year, Russell wrote:

> What might not be pardoned to Mr Cook's Tourists, who were in full cry up the river after the Prince and Princess? Some of our companions had come from Brindisi with the British caravan, and gave accounts which did not tend to make us desire a closer acquaintance. Respectable people – worthy – intelligent – whatever you please; but all thrown off their balances by the prospect of running the Prince and Princess of Wales to earth in a Pyramid, of driving them to bay in the Desert, of hunting them into the recesses of a ruin – enraptured at the idea of being able to deliver 'an address' in the Temple of Karnak.

Outraged when some of Russell's derisory comments appeared in *The Times*, Thomas wrote to the Prince himself – not forgetting to publish a copy of the letter in the *Excursionist*.

TWENTY-SIX

Jerusalem, Jerusalem

It was five o'clock in the morning. Thomas rose from his bed and went outside his tent. It was cold in the desert at dawn. The eastern horizon was already tinged with gold, though the western horizon remained grey. He looked for signs of an omen guaranteeing the success of the project ahead, for on that day they would proceed to Jerusalem overland in a caravan of sixty-five horses, eighty-seven pack mules, tents, beds and field kitchens to prepare hearty breakfasts of boiled eggs followed by chicken and cutlets, and dinners of seven courses including wild boar and mutton.

The previous afternoon, just before sunset, they had pulled up to camp and the accompanying Arab servants had set up twenty little iron bedsteads with soft mattresses and clean white sheets in tents. As if out of nowhere carpets were unrolled and pitchers, canvas basins, soap and towels produced so the honoured tourists could wash and dress for dinner. Some of the tourists were up early to pick desert flowers to press in their Bibles to take home, to which would be added bottles of holy water from the Jordan. The party Thomas was taking through Jerusalem, Bethlehem and Jericho was the first of thousands yet to come. Thomas showed his regret that previously he had been dissuaded by Silk Buckingham from venturing to the Holy Land:

It is a great consolation that at the present time there are no serious impediments to Palestine travel. The country is remarkably free from epidemics, and the tribes are at peace . . . The lack of smooth roads and easy roads is the chief difficulty. Sometimes travellers fall into the hands of haughty, imperious dragomans, who lord over them with almost unbelievable hauteur, and as none can travel alone here, all have to submit to

172

this disagreeable necessity . . . A tour is proposed, horses, mules, tents, provisions of all kinds are arranged, and the traveller is committed to the care of his dragoman for 20, 30, or 40 days, for which payment must be made, whatever happens to the tourist.

Most of all that day would be the longed-for moment of Thomas seeing the cradle of Christianity, Jerusalem. He was arriving at the right time, for until just over a decade earlier the activities of Protestants, especially British or American Nonconformists, had been proscribed, neither could they build churches. This had changed after Britain had helped the Sultan defeat the Russians in the Crimea War and British politicians had negotiated wider rights for both Christians and Jews. Thomas knew that faith was deepened when biblical stories were relived. For him the existence of God based on the history of the Old Testament and the Gospels could not be proven, but the effectiveness of religious practice was obvious.

Thomas was overwhelmed at the sight of the Promised Land. He saw a few well-terraced and cultivated areas, which grew grapes, olives and figs; the meagre tracts where wheat had once grown now appeared desolate and stony. Arab women intermittently passed by with their goats.

This trip combined Thomas's religious mission with business. He had been warned by *Baedeker's Guide* that the pleasure of trips to the Holy Land depended 'on the health and energy of the traveller, on the weather and on a host of incidental circumstances which do not occur in Europe'.[1] It also required being good in the saddle, and many of the tourists, like Thomas, had not been trained to ride. When someone fell out of their saddle he jokingly called it 'saluting the ground'. They had to learn to control the animals because the dragomen let off their rifles and a trumpeter sang wild songs when the party went into certain areas of Bedouin territory.[2]

The new road, built in 1867 along the ancient route of Motza to Abu Ghosh to Bab al-Wad, made travel much less arduous and increased the tourist trade, but winter rains created huge potholes and washed away chunks. Patrols against highwaymen and Bedouins were also improved, but tourists still usually travelled in parties, almost in the form of a caravan. Five years before the Jaffa–Jerusalem road was started, the first carriage road in all Syria had been built between Damascus and the port of Beirut.

One of the insurmountable hurdles, which lingered on well into the twentieth century, was the woeful docking facilities for larger ships at Jaffa, the ancient, but shallow, port through which Herod had imported the cedars of Lebanon for the Temple of Jerusalem. As modern ships were too large to tie up at the old wooden jetties, passengers were transferred from ship to shore in rowing boats. When it was rough, which it often is in the winter and spring months of November and May, landing or boarding could be perilous. Summer was too hot and had the added danger of mosquito fevers – malaria was not yet defined. Another deterrent to tourism was also looming – the Russian–Turkish war.

The climax to Thomas's life was arriving in Jerusalem. After eight hours a day on horseback for two days, he saw the dome of the mosque in the distance. From an early age Thomas had been unable to speak the name of Jesus without reverence or awe, so the excursion was far more than sightseeing. Arriving at biblical sites he had visualised since childhood was an intense experience. Sunday school books and prints had fuelled his vision of the Bible lands and merged fact and fiction. There was a huge gap between the idealised illustrations, almost saccharine in their depictions, and the reality of what was before him.

Disraeli, too, had been similarly overwhelmed. His description of Jerusalem in his novel *Tancred* in 1847 reflects how he fell under the city's mystical aura during his visit sixteen years earlier:

> we saw the Holy City. I will describe it to you from the Mount of Olives. This is a high hill, still partially covered with the tree which gives it its name. Jerusalem is situated upon an opposite height which descends as a steep ravine. . . . As the town is built upon a hill you can from the opposite height discern the roof of almost every house. In the front is the magnificent mosque built upon the site of the Temple. A variety of domes and towers rise in all directions. The houses are of bright stone. I was thunderstruck.

I saw before me apparently a gorgeous city. Nothing can be conceived more wild and terrible and barren than the surrounding scenery, dark, strong, and severe; but the ground is thrown about in such picturesque undulation. . . . Except Athens I never saw anything more essentially striking, no city except that whose sight was so pre-eminently impressive.

Thomas longed for thousands to share his own wonder of standing on the Mount of Olives – from where the earthly form of Jesus was last seen by man – and feel the windy gusts while viewing Jerusalem. His tourists could walk on the sacred ground once trodden on by Christ to Calvary, the places where He fell, where He was insulted, where He was nailed to the Cross; the churches and shrines at the sites of Christ's birth in Bethlehem; where Solomon had dwelt; where Abraham had spoken and where walls still stood which had witnessed the spectacle of the Crucifixion.

Regardless of his ecumenical leanings, Thomas would not pray under the majestic mosaics of the Church of the Holy Sepulchre, or kneel beside the alleged location of the empty tomb of Jesus where the Angel had said, 'He is not here! He has arisen.' That, he believed, was a place for Roman Catholics and members of the Orthodox churches. He was dismissive of the kitsch souvenirs and spurious relics sold outside the church.

His two groups encamped just outside the Jaffa Gate at Jerusalem. He preferred the cleanliness of camping to the possible accommodation in the small hotels, religious hospices or convents. Like many Nonconformists he was reluctant to stay in Roman Catholic establishments run by priests or nuns. Besides the tents, temporary stables were set up to shade the horses and donkeys, ready for tours to Bethlehem, Solomon's Pools, Mar Saba, the Dead Sea, the Jordan, Jericho and for Hebron and other places in the south. 'Adroit thieves' was a term used by some travellers to describe the Bedouin, who proved their skill on the night of 24 March, a few days before Easter. The thieves floated through the tents without waking one of the sixty-five British men and women in the camp, plus double the number of Arab servants and horse-handlers. They took £450 cash in gold napoleons and other belongings. Servants were under suspicion and were arrested by the Turkish authorities, but Thomas pleaded their case and they were released.

The year of Thomas's arrival coincided with water supplies to Jerusalem being improved and gas lights being installed. Camels, which for centuries had been such obstructions on the alleyways, were now banned. He had other problems though, including armed bandits, beggars, unpredictable sheikhs, excess baggage, escorting tourists up steep unpaved roads – and too many demands for *baksheesh*. Thomas engaged dragomen as interpreters, guides and bodyguards. Some of them wore the striped kaftan, Arab headdress and a loose belt sporting an ornamental dagger or two and were descendants of the ancient traders, men who knew about frankincense, myrrh, spices, silks and eastern officialdom.

For many tourists, including Thomas, the first sight of the Jordan, like that of Jerusalem, was a moving experience. With white robes billowing in the muddy waters, Thomas let the waters flow around him while he stood in the very place where Jesus Christ had been baptised[3] on this bend in the Jordan by John the Baptist eighteen hundred years earlier. While Thomas would drink water from the Jordan, he considered bottling it for baptisms and christenings both 'superstitious and ritualistic'.[4]

Thomas would later fulfil more of his old ambitions with his 'Biblical Educational and General Tours for Ministers, Sunday school teachers and others engaged in promoting scriptural education'. These focused on the Holy Places, the missions and their schools, and the newly unearthed relics of the past 'Biblical excavations'. He enthused about the pleasure of coming to 'see these wonderful places and countries . . . with the Bible in one hand and Murray in the other, to trace out sites and scenes immortalized by imperishable events'.[5]

Each tourist had a Bible, a hymn book, a guide book and a folding map. On foot, mule, donkey or horse, they sang English hymns or the psalms of David. Once, a clergyman, Edwin Hodder, borrowed a hornpipe and danced the Highland fling at Solomon's Pools. Some wanted wine, but, after tasting it, one tourist quipped that, if it was served to the American public,[6] it would encourage 'total abstinence with enthusiasm'.

On his first trip, sightseeing was interrupted by an unexpected occurrence. At 3a.m. one morning, the aged Mrs Samuels died and the body had to be crated and secretly carried until a suitable place for burial was found. Miss Riggs of Hampstead recounted in her journal:

Arabs have a great superstition with regard to the dead – and as she was to be taken to Jerusalem to be buried, the natives were told that she was ill and she was packed up and carried on a palanquin. A dead person could not be taken from the convent without government permission. So altogether it was thought advisable to act this deception – she died at 3 [a.m.] and was conveyed thither at 6 in the morning and buried that night – eastern burials are so awfully rapid – we all felt the solemnity of the event . . .

The Times, Daily News, Evening Standard and *Pall Mall Gazette*, ignored the death, but wrote detailed reports of the overnight robbery. Miss Riggs's diary recorded every event, such as when each tourist fell off his horse, the sight of naked Arabs along the river banks and the dancing girls 'which the gentlemen patronised'.[7]

In a strange way, Thomas Cook brought tourism full circle. Apart from the number of female travellers, among the unexpected parallels with his tours and those described by Geoffrey Chaucer in the fourteenth century was his choice of Jerusalem as a destination. By looking at Thomas's career, initially propelled by his deep faith, one can see parallels with medieval travel when people set forth on pilgrimages.

Chaucer's Wife of Bath in his classic description of English life, *The Canterbury Tales*, went to Jerusalem three times. In emphasising her journey Chaucer showed both how women travelled then and how popular Jerusalem was as a destination. As the Wife of Bath was a lusty, rather than a saintly type, he also showed that pilgrimages were not only for the pious. Such journeys were so much on the increase that William Wey, a Fellow of Eton, who visited Jerusalem in 1458 and 1462, produced Britain's first proper travel guide, stating the prices of inns in Venice, and what to see *en route*, and how to get an ass at Jaffa.

TWENTY-SEVEN

The Opening of the Suez Canal

On his return to London, Thomas started advertising another trip to Egypt for the spectacular opening of the Suez Canal. On 1 July 1869, he wrote of the 'balm and beauty of the Egyptian night . . . he may watch the moon rising in a silver dawn' and said:

On November the 17th, the greatest engineering feat of the present century is to have its success celebrated by a magnificent inauguration fête, at which nearly every European royal family will have its special representative . . . The canal [of the ancient Pharaohs] is said to have cost the lives of 120,000 slaves who were employed in making it. At first it seemed as if something of the kind was to be repeated in connection with the present undertaking, for originally the forced labour of 25,000 Egyptian fellahs, or serfs, was resorted to, but this, on the earnest representations of England, was ordered to be dispensed with by the Viceroy of Egypt . . .

In the *Excursionist* of 28 July, an advertisement announced the 'Opening of the Suez Canal . . . to leave England on 3rd November and sail from Brindisi on 8th, in the hope to landing at Alexandria on 12th. The canal is to be opened on 17th – fares £35 first class, £28 second class. Hotels and other arrangements to be . . .' In August and September more advertisements appeared for Palestine and the Grand Opening of the Suez Canal. Not enough customers were coming forward – even with an article in the *Daily News* of 5 August which commended Thomas as 'the Napoleon of Excursionists. Last year more than two hundred thousand people travelled by means of Cook's tickets; this year the number will approach, if it does not exceed, three hundred thousand; and from the time of the commencement of the system until now, between three and four millions of tourists have availed themselves of the facilities offered by it . . .'

By 21 October, Thomas's advertisement had an anxious ring: 'The last of the Season! A year ago, we had, as now, completed the summer series of tours; but, on this very date of 1868, we were in the Turkish metropolis, sounding the way for the Eastern expeditions that followed in the early months of the current year. At the present moment the eye looks again to the East, and a new series of engagements loom in the prospects of the future. Our projected trip to the opening of the Suez Canal is but the precursor of a much greater expedition to the East . . . Thousands of anxious eyes are now directed. Kings, princes and potentates of various distinctions, heralded by the enthusiastic Empress of the French, are preparing to join the assemblance which will soon be gathered in Egypt, from all nations, to land the triumphs of science . . . and energy of M. Lesseps . . . hesitancy of the public to advance the necessary deposits of cash to justify any personal responsibilities . . . so few and feeble were the responses that our doubts . . .'

Yet another anxious announcement followed: 'This is Mr Cook's Programme; and all he now adds is, Send The Money and Secure The Remaining Ten Places. First come, first served.' Keen to put Egypt permanently on his timetable, he wanted to lay the foundation with this trip. In the end, only thirty customers paid the fifty guineas.

Wednesday 17 November 1869 was the day set for the opening of the Suez Canal, when the first ships were to sail through the Maritime Canal to the Red Sea. The three pavilions erected along the main quay at Port Said had started to fill, but all visitors were waiting for the Emperor of Austria, the Crown Prince of Prussia and Eugenie. Napoleon III, suffering from bouts of rheumatism and a persistent stone in the bladder, had been too ill to travel. The streets of Port Said, teeming with visitors in turbans, head cloths, fezes and sun helmets fitted with veils, were adorned with a double line of red flagstaffs, brightly coloured banners and lines of red, yellow, blue and green lanterns. On the canal itself, the forest of ships' masts behind the royal yachts became confused and indistinct as the deep glow faded from the sky. The night sky was lit only by moonlight and lights flashing from lighthouses. Flights of rockets ascended into the sky, lighting up the scene with exploding stars, then with showers of falling gold.[1]

On 16 November, watched by the international dignitaries, the canal was blessed by two ceremonies in Port Said, one for Roman Catholic France and one for Muslim Egypt. Escorted by a glittering galaxy of princes and ministers, on board *L'Aigle*, Eugenie, leaning on the arm of the Emperor Francis Joseph of Austria, who rarely left her side, was the star of the show. Next day, she and de Lesseps were together on the bridge of *L'Aigle*, the first of sixty-seven ships, all decorated with flags and bunting, making the historic journey south in the magnificent Steamboat Procession through the canal to the Red Sea. Behind were yachts carrying the Khedive, the Emperor Francis Joseph, the Prince Royal of Prussia, Prince Henry of the Netherlands – and Thomas Cook himself on an Austrian Lloyd steamer, *America*. Crowds waited for the moment when, it was said, the waters of two great seas would merge, allowing ships to take a short cut from the Mediterranean to the Red Sea and into the Indian Ocean. As the decorated ships sailed down the canal Britain, France and Holland literally became closer to their Asian colonies. The canal would also open the whole of Egypt to the Western world, making it truly international.

Thomas and his party then went by rail to Cairo, where, as he related, 'special preparation was made by the Khedive for public dinners, and the free consumption of champagne and other costly wines, which had no attraction for my little teetotal party'. Britain was represented at the dazzling ceremony by only a lowly 'Mr' from the Foreign Office. No members of the British royal family were present.[2] Eschewing the theatre as usual, Thomas had not attended the inauguration of the lavish new opera house, a replica of La Scala in Milan with Oriental additions, such as boxes screened with fretworked wood for the Khedive's harem. Here on 1 November the lush velvet curtains opened Verdi's *Rigoletto*, based on Victor

Hugo's *Le Roi s'amuse*. Despite its lavish Egyptian spectacle, Verdi's later opera *Aida* had no direct connection with the opening of the canal. The work was commissioned in 1870 and first performed at the Cairo opera house in 1871.

Thomas enjoyed the attention given to him and other British businessmen at the ceremonies because of the absence of any famous or distinguished British visitors at the ceremonies. Even though he was well aware of the commercial benefits of semi-official status at such events, the consequences were beyond his wildest dreams. The following year, Thomas Cook & Son were appointed agent for Nile passenger traffic by the Khedive. This not only enabled Thomas to get a firm foothold in Egypt thirteen years before the British controlled the country, but soon the Khedive granted him the exclusive control over all passenger steamboat traffic on the Nile as far as the first and second cataracts. In return, the Cooks had to take risks. For instance, they were obliged to invest in rented steamers, owned by the Khedive, and also to undertake the management of the service at their own expense. After visiting the Pyramids and the Sphinx, tourists would float down the Nile on a luxury *dahabieh* between Cairo and Aswan listening to one of the specially recruited 'experts' telling the history of the monuments. And all this began just seven years after moving into Great Russell Street and living across the road from the largest collection of Egyptian antiquities on show outside Egypt.

TWENTY-EIGHT

Paris: War, 1870

Neither Thomas nor his son would ever have contemplated becoming a soldier, but in 1870 both would be within earshot of the guns, less than half a mile from the front lines of the Franco-Prussian war and the siege of Paris. The initial cause of the war, like so many, seemed trivial. The Spanish throne was vacant because Queen Isabella had been driven out during the 1868 revolution. Prince Leopold Hohenzollern-Sigmaringens[1] was put forward as a candidate, but, in response to France contesting his candidature, had withdrawn his name. France then accused Bismarck of waving 'the red flag before the Gallic bull'[2] by drafting a telegram sent in the name of the King of Prussia, which offended France. Sensing political intrigue by Bismarck behind the move, France, seeing a German prince in Spain as a threat to the balance of power, requested confirmation that the prince would not attempt to take the throne again.

In Paris crowds in the boulevards, responding to the recent anti-German propaganda and the depressed economy, started singing the *Marseillaise* and shouting '*A Berlin! A Berlin!*' People at last had something on which they could vent their anger. War fever gripped the nation. The empress was eager for battle, and the generals confident of victory.[3] On 19 July 1870, Napoleon III started moving troops to the border. So did the Prussians. So great were the numbers of soldiers in Berlin marching to railway stations that the city resounded with the beat of their boots. Troops, closely packed in cattle trucks, with tents, food, water, guns and ammunition, sped to Metz. Others joined at stations on the Leipzig–Dresden line.

In Germany over 1 million troops were on the move with 462,000 being transported to France by train. Railways had been used for war in Crimea, but these men were the first European troops who never had to march to battle. Observers said that travelling to the front by train instead of on foot allowed soldiers to conserve their energy for fighting. Trains also meant that men could be more easily supplied with food and bullets.[4]

Troop movements were disrupting and causing chaos to passenger services on the continent. Tourists everywhere from Oberammergau[5] to Paris panicked. The British rushed home, packing ferries crossing the English Channel. Some, though, hurried in the other direction. Undeterred either by press censure, or by reminders that some spectators at the Crimean war had been killed, John Mason was about to escort a group of men close to the front.

On 30 August, Napoleon travelled by train to Sedan, a fortified town in northern France close to the Belgian border and about 120 miles north-east of Paris. At dawn the next day, 2 September, the Bavarians attacked and the disastrous Battle of Sedan began. French loses were so high that by mid-afternoon Napoleon hoisted a white flag and surrendered to Prussian forces, ending his shaky empire and his twenty-two years in power. France was now a republic-in-waiting. Once it was known that Prussia coveted Alsace-Lorraine, the French would not cede an inch of their native soil. The Parisians, too, like the soldiers at the front, refused to give in to either the Emperor or the Prussians. As the fighting continued, newspapers carried the headline '*Chute de l'Empire!*' Rebellion broke out in Paris.

Thomas himself wrote little about tourism on the fringes of war, but the *Observer* of 4 September 1870 – six days before Eugenie, accompanied by her American dentist, arrived as a refugee at Hastings – criticised him for his 'doubtful taste' in escorting tourists down the Rhine on a steamer *en route* from Frankfurt. The Prussian advance from the east forced the main French armies, about 150,000 strong, to encamp at Châlons. John Mason, though, was nearer to the action than Thomas – probably as close as half a mile to the fortress of Metz where the other main French army was beaten. Most of the French professional soldiers were stationed in Metz, but John Mason departed before the Germans started their siege there on 19 August, only to travel to the edges of another besieged area, Paris, to find that Thomas had got there first.

According to *The Times* of 13 September 1870, Thomas was in Paris at the time when the Prussians surrounded the city. As revolt broke out and the proclamation of the Third Republic was declared, he witnessed the hurried preparations to blow up two bridges on the Seine to halt the Prussian advance, but, anticipating the isolation of Paris, he did not stay for more than a few days. After he departed, the Prussians, seeking to starve the inhabitants of the city into surrender, cut all communications. A vicious and bloodthirsty streak was revealed in Bismarck, who ordered the most ruthless measures to starve the Parisians into submission.[6] They, though, held out. Trees in the Champs Elysées were felled for firewood, the animals of the zoo, even the monkeys and zebras, were stewed and eaten, streets were blocked with barricades, Napoleon's column in the Place Vendôme was crashed to the ground and the Tuileries brought to ruins.

At Metz, the French troops, starving and weak, withstood the siege for ten weeks until 29 October when they were taken into captivity. Paris, though, lasted for another three months. Three days later, on Tuesday 31 January, John Mason was on his way to Paris. When, after arriving on the Newhaven–Dieppe ferry, he found there were no trains, he went via a circuitous route, by horse and foot, eventually walking into Paris 'by the Avenue of the Grand Army . . . During my two days . . . I lived pretty much as the besieged residents . . . My friends told me the bread was at its worst, but I did not consider it much worse than the coarse oat-cake of the Scotch highlands; the horse-flesh soup was excellent . . . My return journey from Paris was made in 30 hours, particulars of which I have given in the London daily papers . . .'

John Mason was only in London a few days before he was ready to depart again with 150 tourists, eager to be on the fringes of the aftermath of war. The visit was fortunately brief, for on 17 March the Parisians began to rebel again, forming the Paris Commune on 26 March. Until June, when the treaty was signed in Versailles, Paris was again cut off and once again the railways were closed to passenger traffic. British and American tourists, eager to get to Paris, found they could go with John Mason, who, once again, using all forms of transport, re-entered Paris on the heels of the French troops.[7]

This war was expected to damage tourism for the Cooks, but, contrarily, encouraged it. The demand for circuitous tickets which allowed travellers to reach the South of France and the Italian Mediterranean resorts by bypassing the belligerent countries was enormous. Archibald Tait, the Archbishop of Canterbury, purchased tickets for this roundabout route to San Remo to convalesce after a series of heart attacks and a cataleptic seizure. Thomas volunteered to escort him. Far from being the stereotypical plump, red-faced bishop, the archbishop held progressive views and had suffered much sadness in his life. Fifteen years earlier, five of his seven children had died from scarlet fever in the space of a month. Now, as the most important man in the Church of England, to be escorted by a passionate Nonconformist was unexpected, but the archbishop's attitude was broader than most of his predecessors. Indeed, five years later he was widely criticised for holding a meeting of Nonconformist ministers at Lambeth Palace.

Tait's sister, Lady Wake, who wrote a biography of the archbishop in 1876, described Thomas during their journey across France to Italy:

a quiet, middle-aged man very much like a home-staying, retired tradesman was pointed out to me, walking up and down the station with his hands in his pocket, seemingly taking notice of no one. He could not speak a word of any language but his own. How then did he accomplish all these wonders? He had agents in every town, and one line from him could always settle every difficulty and arrange every convenience. On our first crossing to Ostend, one of my boxes, not having been put under his care, disappeared . . . after having performed a tour through Europe by itself, it joined us at San Remo, where the whole party in due time established themselves at the Hotel de Londres; and there Cook left us. We found a great difference on our return to England without his magic wand to clear the way . . .

185

At the end of the war John Mason took a party of American freemasons to Paris and began another continuing section of the family business, American tourist traffic.

A consequence of the Franco-Prussian war was the fall of Rome. Napoleon, needing all his army to fight the Germans, had earlier been forced to withdraw his troops from Rome. For centuries Baptists and other Nonconformists had looked away from this papal enclave, but, after the final battle between the Italian troops and the Pope on 20 September 1870, British Methodists had been at the gates, ready to enter with wheelbarrows of Italian Bibles.

Until then, there were no churches of their own faith in Rome. In Italy, by contrast, once the Pope's territories had shrunk to what was behind the walls of the Vatican, a wide range of Nonconformist religions had been able to build churches and run missions.

Rome was now the capital of unified Italy and it was no longer dangerous to be a non-Catholic proselytising another religion. As in the rest of Italy, permission was given for non-Roman Catholic churches to be built, and Methodists, Baptists and Presbyterians, like the leaders of other denominations, rushed to purchase or rent property for church buildings. Christian services were recited in Italian in some churches instead of the Latin of Roman Catholic services.[8]

Thomas, more than proud that he was behind the setting up of the first General Baptist Mission in Rome,[9] described his own role: 'The Mission at Rome was originated by myself, and I was mainly influenced in my efforts in connection therewith by comparing the simplicity of the early Baptist disciples in Rome with the General Baptists of the Midland counties in England.'[10]

At first, though, the Baptist mission was in rented premises. A building boom in Rome following 20 September meant that prices were soaring and buying a property was no longer straightforward as some changed hands so quickly that their titles were not registered properly. Most of the earliest temporary Protestant churches were in the so-called 'Quarter of the Foreigners', which then extended in a triangle from Piazza del Popolo to Piazza Venezia – from the Tiber to the Spanish Steps. These new churches joined the already well established English places which had already become landmarks: Babington's Tea Rooms, the Keats–Shelley house, the Church of San Lorenzo in Lucina, the setting for a scene in Browning's *The Ring and the Book*, the artists' quarter, many British antique shops on Via del Babuino and the historic coffee bar of Café Greco.[11]

Initially, two Baptist missions opened, one in Piazza San Lorenzo in Lucina and the other, with which Thomas was connected, closer to the Coliseum near the Church of Santa Maria Maggiore. The first Baptist missionary to be appointed there, in 1873, the Revd N.H. Shaw, the former pastor of Dewsbury Baptist Church, managed very quickly to convert a Roman Catholic priest, Cavaliere Paulo Grassi, the incumbent of a nearby church, who became known in the mission, somewhat condescendingly, as a 'native preacher'. Thomas described his own role with the Mission in Rome, saying that it

was originated by myself, and I was mainly influenced in my efforts in connection therewith by comparing the simplicity of the early Baptist disciples in Rome with the General Baptists of the Midland counties in England. Having the privilege of attending the Communion Service of the Church at Rome, then under the care of the Rev Dr Cote, and subsequently with the Church formed by Mr Wall, I was impressed with the earnestness and simplicity of manner which characterized the members of those infant Churches; and I then pleaded through the [General Baptist] Magazine and in public associations for the establishment of a General Baptist Mission in Rome. The result of those appeals and efforts led to the purchase of premises, and the erection of a chapel and minister's residence at a cost of several thousands of pounds.[12]

TWENTY-NINE

Around the World

Thomas, as always, encouraged people to have contact with the biblical past, places linked to the lives of the prophets, apostles and Jesus.[1] In Palestine, tourists could touch the ruins of the magnificent buildings put up during the reign of King Herod and see the terraced gardens with their olive trees, wild figs, worn stones, rosemary and vines while on their way to Bethlehem. Visitors to Damascus were reminded that in the Book of Genesis in the Old Testament there is a description of a battle fought there by Abraham. Thomas proudly wrote in his travel newspaper, the *Excursionist*: 'The educational and social results of these four years of Eastern travel have been most encouraging. A new incentive to scriptural investigation has been created and fostered; "The Land and the Book" have been brought into familiar juxtaposition, and their analogies have been better comprehended; and under the general influence of sacred scenes and repeated sites of biblical events, inquiring and believing spirits have held sweet counsel with each other.'

The following year the Palestine arrangements were put on a new basis. An office was set up at Jaffa to receive and make bookings and itineraries for tourists to travel to Jerusalem and other places. Clients had the choice of booking hotels or hiring horses and tents. The new office opened in the modern part of the port, near large shops, a German bank, schools and town gardens with a bandstand. Among the German and Turkish residents were Baron Ustinov (grandfather of the actor Peter Ustinov), who owned the Park Hotel in Auerbach Street with a rooftop overlooking the sea.[2] When the Palestine tours were extended to the Houran and the Land of Moab, Thomas was pleased that they received letters signed by sheikhs,

188

including the Sheikh of Petra, and Bedouin associates assuring the dragoman contractor of the protection and safety of their parties. Thomas also had the offer of a clergyman in the Lebanon to accompany a party to the Houran. Tourists could follow in the footsteps of the Babylonians, Assyrians, Jews, Arabs, Persians, Greeks, Roman legions and Crusaders: '. . . from Cairo to Sinai, and from Petra to Moab and Bashan, the way is open for arrangements under direction of Mr Howard . . .'

On 26 September 1872, Thomas set off on his inaugural 212-day, 270-guinea 'Round the World' tour. With a party of 'four from Great Britain, one Russian, one Greek, and four Americans' he sailed west from Liverpool to New York on a 29,000-mile journey that was to take over six months. A hundred years earlier, during his voyage on the *Endeavour*, another Cook, Captain James Cook, navigator and explorer, had been the first captain to circumnavigate the world in a westerly direction and the first to circumnavigate the world in both directions. Now Thomas would head a tour which would do likewise. The trip also fulfilled Thomas's hope to be acknowledged as a writer as his essays and articles appeared in *The Times* (see Appendix). This enlarged version of the Grand Tour, described by Thomas as his 'crowning achievement', anticipated Phineas Fogg in Jules Verne's bestselling book *Round the World in Eighty Days*, and shrank the horror of distance of crossing oceans, showing that such a trip could become a pleasurable excursion.

When they crossed the United States – by train with a few connecting stage coaches – in one of his regular Sunday letters home Thomas had much to say about his thrifty laundry arrangements: 'My Very own Marianne, I intended to enclose you, as a curiosity, my Salt Lake washing bill but don't know what has become of it. The items were three undershirts, two flannel so called "large articles"; twenty five collars, front cuffs and handkerchiefs – all for the sum of $4.30 . . . . That was my only "wash up" since I left home and I don't think I will wash again until we reach British India.'

189

As he would not be in India until after Christmas and he had left Salt Lake City in late October, this was a gap of eight weeks between washing his clothes. The eight-month trip included a twenty-four-day trip on the paddle-steamer *The Colorado*, crossing the Pacific from San Francisco to Japan, a distance of 5,250 miles. After a quick tour of Japan, China and India, Thomas finally touched down at Aden. Australia was not on the itinerary. Many meant to go, but only the most determined endured the salt beef and the waves before improved liners shortened the distance and passengers did not have to share cabins with cockroaches.

The final leg of the journey took Thomas through the Suez Canal. The Cook office in Cairo was serving the thousands of people who each year were sailing through Suez en route to the East. Cooks offered three routes from London to Cairo: via Gibraltar by sea; via the Orient Express to Istanbul and then by sea; and across Europe to Brindisi by rail and then by Austrian Lloyd steamer to Alexandria. Not all British holidaymakers though travelled with Thomas Cook & Son – one then staying at Thebes was the scientist Thomas Huxley, 'Darwin's Bulldog', promoter of Darwin's theories, who had invented the word 'agnostic'.

In Egypt, Thomas saw that John Mason had established the reputation of Thomas Cook & Son as one of the top tourist operators in the world. John Mason's abilities were also involved in another innovation of Thomas Cook & Son, *Cook's Continental Time Tables and Tourist's Handbook*, which listed, in infinite detail, all the main railway, diligence and steamship routes across Europe.[3]

Other ground-breaking improvements were perfected by John Mason. Inclusive tours paid for in advance together with hotel coupons to cover the cost of hotel rooms and meals made it unnecessary for tourists to carry large sums of foreign currencies. His 'Circular Notes',[4] launched in 1874, were the forerunners of traveller's cheques which allowed tourists to obtain currency in exchange for a paper note. So huge was the demand for these that Cook's Banking and Exchange Department was opened in 1878. Oscar Wilde paid the firm of Thomas Cook the compliment that 'they wire money like angels'.

Thomas certainly admired John Mason's abilities, but he could never go along with his priorities, his intolerance or his temper. They had seen each other often in Leicester, but nothing healed their differences. Now they saw each other in Egypt and it was no better. John Mason, his face flushed with rage and frustration, would raise his voice and tell Thomas that his preoccupation with religion was a handicap to the company. John Mason's temper was illustrated by the story of how he once threw a dragoman off a steamer into the Nile for being impertinent. Neither father nor son would compromise. It had again been agreed that John Mason would take over the entire business, but Thomas continued to meddle. Some of the quarrels demonstrated that he was unable to relinquish his position. Both men would fly into a rage, saying and writing harsh things which neither man seems to have regretted. Even so, Thomas repeatedly staked everything on reconciliation, while John Mason distanced himself.

In Egypt a letter, written by John Mason from his portable writing desk, was opened by Thomas. On the eve of his departure, Thomas wrote telling Marianne about the continuing row: 'I am not going to distress myself. I know my heart is right towards him and towards yourself, and my dear girl [Annie] also, and I shall not be moved from the path of Duty to either Division of my family. He does not like my mixing Missions with business; but he cannot deprive me of the pleasure I have had in the combination; it has sweetened my journey and I hope improved my heart without prejudice to the mercenary object of my tour. I shall neither be expelled from the office nor stifled in my spirit's utterance, and I have told him so very plainly . . .'

Pushing the bickering and wrangling aside, on his return Thomas enjoyed the interest in his trip. In late February he spoke to a packed audience in the Corn Exchange about his world travels; the *Leicester Journal* reported that 'the large audience was held spellbound'.

The row between father and son went on. John Mason insisted that all business arrangements without profit cease. Neither would yield. Thomas could not stop being a Bible-loving Evangelist and a vocal Temperance campaigner, especially when in the previous year there had been a victory for the Temperance movement with legislation that showed the influence of the Temperance movement. The new Licensing Act curbed the drink trade and imposed opening hours on public houses. While the brewers, the whisky and gin distillers, and wine and spirit importers were up in arms, those who believed in Temperance did not think the new laws went far enough.[5]

THIRTY

Grandeur

Thomas, writing regularly in the *Excursionist*, frequently stated that Cook's offered 'to all classes and to everybody the cheapest Tourist tickets ever presented to the English public'. Long and flowery though his descriptive pieces often were, he used restraint when writing about either religion or Temperance in the magazine. It was the same on his tours. Although Thomas himself seldom missed a chance to visit a mission or church and often invited members of his tours to accompany him, he did not pressure them. Whether in New York or Alexandria, he was involved with missions, and the clergy took up not just his time but his money – money which John Mason claimed belonged to the firm. For instance, in Jaffa, Thomas purchased the building for Miss Arnott's mission school; and he also helped other Protestant church establishments in Bethlehem and Jerusalem. Apart from giving financial aid, he tried to visit these missions at least once or twice a year. On one visit in 1874, the harsh winter caused endless problems for tourists, when storms blew up from Egypt, as it could be bitterly cold in the winter months in the hills of Judea and Mount Lebanon. In Hermon, tourists[1] were held up for three days in an Arab village because of unexpected snowstorms. One member of the party told the story of a minister, who, though ill, recovered enough to baptise a fellow traveller in the Jordan, but died in Jerusalem soon afterwards:

November 20: Poor Dr Gale succumbed, entirely losing his mind, and had to be left at a wayside place until a doctor could be sent to him. November 21: Dr Gale brought in by wagon and carried in. He is quite childish – mind gone. November 25: Poor Dr Gale died about 5 this morning. Not been able to speak. Saw him last night and was recognized by him. His effects and burial left to Dr DeAss [De Haas] American consul. Melancholy thought to leave our friend dead and unburied. Got on steamer all right. All thankful to leave Holy Land.

Edwin Hodder, author of *On Holy Ground* (London, 1874) wrote dismissively:

If the traveller told the plain truth and spoke naturally, he would say the first thing that struck him on entering Jerusalem was the number of costermongers selling pistachio and peanuts, the quantities of sherbert consumed at street stalls, the low row of cafés and cigar shops, and the knot of Englishmen (distinguishable anywhere by their hideous costumes) lounging outside the Mediterranean Hotel.

Nothing, though, would discourage either Thomas or the growing number of tourists. Russian pilgrims also increased in number. Prussia, too, made her mark with a Lutheran church built in Jerusalem. A group from southern Germany established new Knights Templar colonies, and archaeologists started searching, among other things, for the lost tomb of the German Crusader, Emperor Frederick Barbarossa. Crates of newly unearthed antiquities found their way to Berlin and other cities. The widening stream of travellers and archaeologists exporting biblical antiquities to European and American museums would later be accused of plundering. In October 1873 Thomas was writing that he hoped to transfer a house in Bethlehem to a religious society. This had been made over in part payment of the money stolen from a tent on his first visit.

Later Cook's set up an office in King David Street[2] in the Old City near the Jaffa Gate, only a few alleyways up from the Holy Sepulchre. Before modern hotels were built, tents were erected just outside the Jaffa Gate. Visitors often wrote of how 'Cook's Tours' supplied them with tents and riding horses for further journeys.

Because the area around the Jaffa Gate was a jumping off place for tours and expeditions, it became known as the 'station', and other tourist agencies set up their headquarters too. Nearby, the family boarding house of Mr E.L. Kaminitz grew into a big hotel in Jaffa Road. Various crafts connected with the new transport industry, such as coach building and repairs, harness and blacksmithing,[3] also sprang up. Similar expansion was taking place at other tourist destinations worldwide.

To cater for the huge increase in international tourism Thomas Cook & Son offices were opened up in many places, including Rome. In 1873, the London office was moved down Fleet Street to Ludgate Circus, where John Mason supervised the building of purpose-built offices, with a goods receiving depot, a branch post and telegraph office, reading room, waiting room and a daily bulletin of weather in Europe and the Middle East. As Thomas explained, 'Our business was growing to such a magnitude, that we were not only justified but bound, to give our patrons and ourselves the best accommodation . . .'

Within a year of the opening of the grand headquarters, Thomas was contemplating a country seat. At the height of the disputes with John Mason, Thomas decided that, if he was to retire from the firm, Melbourne Hall, which was advertised for lease, could be his base. This was quite out of character. Most of his life he remained uninterested in the acquisition of land or trophy houses filled with antique furniture set in rolling acres. Nor did he seek entry to London clubs or gilded salons. Perhaps this was because he knew he would never have been fully accepted into the class that frequented them. Anyway, this one deviation from his usually modest ambitions was rejected. The then owner of Melbourne Hall, Earl Cowper, thought it more appropriate if a true 'gentleman' and member of the Anglican Church was the occupant. This rejection sheds light on both the heightened sense of privilege of the British upper classes in the nineteenth century and the ongoing intolerance against Nonconformists. Relations between the Church of England and the chapels were still, in 1874, when this letter was written, often embittered:

Mr. Cook has applied to lease Melbourne Hall. He would like to make it a shew place with special trains &c and would no doubt make it answer so that the place would cost him little or nothing – They are a great nuisance in grounds of that size & to the place generally & Mrs. Gooch [previous tenant] was obliged to put a stop to them. I have seen Mr. Cook once & he seems to be a highly respectable and intelligent man but he would be sadly out of place at Melbourne Hall – He is a Baptist and here they do great mischief I consider to the place by the narrowness of their views in matters of Education &c. They will not even support the Infants School on which Churchmen and Dissenters join – it is most desirable if possible to have a gentleman and a Churchman in so leading a position – He will be here on Monday & if your Lordship will sanction it I should throw cold water on his application at any rate, but if he would like to take a suitable site on lease for building a good house it would I think be desirable to offer facilities for this . . .

If the rumour be correct will Mr Cook, who has 'personal' experience of trippers, close his portals against the fraternity, or will he nobly disregard the broken bottles and sandwich papers and empty fusee-boxes [match-boxes] and create a rival Alton Towers with its special trains to Melbourne?[4]

Earl Cowper continued in his objections, saying that he did not 'wish by any means that Melbourne Hall should be turned into a show place. If I had understood that this was Mr. Cook's intention I should have written at once to state my decided objection.'

As always when Thomas received snubs and setbacks, he could divert himself with other activities, such as the mission in Rome, which he frequently visited. Here, as seen in his correspondence, he too was capable of religious bigotry. After one visit in the winter of 1875–6 he wrote on his return in February a letter which was published in the *Missionary Observer* in the edition of March 1876:

After twelve days of confinement to my room in Rome, I have managed to work my way back to London by short stages, and rests by the way. My bronchial trouble, which had culminated so fearfully on my arrival in Rome has now left me without articulative power, so that I cannot even dictate the words of a letter, and my only way of communication is to write a few notes, and get them copied by a plainer hand . . .

On my arrival in Rome, I soon found that we were to be the victims of Jesuitial trickery or of ordinary Italian duplicity. The property for which we had engaged to pay, with legal expenses added, about £1,000 sterling, I was told we could not have unless we would take an adjoining café and other property amounting to nearly £4,000 sterling. I would not for one moment entertain this proposal, but placed the matter in the hands of a lawyer to secure for us the one thousand francs fine, which was agreed to be paid by either side that should fail to complete the transaction. Hearing of other properties in the locality that were on sale, Mr. Wall, Grassi, self, and [an] estate agent, started on a tour of inspection; several properties were examined, and on the following day we got an offer of a choice of three lots, which were in liquidation, the bankrupt stock of a society which had speculated in land and houses . . . The report was highly satisfactory . . .

Finally, a property in via Pudenziana (now via Urbana) was purchased for £1,009 5s 2d and Thomas added that 'our freehold was secured before the Jesuits had time to open their eyes or rub their spectacles. I was afterwards assured that the property was worth double. This was a bright spot amidst the gloom of ten days of physical suffering and darkness.' He then went on to describe the locality: 'The via San Pudenziana, with its very old and grotesque little church, and a large convent, take their names from the generally believed site of the house or palace of Pudens, a Roman senator of the time of Paul's residence in Rome. History or tradition tells us that Pudens was a friend of Paul. He is said to have visited Britain in the time of her many kings; that he married a daughter of

Caractacus, who became a Christian, and afterwards was known by the name of Claudia . . .'.

Marianne and Annie were also drawn up in the excitement of the new chapel and prior to its opening spent three weeks preparing it for worship and helping the wife of the minister, the Revd N.H. Shaw, to start mothers' meetings and other social events – and to distribute Bibles in Italian and English. One Baptist philanthropist in Manchester had given 50,000 copies of the New Testament to the Roman mission alone.

THIRTY-ONE

Egypt

Britain had turned down the offer of shares in the Suez Canal and snubbed the opening, but much to France's fury Britain was the country which prospered the most from the speedier routes it offered. Then, almost overnight, six years after it had opened, the British government became the largest shareholder in the Suez Canal Company.

In 1875, political circles were buzzing with rumours about the extravagances of the Khedive forcing him to sell the majority of his Suez Canal shares. In London, Lionel de Rothschild, then an MP, went to Disraeli and confirmed the rumour. Before France had a minute to beat them, Britain, with a loan of £4 million from Rothschild's bank, purchased the Khedive's 177,000 shares, making Britain the controlling shareholder. Disraeli's and Rothschild's swift purchase left the French reeling. Until then France had been the most active European nation in North Africa and revelled in the Suez Canal increasing her economic base. She was encouraged from behind the scenes by Bismarck. Britain's share deal was such a triumph and such a blow against France that, even when Gladstone's Liberals in the Commons attacked Rothschild for charging 5 per cent interest and a 2.5 commission,[1] there was no further outcry.

The Egyptian finances became so tangled with those of the British and French that the revenue of the company was put under the management of Europeans. From then onwards the European shareholders, or 'bondholders', of the canal controlled Egypt. Half of Egypt's revenue paid the public debt. Captain Evelyn Baring (later Lord Cromer) was sent to Cairo as British Commissioner of the Debt and the ambivalent British occupation of Egypt increased – as did the wave of Muslim anger towards foreign occupation. Thomas now had to keep on the right side of British officialdom, Turkish officialdom, Egyptian officialdom and Syrian officialdom. Egypt was still part of the Ottoman Empire, but was also, at the same time, a showpiece of British imperialism.

The year 1876 was a time of renewed links with the past for Thomas. When he visited Melbourne on the fiftieth anniversary of his baptism, his old friend John Earp presented him with a Bible on behalf of the church, and the minister gave him a certificate commemorating his Golden Jubilee. At the same time, Thomas knew that the trouble in the Middle East would seriously threaten his Near Eastern tours. He had to balance personal beliefs and religion. Gladstone was vociferously criticising the Turks and there were demonstrations throughout Britain. Russo-phobia swept across Britain with large crowds gathering in Trafalgar Square waving the Ottoman crescent-and-star flag while singing:

> We don't want to fight,
> But by jingo if we do . . .
> The Russians shall not have Constantinople!

Balancing between being a client of the Ottoman Empire and safeguarding his investments in Egypt, Syria and Palestine meant he again had to compromise when they were caught up in a war that a large number of people, including Gladstone, in Britain did not support. Thomas behaved as if there was no conflict and just wrote when referring to the Russo-Turkish War of 1877–8 that 'despite the "Eastern Difficulty" bookings have been higher than ever to Egypt and Palestine'.

Gladstone brought out a popular pamphlet denouncing the massacre by the Turks of thousands of Bulgarians following the outbreak of a widespread revolt in Bulgaria, which was then, like Palestine and Egypt, still part of the Ottoman Empire. Reports of the numbers of deaths ranged from 10,000 to 25,000. Religious passions were inflamed – over 40,000 copies of the pamphlet sold in a week, mounting to 200,000 copies by the end of the month. Russia threatened to invade Turkey (and finally did so) to protect the oppressed Balkan Christians. In England, the 'atrocitarians', who believed the worst of the Turks, were backed by the 'jingoists', who said that the Russians were using Bulgarian discontent as an excuse to fulfil their designs on Constantinople and ambitions to gain control of the Dardanelles and the Mediterranean. Gladstone whipped up a frenzy of anti-Turkish, pro-Russian sentiment.

William Morris, the artist and designer, disturbed by reports, became treasurer of the Eastern Question Association, a post he held for seven years when he joined the Socialist Party. His fervour was typical of the many thousands of Englishmen who joined together against the efforts of 'Greedy gamblers on the stock exchange, idle officers . . . and . . . the Tory Rump' to drag Britain into war with Russia. The war lasted longer than Russia expected – until June 1878 – when Turkey agreed to the San Stefano agreement, which proposed an enlarged Bulgaria. Seeing this as a Russian puppet state, Disraeli immediately sent the British fleet to the Dardanelles, which provoked the conference in Berlin. Disraeli, insisting that British policy must be based on British national interests, had kept Britain out of the war, but at the Congress of Berlin he gained almost as much as if Britain had taken part, and deprived Russia of the crucial gains from its victory over Turkey.[2]

Thomas's ambivalence to this war and other situations was defended by Edmund Swinglehurst, archivist and a former public relations official at Thomas Cook & Son, and author of two books on Thomas Cook and his company. 'It would be easy to accuse Cook of opportunism, and of looking the other way when his principles threatened his profits, but this would be unfair. Idealist and philanthropist though he was, he was a practical man who saw the world in a broader perspective than does a zealot. He wanted to change it but within the terms of what was possible, an attitude that helped him to build up his travel business without those head-on confrontations that sometimes spell disaster in enterprises.'[3]

In early 1879, six weeks after Thomas's seventieth birthday, John Mason Cook took over the business completely. It was a year of sadness for Thomas, who, now virtually pushed out of the firm, wrote:

. . . a Deed of Partnership was adopted . . . and in the following month a new deed was agreed upon, under which, by mutual consent, the son agreed to take the management of the business founded by his father, thirty-eight years previously, and the latter was to be at liberty to travel or not at his pleasure, still retaining his proper interest in the business of Thomas Cook & Son, under which title all is now concentrated, our American Partnership of six years having been terminated at the close of the season of 1878, since which time our own Agency has been conducted by our appointed Manager in New York, with subordinate Agencies in Boston, Chicago, Philadelphia, and Washington.

The bitterness fills too many letters to recite but they all point to the fact that John Mason was right in predicting that he and his father would come to blows. If John Mason had not returned to the firm, though, it is unlikely that it would have survived.

In 1878 Thomas had written about his half-brother Simeon 'dying suddenly while on a lecturing tour on temperance, at Bridlington in February 1878, while I was staying with my wife, daughter and friends, at Sorrento'. As his other half-brother, James, had also died at the age of sixty, five years earlier, Thomas was now the only survivor of the Cook–Smithard family – and with John Mason out of Thomas's life, Annie now had almost too much attention focused on her.

The confrontations between the British and the Egyptians intensified after the war between Turkey and Russia. Even though the Khedive refused to abdicate, his eldest son, Tewfik, would eventually replace him. Egypt's huge debts to foreign investors continued to be unpaid. In 1880, coinciding with the tenth anniversary of Thomas's tours in Egypt, the Law of Liquidation was passed by five European powers which aimed at ensuring that they were repaid by virtually taking over some of the Egyptian organisations. The growing loathing of the increased British interference – the result of Gladstone being returned for his second term in office, plus a hatred of many of the European officials – turned into a full-scale rebellion. Arabi Pasha, the nationalist hero, demanded a new ministry and overawed the Khedive.

Arabi Pasha's most vocal British campaigners were Wilfred Blunt and his wife, Lady Anne, Lord Byron's granddaughter. They had both learnt Arabic before riding through the wildest parts of the Mesopotamian and Arabian deserts, and their Egyptian home at Sheykh Obeyd, the Arabian horse stud near Cairo, was then nearly as famous as the Pyramids.

In 1882, Thomas Cook & Son had temporarily to suspend trips to Egypt as a result of the tensions, and a massacre of between 40 and 300 Europeans in Alexandria. Arabi Pasha strengthened the fortifications, but the city was plundered and partly set on fire. On 1 February John Mason and his son Frank, who was now twenty, arrived in Egypt. They were hardly in Cairo before a request from the consul, Noel Temple Moore, came to make arrangements for Prince Albert Victor and Prince George, the two eldest sons of the Prince of Wales, to travel through Syria and Palestine. The Prince of Wales (who obviously felt no bitterness towards the Cooks from the encounter on the Nile with William Howard Russell thirteen years earlier) was keen for his sons to have a trip to Jerusalem, as he had had in his youth. Frank Cook, who had only recently left Mill Hill – the first member of the family to attend an English public school – conducted the royal brothers.

The princes arrived at Suez on the *Bacchante* on 1 March 1882, and M. de Lesseps, who was waiting to welcome them, had kept the Canal clear for the vessel, just as he had done for the *Osborne* on a former occasion. Two days later the princes landed at Ismailia and from that time until they returned to the *Bacchante* at Alexandria they were the guests of the Khedive. They climbed the Pyramids, where, at the top, they found the initials 'A.E.' on the south-west corner, carved there in 1868. The princes put their initials next to those of their father.

Looking at ancient Egypt, so closely associated with the Old Testament, prepared them for their more intensive trip in Palestine which would last till 6 May. Years afterwards, when presiding at a lecture in connection with the Palestine Exploration Fund, Prince George said that he recalled with pleasure the year 1882, when he had travelled 'through the whole of Palestine . . . across the country east of the Jordan'. Queen Victoria had expressed a wish to the Sultan through the Foreign Office that access to all the historical landmarks which had been granted to their father in 1862 should also be given to his sons, including admission to the mosques and the Cave of Hebron.

At Jericho, the news reached the princes of Henry Wadsworth Longfellow's death, at the very scene of his poem about Bartimaeus, the son of Timaeus, a blind beggar, who had said to Jesus, 'Jesus, Son of David, have mercy on me.' Before leaving Turkish territory, the princes sent a telegram of thanks to the Sultan and in their journal added, 'We have most thoroughly enjoyed our life in tents and riding, and are as hearty and hard, and strong as possible.' The *Excursionist*[4] discreetly, in a slightly self-congratulatory tone, reported the royal visit:

> Our arrangements were carried out under the personal superintendence of Dr. F.H. Cook, who has travelled over every route in the Desert, Palestine, and Syria (including Moab as far east as Meshita) likely to be traversed by travellers, and who had the honour, of spending 40 days with the Royal party, and had also the honour, through the special firman granted by the Sultan for the Royal party, to enter the Mosque at Hebron (see Palestine Exploration Society's Report for October), a favour which has only once before been granted to Christians, viz., on the occasion of the visit of H.R.H. the Prince of Wales in 1862. The testimonials we have received of the satisfactory manner in which the arrangements were carried out are specially gratifying, as they prove that Her Britannic Majesty's Consul was justified in intrusting such important arrangements to us.

The princes had hardly sailed away before trouble erupted into war. On 11 July the British bombarded Alexandria. Because of disturbances in France, no French troops or ships were sent, but soon British troops arrived from India and England and started crossing the Sinai Desert. They attacked Tel-el-Kebir on 13 September 1882 and quickly defeated the Egyptians, and then moved on to take Cairo. The British were now masters of all Egypt, with the Khedive Tewfik returned to power as their puppet.

A semblance of order was restored, with Britain insisting that its administration was 'only temporary, to secure stability', and that it would work with the Sultan. The Sultan relied on Britain for protection against the Russian bulwark, so he was unable to object.

Even though Sir Garnet Wolseley described Tel-el-Kebir as 'the tidiest little war ever fought by the British army', casualties were relatively high. John Mason took many of these wounded soldiers to Alexandria at cost price,[5] and such a large number of the other soldiers on pleasure trips down the Nile that he was given a 'grand banquet by Sir Garnet Wolseley at the Abdin Palace on the 13th October'.[6]

Tourism regained its impetus only to confront another setback. In the summer of 1883 a severe outbreak in Egypt of cholera killed at least 150,000 people. Everything seemed to settle down again, but there was yet another threat of war. British tourists, though, were fearless and refused to stay away. During all these troubles Thomas Cook & Son could boast that their tourists had travelled unscathed.

In 1884 Gladstone's government suddenly asked the firm of Thomas Cook & Son to organise emergency transport for 80,000 British soldiers down the Nile to relieve Major General Gordon in Khartoum, capital of the Sudan.[7] Gordon, described as 'a Bible-taught Evangelical, fearless, tireless, incorruptible; following the call of duty through fields of desperate adventure',[8] had become a celebrity. Public alarm in London for his safety had reached a climax at the beginning of May. Even though he was in imminent danger of death by the Mahdi, Gladstone's government had so far taken no steps to send a relief force. Vocal protest groups, marching with placards, held a mass meeting in Hyde Park on 9 May, followed by an equally large gathering in Manchester a few days later.

Gordon was no stranger to Cook's, which had earlier transported him to Khartoum. Their paths had also crossed in the Holy Land earlier when Gordon was looking for the authentic site of the Crucifixion while finishing maps for the Palestine Exploration Fund. He rejected many Roman Catholic religious sites, saying they were erroneous.

Again Gordon was confronting a religious group, as the Mahdi, declaring himself the new messiah, had raised the standard of revolt against what he called the brutal and incompetent Egyptian rule. The headwater of the Nile, the lifeblood of Egypt, and the region around it were now in the hands of fanatical tribes under a religious zealot who might at any moment take it into his head to invade Upper Egypt and raise the banner of the Prophet among the fellahin.[9] The rescue plan was unique. Never before had a private company transported the British army on such an expedition. It is often said that the British army engaged Thomas Cook & Son because of their reputation of getting people out of difficult situations. Actually, there was no choice. As John Mason wrote in the *Excursionist* in 1885, Thomas Cook & Son had a monopoly in the passenger traffic on the Nile, so the government had either to give the job to them or to buy them out.

Arrangements were made for the movements of 18,000 troops, 40,000 tons of supplies, 40,000 tons of coal and 800 whale boats. Twenty-eight large steamers and 6,000 railway trucks were required to transport the coal from Tyneside to Boulac and Assiout via Alexandria. John Mason and his Egyptian managers acted as overseers of the entire operation. They relied on the labour of 5,000 local men and boys, and completed their side of the contract in November 1884. But the prodigious effort was wasted, as the expedition arrived two days too late. Gordon had been killed on 26 January 1885, murdered by the troops of the Mahdi on the palace steps. When the news of the catastrophic death of General Gordon reached Britain, the anger and the storm of protest stirred the public in a way that had not been seen for ten years.[10] The Queen 'led the chorus of denunciation which raved against the Government. In her rage, she dispatched a fulminating telegram to Gladstone, not in the usual cipher, but open . . .'.[11] Gladstone was blamed and the government narrowly avoided defeat in the House of Commons. Thomas Cook & Son's failed rescue also put them in a bad light.

The mood in England had changed since the excitement in the previous year with the introduction of the Third Reform Bill, which had given the vote to agricultural labourers, tripled the electorate and established the principle that the vote ought to be given to every adult as a matter of right. The qualifications of property and income

206

were no more. But defeat came to Gladstone's government four months later over an issue close to Thomas's heart – that is, an increase in duties on beer and spirits. The Tories, backed by the brewing industry, went in fighting. On 9 June, amidst scenes of tumult and cries of 'Buckshot!' and 'Coercion!', the government lost by twelve votes. Lord Salisbury became prime minister. By chance, Salisbury, like Gladstone, was a client of Cook's.

In 1885, problems once again threatened the calm of tours in Egypt. Salisbury's Tory government all but decided to evacuate Egypt – the occupation was a legacy from the Liberals, and now was associated with the death of Gordon. Why should it continue? Salisbury dispatched Sir Henry Drummond Wolff to Constantinople to see Sultan Abdul Hamid II – Abdul 'the Damned' – who had come to the throne in 1876. Famed for his wives and concubines (and later by an unexpected devotion to the tales of Sherlock Holmes), he had been disliked by Gladstone, but was now courted by Tories. Despite a new and ambiguous convention, the British occupation continued.

Tourism spread in leaps and bounds – and so did the fortunes of Thomas Cook & Son. Thomas could boast that he carried his 'Temperance Flag pure and unsullied Round the World'. Thomas wrote that in '1879 it was strongly urged upon my son to arrange for opening an Office in Melbourne, in connection with the Australian Exhibition. Under assurances of the support of the Colonial Railways Authorities an agent was sent to Melbourne, an office was opened.'

The heyday of Cook's in the Far East and Australia had begun after the proclamation of Victoria as Empress of India in 1877. Tourist traffic was now two-way. While the Cooks took the British to India, they arranged for what they called 'the wealthy natives of India' – maharajahs, princes and rajahs – to travel to London and on to places like Monte Carlo and Paris. A handful of rajahs were unlikely to make much difference to overall trade, but it was their policy to look for overseas customers to counter the slowing-down at home – part of the knock-on effect of 'the great depression' in agriculture[12] in England, caused, according to some sceptics, by the repeal of the Corn Laws thirty years earlier. Britain's 'commercial Empire' was now also overshadowed by both the United States and the recently united Germany. Another problem was that England had become so densely peopled that the soil could not maintain its population. More imported food had to come in; more manufactured exports and people had to leave. The agricultural depression would linger for another twenty years.

Offices were opened in Calcutta in 1883 following John Mason's extensive visit in 1881. But at home the tensions between father and son, between altruism and commerce, increased. After a short while Thomas ignored it and slipped into his old way of going to the office. John Mason expressed real anger at his father. He went so far as to accuse him of dishonesty in diverting some of the bills for his new house in Leicester, Thorncroft, through the firm. All hope of reconciliation ceased. John Mason believed that Thomas was sacrificing tourism to his religious and philanthropic interests. There were also other deep-seated, unspoken hostilities. John Mason's patience was running out. Finally, they split.

Thomas liked having people nearby and was content to retire to Thorncroft, his two-storey, double-fronted, red-brick villa at 244 London Road, Stoneygate, on Leicester's outskirts.[13] A solid Victorian middle-class suburban family house, with a semi-circular drive and shrubbery, it had no pretence of being a country house. The front door led into a very light, double-storey square hall under a huge Paxton-inspired roof light. Doors from the hall opened into the dining room, breakfast room, drawing room and library. A wide staircase led up to a balcony with a circular landing leading to the bedrooms and bathroom. One visitor, Albert Bishop, recalled:

Mr Cook loved to have his friends round him at the Festive Season. There was a long table in the Dining room, generally full to capacity on Christmas Day. My father was always given the job of carving the turkey (of prodigious size) at one end of the table and generally one of the Mason family was at the other end to carve the huge sirloin of beef . . . We boys used afterwards to be allowed to play at puss-in-the-corner in the hall with some of the younger guests and I seem to remember in the early days Mr. Cook coming out of the Drawing room to watch benevolently . . .[14]

He also remembered his closed-in carriage, 'something like a glorified small bus (without top seats of course), with a seat down each side. The cushions were covered with blue cloth and when Mr. Cook called at our house to take Mother down to chapel, as he sometimes did, I used occasionally to get a ride . . . I felt myself to be a very grand and fortunate person.'[15]

Even after Thomas's retirement, Thomas Cook & Son continued to send tens of thousands of budget tourists to Jerusalem. Thomas kept up a correspondence with his agent, who ran the Jerusalem office with its reading room on the corner from the Souk and the Oriental bazaar. His old house, though, outside the old walled city, near the American Colony, became but a storeroom for the expanding camping paraphernalia needed for elegant tours.

THIRTY-TWO

'My God, My God, Why Hast Thou Forsaken Me?'

There was much fashionable interest in embroidery in the 1870s and 1880s. William Morris had encouraged the women in his family, and his female friends, including Georgiana Burne-Jones, to take up needlework. After the Royal School of Needlework was founded in 1872, Morris's sister-in-law, Bessie Burden, became its chief instructor. Another skilled embroiderer was W.B. Yeats's sister, Lily, later employed by both Morris and his daughter May. So when Annie Cook started a sewing circle on Saturday nights in Leicester she was taking a small part in what would soon be called the 'Arts & Craft Movement'.[1]

Running the Cook accommodation establishments and helping her father with tours to France and Italy had not been a sheltered life for Annie, but romance came late to her, at the age of thirty. She was now 'spoken for' by a young man, and had become secretly engaged to Mr A. Akin Higgins, a clerk in Ludgate Circus. The previous year when John Mason had heard of this he was furious, and said, 'I could not have a brother-in-law a member of my staff.'[2] Higgins had to resign. As a proof of his devotion, Higgins followed Annie to Leicester to 28 Pocklington's Walk in the town centre and managed to get a job as 'a stock and share broker and general agent'. Marianne did not encourage the romance, and how often and where Higgins and Annie met is not recorded. Indeed, so little about him has survived that now no one knows whether he was lively and dashing, handsome or plain.

Annie returned home from a sewing class on Saturday 8 November, had supper with her parents and announced she was going to have a bath. She went upstairs and turned on the recently installed new-patent 'instantaneous' gas water heater. An offensive odour from the geyser caused her to go downstairs to ask her father to check it. The time was then about 11p.m. When he came upstairs Annie also pointed out to him black specks in the water. Having learnt to trust his judgement, she had confidence in him when he assured her it was nothing. She ran her bath.

On Sunday mornings Annie was in the habit of bringing her parents tea on a tray first thing. When she did not come, Thomas went into her room. Her bed was empty. He went to the bathroom; the door was locked. Why had she locked it? Using all his strength he forced the door and found her dead in the white enamel bath, purple in the face. Victorian baths were particularly deep and long, so she had slowly sunk into the water and drowned.

Had he miscalculated the danger of the fumes, or was there another cause? Dr Lankester rushed to the house. Rumours persisted that the love affair of this 34-year-old had taken a toll and that it may not have been an accident. Suicide, considered the greatest sin, was usually out of the question for anyone deeply religious. As Annie had been the best of children and would not have done something which would have given her parents so much anguish, the balance of probabilities is against suicide. At the inquest, Thomas admitted that he knew of the situation with the gas appliance before retiring.

A shadow fell across Thorncroft and its two occupants. For evermore a feeling of sorrow filled the rooms. Annie's ghostly footsteps could almost be heard coming from the shadows. Whenever she spoke of her, Marianne had tears in her eyes.

The funeral took place on 12 November 1880. So many people were overcome by the tragedy of this girl who had devoted so much of her life to the Sunday school that her funeral and burial were attended by a large number of civic dignitaries, including the mayor, John Bennett, member of the United Baptist Chapel, who sat on the front pew.[3] The chapel was too small. At 2p.m. the Baptist minister read the first prayers of the burial service to the crowded congregation and to those jammed along the pavement and road outside. It was if a thousand voices were raised to sing the 23rd

Psalm, 'The Lord is my shepherd, I shall not want. He maketh me to lie down in green pastures: he leadeth me beside the still waters . . .'

There were emotional scenes; some quietly sobbed, while others openly wept. On they went, hymn after prayer, prayer after psalm. Then began the long procession accompanying the corpse on its last journey. At last, the melancholy cortege in silence arrived at Welford Road cemetery, the 28-acre municipal burial ground on the edge of Leicester opened in 1849.

Annie was the first of the family to be buried here. The sods of earth, damp from recent rain, had been piled around the newly dug grave, six feet deep, six feet long and three feet wide. More words were said, more amens chorused, more prayers offered. The minister quoted St Peter: 'For all flesh is of grass . . . the grass withereth, and the flower falleth away . . .'. The little children from Annie's Sunday school wept at her graveside.

Then came the final moment when the coffin was lowered. A solemn hush. Spades shovelled the sods of earth upon the coffin, made of English elm, which would not rot for centuries. More eyes were red with tears. Voices were low. Before they departed every hat was lifted, every bare head was reverently bowed, including that of Higgins, who had hoped to be her husband. He then vanished from the life of the Cooks; there is nothing more about him in the records.

The rumours never died down, but in a way they protected Thomas, whose misjudgement about the gas heater may have caused her death. At the inquest, the witnesses were Thomas, Lankester and Mr Akin Higgins; a verdict of 'death by drowning' was returned. *The Times* obituary was a little ambiguous:

and when the fatality occurred it [the heater] had only been used three times. On a previous occasion when the deceased used the bath she complained to an intimate friend [Higgins] that when in the bath she lost consciousness and that she hardly knew how she recovered herself, as she felt on the verge of death. She, however, had not complained of this to her father or mother. On Saturday night Mr. Cook noticed a very disagreeable smell after the apparatus had been lighted. No more, however, was thought of the matter until Miss Cook was found dead in her bath. Dr. Henry Lankester, who was called, said he found evidence which showed that there had been an exceedingly high temperature in the room, and this together with the offensive odour from the gas apparatus induced syncope [fainting] and Miss Cook was drowned. The room was fitted with electric bells, so that the deceased, had she had the power, could have called assistance at once.

Thomas's pamphlet, 'A Father's Tribute', was never published but was circulated privately – the only surviving copy is in the Leicestershire Records Office. He describes that fateful night and says, 'My only bitter reflection on myself is that I did not turn off the gas and close the door.'[4] There is also the possibility that Annie may have had an undiagnosed heart problem and excessive heat in the bathroom may have caused her to black out and drown. Indeed, Higgins had said in the inquest that she had confided in him about a previous blackout.

The Archdeacon Lane Sunday School in the poorest area of Leicester had been central to Annie's life, so at the cost of £7,000 Thomas built the Annie Cook Memorial Hall, complete with classrooms[5] close to the Baptist chapel where she had taught some of its 900 pupils. The Italian sculptor who chiselled a marble bust of her to be placed inside portrayed her looking demure in a finely pleated, high-necked blouse, but her eyes have a half-tender, half-tortured expression.[6]

Thomas's happiest years had passed. The happiness he had anticipated had dissolved. In five years, one by one the members of his immediate family fell out of his life, like targets in a shooting gallery, leaving Thomas to spend his last eight years alone. It was as if he had not had any children. John Mason had been the first to step out of his life, then Annie. Next would be his wife Marianne.

It might have been better if Thomas and Marianne had moved out of the house, as there could never be true happiness there again. Marianne fell into the role of invalid, her bouts of physical exhaustion and depression becoming more frequent. She had not settled into the life of retirement well, but now it became much worse. Thomas took her to the old spa and seaside holiday resorts, but she declined further. Thermal baths in Bath were of no avail, nor were sea baths in Bournemouth and Worthing. In February 1883, extra staff had to be employed to augment the coachman and the usual live-in servant. For three months Marianne had to be carried from room to room. As Thomas wrote in one of his innumerable short memoirs, which he entitled *In Memoriam, Brief Notes on the Life, Labours, Sufferings and Death of Mrs Marianne Cook*, her last year was a 'time of extreme trial'. In June she had recovered enough to be able to 'occupy a through saloon carriage to Worthing', returning home in July, and going back again to Worthing in September, again returning the next month, only to pass 'from Time to Eternity at six o'clock in the morning on the 8th of March'. It had taken three-and-a-half years from Annie's death before she joined her in her grave.[7] Again John Mason was away for the funeral, this time in Egypt with Frank, one of his sons.

Thomas and Marianne had been together for over fifty years but Thomas had been absent much of the time. Whether they spent more nights together or apart, or really cared, is not easy to decipher, but their letters reveal a sunny relationship. She had always been there when he came home, had kept up a steady income from the hotels and had pleased him with her unrelenting thrift. Occasionally, she had accompanied him on trips, as she had to Rome, where she had helped with the Baptist mission.

Thomas's dotage was sad as, not having lived alone before, he found it difficult. He was often in an armchair beside the coal fire. The long dark candleless nights of his youth returned; reluctantly he caught up with all the sleep missed in those years of back-breaking labour.[8] 'It almost nightly happens that in the first part of the night, while I sleep somewhat heavily, I am engaged in my dreams in various matters of work connected with tours and travel, and I make many trips through dreamland which leave an impression upon me in the wakeful hours of the morning . . .' In vain he tried to forget Annie. Gradually he had to accept that he could no longer read properly. For fifty years Thomas had led a restless, unstructured life, dashing here and there, adapting to meals and beds in different places and times. Now he was nearly blind, alone and enfeebled – difficult for someone used to being centre stage.

Interfering in the firm was out of the question. He would just receive another knuckle-rapping from John, who would remind him how much more profitable Thomas Cook & Son was now that *he* was running it *his* way. Nothing could obliterate the pain of rejection and the boredom of being solitary. There was the housekeeper, but she lived her own life with her own family.

Prayer did not fill the vacuum. Unhindered by his physical impairments and lack of sight, Thomas continued to push himself. Lankester often came to see him and accompanied him to Temperance meetings. A welcome addition to the movement at that time was Rosalind, Lady Carlisle, the formidable wife of George Howard, 9th Earl of Carlisle, and close friend of William Morris. She added a similar aristocratic glamour to Temperance as Selina, Countess of Huntingdon, had done for Nonconformity a century and a half earlier. Rosalind used her influence to close down pubs or convert them into Temperance hotels or coffee houses. As president of the British Women's Temperance Association in 1881, she campaigned widely and founded a Band of Hope at Brampton, a mining area near her, a place with a wretched reputation for drunkenness. In Leicester, Lankester fostered similar activities. He was president of the Leicester Band of Hope, a director of the Leicester Coffee and Cocoa Company, president of the Ragged School and in 1889 mayor of Leicester.

Meanwhile John Mason was becoming a legendary figure. From his head office beside Shepheard's Hotel in Cairo, branches were opened in every main town in Egypt. In an article in the *Excursionist* in 1888 it was announced that Egypt had grown to be the mainstay of their worldwide business. The impact of the Cooks on the Egyptian economy was described by one tourist: 'Those donkeys are subsidized by Cook's; that little plot of lettuce is being grown for Cook, and so are the fowls; those boats tied up on the bank were built by the Sheikh of the Cataract for the tourist service with money advanced by Cook.'[9]

In November 1888, John Mason purchased the funicular railway up Mt Vesuvius, which had been opened eight years earlier[10] to a wave of international press attention and the celebrated song 'Funiculì-Funiculà'. It brought enormous numbers of customers, but it also brought problems. When the demands of local guides were not met, John Mason found he had a burnt-out station, a cut track and a carriage cast down the abyss.

Before Thomas returned to the Nile in 1888, he wrote to John Mason saying, 'I do most earnestly desire to go up the Nile as far as Luxor or Aswan. I hope . . . that I may have the pleasure of one trip more, in the course of which I can tell my friends where they land and what they should see, for . . . I feel as if I know everything by heart and memory.' Accompanied by another staunch Temperance supporter, Miss Lines, who had been with him on his trip to Egypt eighteen years earlier, plus another old-timer, Miss Frewin, who had also gone with him to Palestine during the early years, as well as her sister and his 'friend and neighbour Mr. Glasgow', Thomas, at the age of seventy-seven, now made his last trip to Jerusalem. His friends, he said, 'considering my impaired sight, thought it almost reckless for me to take a long journey into foreign lands'. It was his farewell to his beloved Palestine and Egypt.

Having travelled by train to Venice, the trio then sailed over the Adriatic and Mediterranean to Alexandria, where Thomas was pleased to have 'a pleasant interview with the Khedive'. They eventually landed in Jaffa on 1 April ready to be present at the twenty-fifth anniversary of Miss Arnott's Tabeetha Mission School, for which Thomas had done so much. They then proceeded to Jericho, the Jordan, Bethlehem and Jerusalem for two weeks. Even though Thomas's face was now wrinkled and craggy and his gait slow, all the locals recognised him, rushing up to him with enthusiastic greetings in Arabic.

Then the sad day came when Thomas knew he had to bid goodbye to Jerusalem forever. Often groping his way in the grey darkness of his diminishing sight, he had to step back, but never was an exit more reluctant. With sadness, he left the familiar and spacious area around King David's Tower close to the Jaffa Gate, near Jerusalem's ancient walls. No more would he hear the echoing chants of the muezzin calling Muslims to prayer five times a day to the many mosques, nor the clatter of hooves of the donkeys on the steep cobbled paths. His last souvenir was a wooden crate of simple biblical fruit for the children at the Baptist Sunday school in Archdeacon Lane, Leicester, so they could eat 'figs from the Holy Land'.

From the Mount of Olives, where tourists go to view the entire city, he looked down over the Old City of Jerusalem, but all beyond were blurs and hazy shapes. In his mind, though, he could still see everything; the glistening dome of the Mosque of Omar, the crenellated walls with their twelve gates and the ancient gnarled trees. He would return via the Jaffa Gate, not the closer Eastern Gate, which had remained shut for over 2,000 years. Then the party rode down the steep winding hills to Jaffa. The weather was unusually stormy for April, as Thomas wrote: 'we had to remain a week in consequence of stormy weather, which prevented our embarkation.' He then described a young Arab girl, Labeebeh, whom he befriended: 'The week was profitably spent in many ways, and . . . I made the acquaintance of an interesting Syrian maid, who had been taught and was now a teacher in Miss Arnott's School. This young lady expressed a strong desire to see England . . .' Having booked her onto one of the 'great Orient Steamers', he then returned to England via Athens, Corfu, Trieste and Venice to Mayence, where his party took a steamer on the Rhine, and landed at Cologne, and then travelled to England via Calais.

Thomas was hardly home before he was off again, on his 'annual visit to the Highlands' with different friends. Labeebeh arrived in Edinburgh in early June and would stay by his side for nearly six months. Some people might think that taking a pretty young Syrian girl home was an old man's dream, but in reality it was the gesture of a Christian, and his longing to bring a little of the Holy Land back to Leicester. Many a traveller before, including Captain Cook, had brought home a 'sample native'. Labeebeh appears to have been a brief attempt to find a stand-in daughter.

Labeebeh and he went everywhere from Oban, to Iona, to Inverness, to Perth. Before crossing the border they visited Sir Walter Scott's house, Abbotsford, before returning to Thorncroft. In a circular sent to 'numerous friends, especially those who were with us in Scotland', he announced celebrations for his eightieth birthday:

> On 12th of November, it is my intention again to take Labeebeh to London, and offer to friends there the opportunity and privilege of meeting her on that day at Parson's Temperance Hotel, 59, Great Russell Street. Invited friends and guests will take tea together there at six o'clock on the evening of that day. The chief part of the following day will be spent in London, and we then return to Leicester. The remainder of the week will be devoted to a Conversazione at the Memorial Hall, which was built in memory of my departed daughter . . . During the time allotted to refreshments some beautiful specimens of Needlework executed by Labeebeh during her visit to Thorncroft . . . will be shown in the Memorial Room; and there will also be shown specimens of Agricultural Implements used in the East, which have been manufactured by a youth in connection with Miss Arnott's School. At seven o'clock addresses will be delivered by H. Lankester . . . Suitable hymns will be sung. Wednesday, November 21st will be spent at my home at Thorncroft, and the eve of my 80th birthday will be spent in suitable exercises. On Thursday, November 22nd, I propose, with a few friends who may choose to accompany me, to go with Labeebeh to Liverpool, and see her embark there for Jaffa on board the S.S. *Britannia*, which is advertised to sail on the 23rd inst.

Activities filling Thomas's months and days for the next two years are not recorded – his diaries have disappeared. But much time was spent doing what he could to help the Baptist Union and spreading 'the word'. He also had the satisfaction of seeing the youngest of his three grandsons educated at Mill Hill school in London, but sadly he did not spend time with them or his two granddaughters.

The year 1891 was marked by three remarkable achievements. First, in July the Golden Jubilee[11] was celebrated to mark the fiftieth year of Thomas Cook & Son; secondly, over sixty years after he had left Melbourne, Thomas unveiled the memorial cottages there, bringing his life full circle; and, thirdly, his *Cook's Tourist Handbook for Palestine and Syria* was published, with its references to biblical sites and their scriptural references, designed to be read on horseback or by a flickering lamp in a tent.[12]

Thomas was not one of the 300 guests in London at the lavish celebrations at the Hotel Metropole for the Jubilee banquet. Excuses were given. Presiding over the long table and its silver table centre, with the loftiness of an aristocrat, John Mason gave a speech in which he told of Thomas's frailty. This, though, was dramatised and inaccurate. His remark that Thomas had not recognised John Mason's voice implied that Thomas may have also been suffering from failing mental powers, but this was not the case. Thomas travelled frequently to Melbourne and wrote or dictated an admirable series of circulars and reminiscences.

Then, as always, the problem was that John Mason, a man who always liked being in full control, never liked sharing the limelight with anyone, let alone his father. In one of the speeches he boasted how his personal management had been the turning point in the firm's fortunes: 'In 1865 the whole personnel of the business consisted of Thomas Cook, myself, two assistants and one messenger . . . In 1880 we had a staff of 1,714 permanent salaried members. In addition it required 978 persons, chiefly Arabs, to work our business in Egypt and Palestine . . . we have 45 distinct banking accounts; and either as our own property or under rental or lease we have 84 offices worked by salaried staff of the firm, and in addition 85 agencies.'

An extract from a letter from Gladstone was also read out aloud. Having given excuses for being unable to attend he wrote: 'I do not regard your festival as a mere celebration of commercial success . . . I conceive that the idea which your house was, I believe, the first to conceive and patiently to work out, has distinctly placed you in the rank of public benefactors; and the competitors who have sprung or may yet spring up around you are so many additional witnesses to the real greatness of the service you have rendered . . .'

Regardless of his diminishing sight and physical infirmities, Thomas's last autumn was happy. Although the rift with his son was still there, the bitterness lessened. The return of the old injury from childhood to his leg caused possible gangrene and much pain, so that he was seldom able to take long walks, but he managed to get around. Gladstone was setting a remarkable example of being sprightly at a year younger than Thomas. He looked as if he would be celebrating his eightieth birthday at 10 Downing Street, as once again the whole country was split over Ireland.

Old age had not dulled Thomas's desire to help the poor. Far from forsaking his roots, he enjoyed the role of the local boy made good when he returned to Melbourne. Following philanthropists who had built tenements in London, he started planning a project on the hill, just two streets away from Quick Close, at a slightly lower level than the High Street but above green fields. Land was purchased and an up-to-the-minute architect was engaged to make drawings for a block of fourteen memorial cottages, a Baptist mission hall[13] and four holiday flats for Baptist ministers, with a bakehouse, laundry and wash-house and a spacious mission hall on which a pale green and cream 8-inch-wide border below the ceiling was painted and stencilled with a William Morris-inspired motif. Each flat would be furnished and fully equipped and rented at fourpence a week to 'poor and deserving people belonging to the Baptist denomination'. Another flat was for a caretaker and another three, named the Houses of Call, were reserved for Thomas and friends when visiting Melbourne and as holiday homes for pastors and their families – with the proviso that they conducted services in the mission hall.[14]

Before the building was finished, a lovely garden was planted in the front, crowded with hardy flowers, such as hollyhocks, roses, campanulas, peonies, pinks, Michaelmas daises and polyanthus. An organ was then installed so there would be always be music to accompany hymns. Bearing the names of his daughter and his wife, the cottages are also an unspoken memorial to his youth. The circle of his life was now complete. At last he had a bed and base, a little home of his very own, in Melbourne. And it was all new, clean, warm, modern and up-to-date.

Every detail was arranged by Thomas. He was giving something back to the church which had encompassed every part of his life. The *Barton Church Magazine*[15] described the gala opening on 10 March with a description of weather which must have reminded Thomas of the hardships of his youth: 'a keen wind and numberless snowflakes dancing in the air – the outermost fringe of the fierce blizzard then ranging over land and sea.' His old friend John Earp, who had climbed through the chapel windows at dawn with him over fifty years earlier, was there. Like Thomas, his career as a preacher had also been brief, but it had given him the confidence to become a wool buyer and maltster. The old Baptist chapel down the road was not forgotten. As a former printer and publisher, Thomas gave a tall bookcase similar to the ones he had already given to the chapels at Barton and Market Harborough.

Thomas's support of the Liberal Party was constant. The National Temperance Federation, which had been formed in 1884, was becoming more and more closely associated with the Liberals, whereas the Conservative Party still appeared to be aligned with the interests of the drink trade. Thomas hurried from his flat in Melbourne to Leicester on 13 July 1892 to cast his vote at the polls for the local Liberal candidate.[16] Two days later, on 15 July, Thomas Cooper, one of the old leaders of the Chartist Movement, died in Lincoln. Three days after that, on 18 July, Thomas lay on his deathbed at Thorncroft, London Road, Leicester, aged eighty-three. 'My flesh and my heart faileth; but God is the strength of my heart, and my portion for ever' (Psalm 73: 25). Comfort came from the words of his favourite hymn, 'Forever with the Lord'. A sudden pain and paralysis on his side hit him after supper around 8p.m. Friends and staff passed in and out of the room. Lankester was called.

Thomas left the world with a prayer in his heart and, one assumes, the knowledge that 'man has been brought nearer to God', with a vision of Jerusalem and the Jordan.[17] An obituary in the *Leicester Chronicle* made the pertinent remark, 'The total blindness which overcame him did not affect his spirits or prevent him from making an excursion to the Holy Land.'[18]

The son of the minister, Albert Bishop, described the music and gloom in the dark chapel after mourners had filed past Cook's coffin on 25 July in the Archdeacon Lane chapel: 'I could almost hear the beat of the wings of the Dark Angel of Death and catch a glimpse of the white wings of the Angel of Light as he carried the soul of the Departed to Him who made us all leave this Earth-bound place for another life elsewhere.' The minister, remembering Thomas's soup kitchens and cost-price potato seeds for men with allotments, emphasised that he had become a champion for the weak and poor 'in the times of terrible distress in Leicester fifty years ago'.[19]

The draped hearse was drawn by six black horses adorned with plumes of black feathers. Behind, the mayor, Alderman Thomas Wright, headed the procession of twelve horse-drawn carriages. Making its way to the north-east corner of Welford cemetery, the mourners were led by the Cook family, headed by three grandchildren. John Mason, though, was absent. His excuse was that he could not return in time from a trip to Norway, although there was a gap of nearly a week between the death and the funeral. Thomas had eschewed being buried with his parents in the chapel yard in Melbourne where the soft green grass, violets and daisies grew over the old coffins. In Leicester, marble covered the tomb of Annie and Marianne, giving an air of perpetuity and importance – as did the nearby tombstones of Thomas's old mentors – Winks was just 30 yards away and Ellis was 50 yards away. Only Annie, Marianne and Thomas lie there together. When John died nine years later, he chose to be buried in a vault lined with ivy and white lilies in the Anglican section on the other side of Welford Road Cemetery. He had become a member of the Church of England. In a similar way to the children of so many financially successful Nonconformists, he enjoyed the status of being a pillar of the established Church.

Thomas might have been the world's best-known railway excursion and tourist pioneer, but he was no millionaire. Time after time, profits had been given away to the poor or to religious establishments and he had subsidised many of his beloved tours to the Holy Land. He had handed over more money than he saved. Having also in 1879 let John be the 'holder of all the capital in the business', he left just £2,731 gross. His home in Leicester was sold to a member of the Ellis family.[20] When John Mason died seven years later he left an estate of around £700,000 – another example of the triumph of town over the country, of industrial riches over land.[21]

The *Leicester Daily Post* of 20 July reported that Gladstone, a man also driven by religious conviction, praised Cook: 'thousands and thousands of the inhabitants of these islands who never would for a moment have passed beyond its shores, have been able to go and return in safety and comfort, and with great enjoyment, great refreshment, and great improvement to themselves.'[22] A few days after Thomas's death, Gladstone, the old warrior, won the general election, becoming prime minister for the fourth time. Gladstone's cabinet contained two of Britain's first Nonconformist prime ministers – Henry Campbell-Bannerman as Secretary for War and Herbert Asquith[23] at the Home Office. Another Baptist, David Lloyd George, the MP for Caernarvon Boroughs, who was waiting in the wings, would be Britain's third Nonconformist prime minister.

Thomas had received no state honours during his lifetime, and there were none now. But he had founded both a dynasty and the most familiar name in the British travel business. It is strange that he is seldom grouped with other self-made Nonconformists of the mid-nineteenth century who set up companies which continue today, such as Boot (chemist shops), Cadbury (chocolate), Fry (chocolate), Wills (tobacco), Rowntree (toffees and sweets), Morley (hosiery), Clark (shoes), Barclay (banking) and Lever (soap).

Unlike many newly enriched tradesmen in industrial England who were not satisfied until they found themselves accepted by the gentry, Thomas had remained a strictly urban man, ignoring the process of gentrification. He never got beyond the lower middle class. However, by breaking down 'the barriers of prejudice'[24] and using class boundaries as hurdles to be leapt over, he had opened the doors for people from every walk of life to venture out on Grand Tours, making travel no longer a daunting experience.

His lasting memorials are worldwide and his face is on all Thomas Cook traveller's cheques, although it is usually his name that is remembered, not his face. Just over a century after his death in Leicester, a bronze statue of Thomas wearing a frock coat and carrying a rolled umbrella and suitcase was erected outside London Road Railway Station.

A month after Thomas's death two things occurred that would have given him pleasure: John Mason became president of the Leicester Temperance Society; then in August, tours to the Holy Land were given another boost when the railroad from Jaffa to Jerusalem was completed. Trains ran in each direction daily, and carried an increasing number of pilgrims and tourists.

Thomas made travelling easier and cheaper for Europeans, Americans, Indians, Australians and New Zealanders of all classes. There had been tours before but few which included advance tickets for transportation, food and sightseeing for such large numbers. As Clement E. Stretton said, Thomas was 'the first person to hire a special train at his own risk, sell railway tickets to the public, and personally travel with the train to look after the comfort of his passengers'.[25]

When Thomas was born, most power had rested with the upper classes, but now the new middle classes were snapping at their heels. Class divides were lessening. The two-party system had emerged, and both parties drew their voters from across all classes.[26] Nothing exemplified the new tolerance more than the larger-than-life bronze statue of the old champion of the Dissenters, Oliver Cromwell, unveiled in 1899 outside the House of Commons. He was now also seen as a champion of parliamentary democracy – part of the new Liberal interpretation of history. Plans to erect the statue had been passed during the premiership of Rosebery, the second Liberal prime minister, who was also said to have secretly paid for it.

Thomas would also have been pleased to witness another milestone in the long struggle of the Nonconformists. In 1900

Joseph Chamberlain, the Unitarian MP from Birmingham, became the first chancellor of a university[27] in England not to have been a member of the established church. Chamberlain was also the first commoner in 240 years to hold such a post. With the election of the first Nonconformist prime minister in Britain, Sir Henry Campbell-Bannerman, in 1905, the long struggle for the Nonconformists was over. The sharply defined religious beliefs that had so divided the nation were disappearing. But even though people now accepted that social and economic inequalities were not really part of a divine plan, they still existed. The earlier persecution of the Nonconformists, which had made so many of them champion wider freedoms, was gone.

Epilogue

It is difficult to visualise how Thomas would have responded to his obituary in *The Times*. It praised his ability to 'organize travel as it was never organized before', but revamped the old snobbish refrain. Out came the clichés that there were too many of his uncultured tourists filling up destinations which, until recently, had been exclusively for the upper and middle classes. They complained that they were being forced to mix with sight-seeing compatriots they considered to be less congenial: 'The world is not altogether reformed by cheap tours, nor is the inherent vulgarity of the British Philistine going to be eradicated by sending him with a through ticket and a bundle of hotel coupons to Egypt and the Holy Land . . . If only Messrs Cook could guarantee a benefit to mind and manners as easily as they can guarantee a comfortable journey!'[1]

Cook's had a monopoly of the boats on the Nile, and, during the first twenty years of conducting passenger traffic on it, 'from three to four millions Sterling (pounds) had been circulated in Egypt by travellers'.[2] In 1894 the Egyptian side of Cook's business was shifted into a company registered as Thos. Cook & Son (Egypt) Limited, with nominal capital of £200,000 divided into 20,000 shares of £10 each, John Mason holding nearly two-thirds. Anxious to reassure old customers, the *Excursionist* explained that management was still in the hands of Thomas Cook and everything was the same as before. Cook's had already made Egypt's share of the global tourist market significant. By the end of the century the firm had annual net profits of about £82,000 in Egypt with almost half of the enterprise's revenue coming from their Nile fleet. An adjunct of empire though they now were, nowhere was their 'presence more conspicuous and welcome than on the tawny bosom of old Father Nile.'[3] In 1896–8, Cook's Nile steamers were again used as military transport, this time to move General Kitchener and his troops south to the Sudan, to defeat the Mahdi's successors.

Thomas would have been pleased that his special low-price excursions to the Holy Land continued. Tours to the Middle East were booming. Clients now ranged from most of the British royal family and the Kaiser Wilhelm II to the new Tsar, Nicholas II, who became the Emperor of Russia in 1894. One advertisement promoted £60 trips from Liverpool: 'Once in two weeks, a special boat will leave Liverpool bringing tourists to visit Italy, Egypt and Syria, Asia Minor and Greece, and returning home sixty days after their departure. The journey will cost £60, one pound per day . . . reduced the price almost by half, in the hope of bringing many more tourists . . .'[4] The following year, in 1898, when John Mason escorted the German Kaiser, more than 3,000 tourists flocked to Jerusalem with Thos. Cook. But just after this trip, seven years after Cook was buried, the year after Victoria's Diamond Jubilee, John Mason died of a disease. He had, as on his earlier trips, drunk the local water instead of wine. Two of his three sons, Frank and Ernest, took over the business until 1928, when they sold it to the International Sleeping Car Company, Wagons-Lits of Belgium.[5] Ernest, who had presided over the banking and foreign exchange business of the firm, died a bachelor in 1931 and left £1,054,769 6s 4d, most of which, along with his 21,000 acres of estate, went into the Ernest Cook Trust. Money from the Trust supports educational and research projects relating to the countryside, the environment and architectural conservation. He also left his collection of paintings to the National Arts Collection Fund for provincial galleries.

In 1975 Thomas Cook's grave had a marble table in the shape of an open book[6] placed on it, with a commemorative inscription, finishing with the epitaph 'He brought travel to the millions'.

A more stately tribute is in Norfolk. Four generations of Thomas's descendants have lived the life of country gentlemen at Sennowe Park, near Fakenham in Norfolk. More a palace than a country house, Sennowe is surrounded by an eight-acre lake, clock tower and a garden with elaborate terraces. Inside, the grand, oak-panelled dining room, a portrait of Thomas, painted forty years after his death, surveys the opulence.

Appendix: Three Cook Letters

FIRST LETTER
WRITTEN AT SAN FRANCISCO
A 'CIRCULAR TOUR'

We have been favoured by Mr. Thomas Cook, the enterprising organizer of Tours, with the following interesting letter, the first, we hope of a series. The letter is dated 'San Francisco, Oct. 31, 1872': –

Before leaving England on this greatest tour of my travelling life, I was pressed by many friends and by many inquiring correspondents to furnish particulars *en route* of my observations and experience of countries through which we passed, and the various travelling and other accommodation essential to the comfort and convenience of a journey of over 25,000 miles. I promised to adopt the best medium of communicating with friends and the British public on these topics, in the hope that I might be able, from certain points of greatest interest, to write letters which might, by your courtesy, find access to *The Times*, and thus obviate the necessity of writing many letters to individuals or to papers of local and limited circulation. On these grounds I ask your indulgence, under a conviction that tours round the world will soon become a popular and instructive recreation to those who can command the necessary time and money.

The season selected for this pioneering trip is, I believe, the very best that could have been chosen. Had we started one week earlier, we might have visited from this point the wonderful Yosemite Valley and the big trees – one of the greatest of American attractions; but for all other points and countries we seem to be just right. We have crossed the great American Continent under the genial climate of the

Indian summer; we are at San Francisco at the commencement of the winter season, under the genial rays of a lovely and brilliant sun, the thermometer ranging at about 70 degrees; earth, air, sea, and sky alike attractive; the forests presenting their richest and most varied hues; the plains, prairies, and mountain slopes glowing with auriferous tints, and the markets of this 'golden gate of the West' teeming with the richest and most delicious fruits, including fine strawberries, grapes, apples, pears, plums, &c., in endless variety. In the vegetable markets are green peas, French beans, and other productions of British summers, and it is hard to realize that we are entering upon a Californian winter. Looking ahead, over that sea which seems worthy of the name of Pacific, we are anticipating a good time in Japan and on its famed inland sea; in Hongkong and one or two other places in China; in India in the very best month of the year (January); and then we shall be just right at Suez and Cairo for the Nile, and afterwards for Palestine, Turkey, Greece, Italy, &c.; all to be completed before the middle of May, when a detour may be made to the Vienna Exhibition before returning to London.

My pioneering party is not large – eight to-day, and may be eleven when we sail hence to-morrow; but we represent, in pleasing harmony, England, Scotland, Russia, America, and Greece, and it has been our pleasure to fall in with several English and American ladies and gentlemen who bid fair to be pleasant companions. We also sail across the Pacific with a party of Japanese, who have spent five years in England, one of whom is a Prince of close relation to the ruling Mikado, and second in succession to the throne of Japan. In a splendid and powerful steamer, and with such variety of companions, we anticipate a pleasant voyage of about 22 days across the Pacific.

Our journey to this extreme point of the American Continent has been all that could be reasonably desired. True, we had to contend against hard gales and strong head winds in crossing the 'Atlantic ferry,' but our voyage was made agreeable by the mutual accord and pleasant arrangements of the cabin passengers, and the uniform kindness and courtesy of the commander and officers of the Oceanic, of the White Star Line. The excitement in the English Press just before we sailed from Liverpool about the accommodation for steerage passengers led me to examine rather closely the ship's arrangements for the 778 of this class that we had on board. I was permitted to go through the various departments of the ship, and I conversed with many of the most intelligent and rational-looking of the passengers, and I was almost surprised to find how few were their complaints, notwithstanding the close contact of 367 English men, women, and children; 124 from Ireland, 184 Germans, 54 Swedes, 44 French, and 3 Italians. With the exception of the beef being too salt and too hard, I scarcely heard a complaint, and the sleeping arrangements separated men from women, and married women and children from single women. When the whole 'marched past' the examining medical officers at the New York quarantine station, I thought I never saw a more healthy or pleasant crowd of mixed nationalities; and, considering the price paid for the 13 days' passage and food (six guineas), I could not but congratulate them on the facilities afforded to them for crossing the Atlantic. In the cabin there were 117 passengers – two-thirds Americans – and the officers and crew numbered 146; thus making a total of 1,039 souls.

Our stay at New York was limited to five days, quite sufficient for the general purposes of sight-seeing. The great railway trip from New York to San Francisco can be accomplished without difficulty in seven days and nights, but we broke the journey at the Falls of Niagara, at Detroit, at Chicago, and at Salt Lake City, and only required sleeping-berths for five nights. We selected the Erie Railway from half-a-dozen or more routes to Niagara and Chicago, and our ride in one of Pullman's drawing–room cars, by the course of the Delaware river, was extremely interesting. After visiting all the points of interest at Niagara, we took the Great Western Line of Canada to Detroit, and thence to Chicago by the Michigan Central Line. Our stay at Chicago for three days gave us ample time to see the phoenix-like restoration of this astonishing city, where there remain but faint traces of the devastation of twelve months previous. Every public building, every church, every hotel, and every mercantile establishment is completed, or in course of completion, on a larger scale than before the fire. As we happened to be there a few days after the anniversary of the fire, which had been celebrated, or commemorated, in churches and by public papers and associations, we heard and read much of the destruction and the recovery of the city; but among the strange and thrilling recitals of suffering and heroism, I neither heard nor read of any more touching incident than was recorded in the Chicago *Tribune* in reference to the proprietors of the Sherman-house, where we were located. I copy from the anniversary double number of the *Tribune* the following paragraph: –

The ruins of the Sherman-house were still smoking on Monday morning, and the three dispossessed proprietors – Messrs. David A. Gage, John A. Rice, and George W. Gage – were sitting together on a rescued trunk in the doorway of the residence of the latter, on Michigan avenue. The city was in horrible confusion, and the red tide of the fire was still sweeping on its course in the northern division. The question these gentlemen was asking was the question of the hour, asked by 70,000 business men in Chicago, 'What shall we do?' Now, W. P. Gates had built a large brick hotel on West Madison-street, near the canal, just furnished before the fire – commodious, well-constructed, ready. 'We must buy the Eagle Hotel.' Out came the carriage and horses of George W., and away went the partners south to Eighth-street, thence west over the bridge. They had energy, capital, and a purpose. But as they turned into Canal-street, George W. burst out, 'This won't do. These people on the north side are starving. I have oceans of milk on my Brighton farm. You go buy this hotel, David and John; I'll slip down and get a waggon load of milk.' On he went, and while the partners were closing the instant purchase of the Eagle Hotel, at 175,000 dollars, George W. Gage, without a licence, except from Him who said, 'Inasmuch as ye have done it to the least of these ye did it unto Me,' was peddling Brighton milk, without money or price, among the suffering, hunted, and distressed pilgrims of the north side, to which purpose he gave up a day of vast importance to his firm's interests. The Sherman was furnished in ten days and opened at the old rates. It has made thousands of its old patrons happy, and has since been forced at times to turn away nearly as many as it accommodated.

The Great Pacific Hotel, now re-erected, the largest hotel in the world, is to be opened by those brave citizens on the 1st of March next. They will have their reward. From Chicago we took the Burlington route to Omaha, traversing the rich prairies of Illinois, crossing the Mississippi and the Missouri; from Omaha, still running over the prairies, and gradually ascending the long eastern slope towards the Rocky Mountains, until we reached the highest point of the road at Sherman, 8,242 feet above the sea level. But it was difficult to realize the fact of this great elevation, the ascent from Omaha being gradual most of the way. Prairie fires on all sides, antelopes, wolves, and Indians kept us in a state of almost constant excitement. The Sioux tribe were evidently on the move to southern quarters, as they were mounted, in great force, on both sides of the line. They were supposed to be 500 at least, all mounted on very fine horses, gaudily dressed, and armed to the teeth. Had they been hostile, they might have troubled us by closing in their extended lines; but they gave evidence of friendship by cheers and actions, waving of caps and other signs of mirth. The Union Pacific line extends from Omaha to Ogden, a distance of 1,032 miles; and the Central Pacific, which meets with the Union at Ogden, extends to San Francisco, 881 miles. The total distance from New York the way we took was about 3,300 miles, and the detour from Ogden to Salt Lake City is about 37 miles. That detour we made, and spent two days among the Mormons, besides passing several of their settlements in the Rocky Mountains, all of which had a very clean and thrifty appearance. All of my party were surprised at the magnitude and business characteristics of Salt Lake City, which is rapidly filling with a smart Gentile population. The recently-discovered silver mines in the locality are attracting speculators and miners, and it will be difficult for Brigham Young and all his apostles and bishops to maintain the former exclusiveness of the city. But, apart from all religious considerations, the Mormons have done a great work in cultivating the plain and its tributaries, and it would be a sad day if this colony of early and industrious settlers should be depopulated, or their homesteads be forcibly taken from them. Every one feels that there are great changes, and the question will soon be tested as to the existence of such a peculiar organization in the midst of a mixed population of traders, adventurers, and speculators of all classes. My party visited Brigham Young, and most of them also visited the military camp which is located within a short distance of the city. We went through and on to the roof of the great Mormon Tabernacle, which is capable of seating 14,000 people, and is frequently filled. We also saw the commencing work of the great Temple which is slowly rising from its basement; and several Mormon families were visited. I called to see one of my once near neighbours at Leicester, who left his home and friends 19 years since, as a journeyman carpenter. At my request he showed the produce of his farm, which was perfectly astounding. A plot of five acres had yielded 100 bushels of wheat, three waggon-loads of squash for feeding cattle, 150 bushels of potatoes, and 20 waggon-loads of Indian corn. A two acres and a half plot had yielded 30 bushels of wheat and six loads of hay, and he was able to keep one cow, one heifer, a 'span' of horses, five pigs, a score of chickens and other poultry. His homestead of over an acre yielded great quantities of fruit and vegetables; and being 'the husband of one wife,' he really appeared to be in circumstances of strong attachment to the place; and thus it is with great numbers of industrious settlers, and it is earnestly hoped that they will never be disturbed in the possession of such honourably-acquired wealth, for wealth it really is of the very best kind. It is not my purpose to discuss at all the vexed questions of 'celestial marriages,' or any of the peculiarities of the Latter Day Saints. It is unquestionable that Brigham Young and his adherents have raised a city, cultivated the greater part of the territory of Utah, constructed railways, and executed other public works, and have pioneered the way to the formation of another State of the Union.

We stayed at the Walker-house, a very large and beautiful hotel, which is doing a flourishing business. The brothers Walker, who built the hotel, have made a large fortune in the city, and are proprietors of an immense store of goods of almost every description. I could add very many interesting particulars, but shall run a serious risk of having this letter rejected for its length.

The last stage of our journey was intensely interesting. The Rocky Mountains disappointed us, but the Sierra Nevada was 'no mistake,' only that many of its great features were hidden by about 45 miles of most elaborately constructed snowsheds. The glimpses we got were grand beyond description, surpassing in some respects the greatest of our Alpine roads on the Continent of Europe. We had fine views of the important gold mines and works between the summit of the Sierra Nevada and Sacramento, and the recollections of the reports of the last 20 or 30 years added greatly to our travelling interest.

I am afraid to add to the length of this letter, or I should like to tell strangers to America of the peculiarities of the railways and the hotel systems of the United States. As it is arranged for the Pacific steamers going west and coining east to meet and transfer mails on the Pacific, if the sea does not dishonour its name, I may be able to add a few items to these hasty notes, with the view of showing the cost, the conveniences, and the inconveniences of American travel. We have now completed about a fourth of our tour in distance. We have been coursing the 'far West' for about 6,300 miles. We have gone with the setting sun until my watch, which still adheres to Old Country time, points to 5 a.m. to-morrow, it being here but 9 p.m. I expect somewhere in the middle of the Pacific to lose a day, and then our next land will be that of the rising sun, travelling in the course of which we will regain the losses of his decline in the west.

SECOND LETTER
WRITTEN ON THE PACIFIC OCEAN

Mr. Thomas Cook, writing on board the Pacific steamer Colorado, under date Nov. 6, 1872, continues his interesting account of the journey now being taken round the world by a party of tourists under his guidance: –

Assuming that my letter from San Francisco reached you and was honoured with a place in *The Times*, I avail myself of the tranquillity of the Pacific and the expectation of meeting a returning mail steamer to add a few particulars on American travel, which I think will be of service to strangers visiting the United States, especially those who contemplate a tour round the world. Railroads and hotels are the two great essentials of ease and comfort in American travel, and these institutions differ in their management and provisions from European accommodation. I will endeavour to note some of the most prominent advantages and disadvantages of American as compared with English railways.

The open cars of the American lines afford facilities of contact, and meet the necessities of long journeys far better than the sectional and boxed-up system of English carriages. Conductors have thorough command of trains, and can meet any emergencies of travellers without difficulty. Passengers, too, are provided with many conveniences which cannot be afforded under the English system. The sleeping car and toilet arrangements are necessary adjuncts to a railway ride of one to three thousand miles; and the baggage arrangements are perfect, though a little expensive in the transfer department. Nevertheless, when work is well done most travellers are willing to pay liberally for its performance. When you leave the hotel a Baggage Express Company take charge of your trunks, &c., and you may walk or ride at discretion to the railroad depôt, where luggage is checked by a strap and brass indicator being attached to it, a corresponding brass check being given to its owner. When nearing the place of destination, an agent of the Express Company comes through the cars, takes the brass check and gives a receipt for it, and the luggage is promptly taken to the hotel or other address where it is desired to have it delivered; or, if the traveller wishes to go forward by a following train, a transfer is effected, and a new check given. Baggage not wanted can be left at the depôt by merely withholding the check until it is claimed. The 'lie-over' system is also a great advantage. A traveller takes a through ticket as far as he wishes to travel, but he can break his journey at any intermediate station, by simply asking the train conductor for a 'lie-over ticket,' and this may be repeated as often as is desired. With our through tickets from New York to San Francisco, we tarried a day at Niagara Falls, a day at Detroit, three days at Chicago, and three days at Salt Lake City, and we might have stopped at 50 or 100 other stations if we had desired. The speed of trains is not equal to that of the English lines. The Pacific express of the Union and Central Pacific lines, in connexion with the fastest trains east of Chicago, only attain an average of about 19 miles per hour between New York and San Francisco, including short stoppages of 20 or 25 minutes three times a day for refreshments, and longer delays at the junctions of lines. It takes about 170 hours to go 3,300 miles, and that includes seven nights in succession in the sleeping car. The ascent of the Rocky Mountains to the height of nearly 9,000 feet, and of the Sierra Nevada to about 8,000 feet, naturally reduces the general average of speed; but the through journey is a wonderful achievement of science, energy, and capital, and our trains consisted of four great sleeping cars and four or five ordinary cars, all full of passengers.

Hundreds of Americans, with whom it has been my privilege to travel in Europe, have extolled the American system of railroad travelling for its cheapness and equality. But these are, to say to the least, very questionable advantages over our own system of selection and fares. The through fare from New York to San Francisco is about £27 sterling – a fraction under 2d. a mile. A second-class fare is quoted at about £21, nearly 1½d. per mile. But to this first-class must be added 21 dollars, or about £4, for sleeping cars; and second-class passengers are not permitted to take sleeping car tickets – a species of exclusiveness which does not comport with Republican equality. Sleeping in cars is not nearly as easy and pleasant as in the state rooms of the Colorado on this Pacific Sea; and the admixture of strangers and sexes is very repulsive to English travellers. The second-class and other travellers not provided with sleeping car accommodation must have a weary time of it, as their seats afford no support to the head and shoulders, and though a seat designed for two may have but one occupant, it is too short for horizontal repose. There are no second class cars, but the holders of second-class tickets for the Pacific route are generally restricted to the use of the cars appropriated to smokers. The sleeping and drawing-room cars are the property and under the management of an 'outside' company, except on the Central Pacific Line, from Ogden to San Francisco, where they are owned and worked by the railway company. In other cases the Pullman Company provide the cars, and work them on their own account. The railroad companies run the cars and have the advantage of the seats in the day time, the Pullman Company charging three or four dollars extra per night for the sleeping accommodation. On the Erie line we travelled from New York to Buffalo, in a really pleasant drawing-room car, beautifully carpeted, and furnished with elbow chairs, mounted on columns, and capable of being turned about in any direction. This was our pleasantest ride in the 3,300 miles, for which we paid two-and-a-half dollars extra (about 10s.) each passenger. It is thus by a double arrangement that a select first-class distinction is sustained.

The third-class arrangement of the American lines compares very disadvantageously with the English third-class. The emigrant train is worked separately, or consists of cars attached to freight trains, and the time allotted to the journey from New York to San Francisco is about 14 days. 'Hard lines' for poor settlers who have perhaps sold all they possessed, or borrowed, or depend on charity for the means of getting to a country which owes much of its prosperity to settlers from other lands. We saw an illustration of the troubles of this class in the case of a poor woman and child, who were turned out of the car in which second-class passengers were riding, and would have to wait at a way-side station nearly a day for the emigrant train. Many such, with children, have to spend wearisome days and nights on hard boards, with perhaps scanty food, before they reach their destinations in the Western States, where they are going to enrich railroad companies by the cultivation of their lands and the new territories of the States. In reference to this class of travellers, and to all the humbler classes, the English system offers decided advantages over the American. The spirited example set by the Midland Company last April, and copied by nearly all others, of 'Third-class by all trains,' has been the greatest boon ever offered to the large class of travellers whose time is equally as valuable to them as that of the wealthy, and who have less money to spend in necessary refreshments on a long journey. This is a matter that must soon engage the consideration of American railroad companies, and they cannot afford to risk their popularity and good repute by allowing John Bull to keep ahead of them. In the matter of passenger fares, England, with its three-fold system, is quite as liberal as America. There are local rates in America of 2 cents (1d.) per mile, and there are rates of 7, 8, and 9 cents. The short line from Ogden to Salt Lake City – about 35 miles – is charged two-and-a-half dollars (nearly 10s.), with no return tickets. Verily it is almost as bad to go to the city of the 'Latter-day Saints' as it used to be to go to Rome in the 'Holy Week,' when the most exacting charges were made on visitors. In winding up these notes on railway accommodation and charges, I think the companies on both sides of the Atlantic may learn lessons of mutual advantage.

The transition from railroads and steamboats to hotels is, in many American cities, a very expensive affair, and requires travellers who wish to be economical to be wide awake. On our landing at New York the proprietor of the coach that works in connexion with our hotel, wanted 3 dollars a head for my party, and would not accept 2 dollars – nearly 8s. But we engaged an express waggon to take our baggage for six persons for 3 dollars. We walked across the streets from the Ferry to the Broadway, and there took an omnibus for 10 cents (5d.) each. An 'independent' gentleman who went from the same steamer to the same hotel, ordered a coach, and was charged 6 dollars. At San Francisco 2½ dollars was charged to each from the ferry boat station to the hotel; in returning we paid a Transfer Company 4 dollars for baggage, and rode in street cars for 5 cents each. A carriage for four persons for a single hour was charged 3 dollars and 2 dollars an hour afterwards. In England we can get carriages for 2s. 6d. or 3s. an hour, and in Rome or Naples we can hire beautiful open carriages, with a pair of horses, for a day of nine hours, for 20 francs. Thus, a franc in Italy and a shilling in England are about equal to a dollar in America for carriage drives. The only drawback in the case of London is that it is the worst provided city in the world for this class of sight-seeing conveyance.

We have given a fair trial to the hotel and refreshment room arrangements between New York and San Francisco, and for various reasons I give the preference to American hotels over those of other countries. The prices paid have varied from 3 to 4½ dollars a day at the Grand Central, New York; the International, Niagara; the Russell, Detroit; the Sherman, Chicago; the Walker, Salt Lake City; and the Grand, San Francisco. The supplies of food at all these houses were simply enormous, and our greatest difficulty has been to select what to eat and what to avoid from bills of fare showing from 50 to 100 varieties. The American plan is to order about a dozen dishes of fish, meats, vegetables, pastry, &c.; a small portion is eaten from each dish and the 'leavings' go no outsider can tell where. This service is repeated at least three times a day, besides which a supplement can be had in the shape of tea or coffee, cakes, fruit, &c., for supper. But the best feature of the American hotel tables is that relating to drinks. On every table large jugs of iced water are placed, and tea and coffee can be had with every meal; but though the bill of fare generally has a wine list printed on the back, there is no positive obligation to drink, and custom does not sanction the habit of taking wine and strong drinks with meals. The bar is quite a separate arrangement of the hotel, and frequently in the hands of another proprietor. Americans, if they drink at all, frequently 'take a drink' at the bar counter before they go into the dining saloon; but the dinner table is free from that slavery and exaction often seen and felt at English tables, where some old 'heavy wet' manages to get in the chair, calls for wine and holds all responsible for payment of equal shares; and if any one dares to object he is regarded as mean and exceptional. I saw at the dinner of the Grand Central Hotel, New York, about 200 ladies and gentlemen seated at tables, and I could only see a single glass containing beer, and not a bottle of wine. I asked an intelligent waiter what was thought of such exceptional drinkers. He replied, 'They are either English or come from the south.' The young lady who had that odd glass of beer had an English face, and she did not continue long at the table. The same general absence of strong drink characterized all the hotels we visited; and I felt that it must be a great relief to strange travellers to be freed from the feeling of obligation to drink 'for the good of the house,' or to avoid the trouble of being exceptional. Those who think they 'cannot live without it,' can get 'the drink,' though in its use they constitute the exceptions. The Americans are free from the slavery of the drinking customs of the table. I heard an English gentleman ask an officer of this steamer to drink wine with him, and the reply was, 'I never drink wine at the table.' This strong anti-drinking sentiment is powerfully aiding the authorities of Chicago in their determination to enforce the law against the opening of the drinking saloons on Sundays; and the same influence of sentiment is felt in San Francisco, where, on one of the days we were there, a saloon-keeper was fined, and, not paying the fine, thrown into prison for selling drink to boys under 16 years of age. While passing through the States, I have seen numerous reports of cases where actions have been brought against drinksellers, for losses and damages to families occasioned by their supplying drunken husbands and fathers with liquor. The respectable hotel-keepers of America are generally clear of all such charges, as they offer no inducements to drink at public tables, and never treat with disesteem those who altogether abstain.

In American hotels, great attention is paid to the privacy and comfort of ladies, for whom large and elegant drawing-rooms are provided, with separate entrance and staircase, available also for gentlemen with ladies. The first floor is generally appropriated to dining and breakfast saloons and drawing-rooms, for which no extra charge is made. The ground floor and basement are appropriated to the business offices of the hotel, post and telegraph offices, railway ticket office, newspaper and book stands, barber's shop, smoking-room furnished with desks for correspondence, lavatory, shops for the sale of travellers' requisites, man millinery, pharmacy, and – generally in the most remote part – a drinking bar. Every guest on entering the hotel is required to enter his name in the register on the counter, and then, and not till then, a bed-room is allotted, and the number of the room is entered by the clerk in the register, which is open to the inspection of visitors and inquirers, the lobby, or central court, being open to the public. Private sitting-rooms are seldom required, and thus the expense of selecting accommodation is saved. Washing and ironing arrangements are generally connected with the hotels, but in this department care is necessary, as washing bills are generally very high. At Salt Lake City I paid 4½ dollars (nearly 18s.) for washing and 'getting up' 30 articles, 25 of which consisted of small pieces, such as collars, cuffs, pocket handkerchiefs, &c. In other places the charges are nearly equal to those of Salt Lake City.

The refreshment rooms *en route* between the Atlantic and the Pacific are generally well supplied with every variety of the best food, fruits, &c., and the attendance is of the very best character. Along the line of railway over the prairies, the Rocky Mountains, and at the summit of the Sierra Nevada, we were astonished to observe the amplitude of the supplies and the smart activity of the waiters of all kinds and colours – American and English white men, decently attired and becoming maidens, negroes of every shade of colour, and Chinamen clothed from head to foot in frocks of snowy whiteness. The refreshment car was only attached for two meals, on the Burlington and Missouri River line, but the three appointed stopping places for the day were generally well-timed, and we had always a clear 20 or 25 minutes for a meal, the charge for which was a dollar or 75 cents., but most frequently the former amount.

On the steamers our meals are served with the utmost regularity, and all our waiters are China boys, quick of perception, cheerful in their services, and quiet as lambs. Those who turn out early in the morning can get coffee from 7 to 8 o'clock; at 9, a substantial breakfast is served; lunch at 1; dinner at 6, and tea at 8.30. With the thermometer at 66 to 72, it's pretty hard work to respond to all the calls of the gong. Our life on the Pacific is very monotonous; not a sail of any kind has been seen since we left the Golden Gate of California. Flocks of strange birds, with wings at least six feet from tip to tip, followed us a long way, but have given up the chase; half-a-dozen sharks tried once their swimming powers against the Colorado, but we beat them. For three days we have made just the same gentle speed of 206 miles a day; all is tranquil and serene, and in five times 24 hours we have made 1,030 miles out of the 4,780, on a straight line to Yokohama. Our monotony has been twice broken by cries of 'Fire!' but these cries have only been uttered to call up the officers and crew for exercise; and it is quite amusing to see the China boys rush out from hatchways and every available porthole and take up hatchets, buckets, and apply the hose, fore, aft, and amidships. Our good Captain Warsaw combines humanity with stern discipline, and every morning and evening inspects every part of the ship with the keenest eye for dust or irregularity. But of all scrubbers and dusters I never saw the like of John Chinaman. In addition to our 50 cabin passengers, including the Japanese Prince and party lately in England, we have about 550 steerage passengers, most of whom are Chinese, returning home to live on the 300 or 400 dollars they have made by gold washing, mining, clothes washing, ironing, and other domestic engagements. All are quiet and gentle, not a rowdy fellow among them.

In a week or ten days more we expect to reach the 180th degree of longitude, when London will be under our feet, and a day will mysteriously drop from the calendar. But this going round the world is a very easy and almost imperceptible business; there is no difficulty about it, and but for the discrepancies of watches, the daily log of Captain Warsaw, and the salubrity of the climate in November, we should not realize our approach to the meridian line, or suppose it possible that the next land we see will be that of the rising sun, from which point I may possibly send a few additional notes of our progress for the information of home friends who read *The Times*.

THIRD LETTER
WRITTEN AT YOKOHAMA

Mr. Thomas Cook writes to us from Yokohama under date November 28, 1872: –

In crossing the Pacific from San Francisco to Japan we are almost assured that we shall meet one of the Pacific mail steamers in mid-ocean, when mail bags will be transferred and we may be able to communicate once or more during the voyage with friends at home. But in our voyage of this month, from the 1st to the 26th, three of the company's steamers passed eastward and were not seen. I had written at sea a letter to *The Times* on railroad, hotel, and other accommodation, of interest to travellers crossing the American continent, but that letter is quietly reposing in the American post-office here, waiting for the next steamer, on the 7th or 8th of December, and, as there is a chance of the Sierra Nevada and the Rocky Mountains being snow-blocked in mid winter, it is probable that this communication by the English mail of the 3d proximo may reach you before my letter from the sea. But, as this is a point of great interest in a tour around the world, I presume to trouble you with another letter.

I believe we are now about midway on our tour, unless Shanghai should prove to be the culminating point. The distance we have come has been about 12,000 miles, 8,500 by sea, and 3,500 by land. A voyage across the Pacific from San Francisco to Yokohama by the direct line is about 4,700 or 4,800 miles; but at this season our captain steered southerly some 10 or 12 degrees of latitude to avoid northern storms, and the ship's log showed a total distance of 5,250 miles, which occupied 24 days and four hours from port to port.

A fraction over nine miles an hour on a Pacific sea is slow progress as compared with Atlantic voyages between Liverpool and New York; but the economy of coal for a voyage of over 5,000 miles is a serious consideration when at least 1,400 tons have to be provided for the voyage, and if by any accident or detention the supply should run short there is no intermediate coaling station. Over that vast expanse of waters we never caught sight of a sail or craft of any description, and for 580 hours the engines never stopped or lost a single revolution; and we made our best progress when the sea was most disturbed, although the wind could seldom be called 'fair.' When the Colorado (our steamer) made the pioneer trip of the company, in 1866, on arrival at the port of Yokohama British sailors exclaimed 'What a mountain!' Her bulwarks, 18ft. or 20ft. above the water, with huge paddle-boxes, and the great works of the engine high over all, like those of the New York ferry steamers, contrasted strangely with the steamers of the Peninsular and Oriental Company, and a steamer so bulky had not before been seen in the Gulf of Yedo, and old salts wondered how such a mountain had been sustained in her passage over so wide a sea. But seven or eight similar craft have continued to cross the Pacific twice a month each way with very great regularity, and the impression of 'slow and sure' reconciled our voyagers to the moderate speed of 200 to 280 miles a day. Had not American navigation been clogged by laws of 'protection' our naturally fast neighbours would long before now have had not one fleet only of iron screw boats, but would have run sharp races over this and other seas with their elder brother east of the Atlantic. But light is breaking in upon the Legislature of the United States, and their free trade in tea is teaching an invaluable lesson. The chief traffic of the Americans with the East is in tea, the cargoes of which, with silk, fill these great ships from hold to cabin. Tea, silks, and coolies constitute the chief imports of this Pacific line. Of the latter we had about 550 returning to their country to live on their 300 or 400 dollars that they had earned by various industries in the States; and thus it is with most west-bound steamers, while those going east frequently carry nearer 1,000 than 500 steerage passengers. These Chinese coolies are so patriotically and reverentially attached to their fatherland that they try in every conceivable way to get the bones of their relatives carried back, and a case was discovered in our ship in which a Chinese coolie was conveying his father's bones in a bag which he used as a pillow. Of course this scheme was frustrated when discovered, but what became of the bones I cannot say. Should a Chinese passenger, however poor, die in the passage, provision is made by a Chinese organization to provide a coffin and for the embalming of the body, so that not one is thrown into the deep. It was rumoured on board that there were many embalmed bodies being conveyed from California in the hold of the Colorado. Thus it is seen that 'celestials' appreciate the dollars, but will not leave their relatives and countrymen to mingle with the 'sordid dust' of a 'barbarian' land.

Our cabin passengers consisted of about 50, representatives of I can scarcely tell how many nationalities. We had with us a Japanese prince, with eight or ten attendants and friends, returning from a sojourn of several years in England and America, where they have been studying the English language and social and political constitution and habits. My own little party of ten included four from Great Britain, one Russian, one Greek, and four Americans. We were also accompanied by two missionaries and their wives, returning to spheres of honoured labours, one of whom was a coadjutor with Dr. Judson in Burmah, and the other a talented translator of the Scriptures into the Assam language. The latter gentleman preached on three Sundays, and on two evenings lectured on Indian mythology, customs, and habits. In many ways the monotony of a voyage of nearly a month was relieved of weariness and rendered interesting and profitable. The actual loss of a day in the middle of the Pacific has puzzled many travellers, but it is a *bonâ fide* [sic] fact that the 16th November was dropped from our calendar. It is in this way. On reaching the 180th degree of longitude we are at the antipodes of Greenwich, and London time is 12 hours in advance. We then take a leap of 24 hours, leaving Greenwich 12 hours in our rear; but crossing the meridian line we put back our time an hour for every 15 degrees, and by the time we reach London the clocks and time will have righted themselves. The steamers of the line, on their return trip, get two days of the same date, and thus regain their loss. It certainly was curious that we should turn into our berths on Friday night, November 15, and all wake up on Sunday morning, the 17th. But it is more curious still, and a study for Sabbatarians, that on one of the Pacific islands Saturday is observed as the Christian Sabbath, and on another island, on the opposite side of the Line, Monday is kept as the Lord's day, Sunday being the dropped day. I quote this on the authority of Dr. Prime, of New York, as stated in his *Voyage Around the World*, recently published.

But enough of this steamboat trip across the Pacific. We are glad to find ourselves in a land of extraordinary interest, natural, historical, political, and social. All that has been told us recently of Japan is abundantly confirmed by observation and experience. The land is one of great beauty and rich fertility. The inhabitants and the

Government are rapidly transforming into enlightened, peaceful, and cordial citizens. The Mikado has emerged from seclusion, and the day before we arrived here showed himself openly on sea and on land at a naval and military review in honour of the visit of the Russian Prince Alexis, and on other occasions he has mingled with his people. The recent visit to Europe of Japanese Embassies and Princes, and of Government enquirers, all have a serious purpose for political and social objects. The railway and the telegraph are teaching the people great lessons of social reform. The two-sworded warriors are scarcely to be seen, and there are substituted for these desperadoes an improved system of police. It is encouraging to read Government notifications like the following: –

Trafficking in human bodies, or entering on employment; in which the master's will is absolutely submitted to, either for a lifetime or for a period of years, being a wrong thing, and contrary to the principles by which the social relations are regulated, has from ancient times been prohibited. The practice of forcing individuals to go into service under such names as 'service for a period of years,' &c., which has hitherto existed, being an abominable thing, which amounts to trafficking, is henceforth rigidly interdicted.

It is freely permitted to take pupil-servants (apprentices) to be instructed in farming, or in any trade or handiwork, but the period must not exceed seven years. The period may, however, be extended by mutual agreement.

Ordinary servants shall be engaged for one year, and if a person continues for a longer term, the agreement must be renewed.

Prostitutes, singing and dancing girls, and all other persons engaged for a term of years shall be set free, and no complaints about money lent or borrowed will be entertained.

The above having been determined must be rigidly obeyed.

Notified from the Council of State, November 2, 1872.

The following statistics will show how the foreign element is appreciated in the government of the country: –

In the department of the Imperial Government proper 214 foreigners are employed, on salaries ranging from 480 dollars to 16,000 dollars per annum. Perhaps the rumours of such salaries as 36,000 dollars may be true, but the statement does not appear in the Japanese official print. The nationality of the *employês* referred to is as follows: – English 119; French, 50; American, 16; Dutch, 2; Prussian, 8; Chinese, 9; Indian, 2; Danish, 1; Italian, 1; Manillan, 4; Portuguese, 1; Paraguayan, 1. In the Fu, or Imperial cities, and in the Kens, provincial local authorities, in all, 164 foreigners are employed. Of these, 50 are English, 19 French, 25 American, 9 Prussian, 15 Dutch, 3 Manillan, 42 Chinese, and 3 Arabian (as sailors). It would appear from the record that there are over 100 foreigners living in the interior, as teachers, surgeons, engineers, &c., &c.

Great Britain holds an enviable position in this category of officials, and British influence is seen all around. Many official notices are published in English, and the English language predominates on the new railway. I travelled yesterday with a polite conductor of a train who came from Devonshire, and a friend of mine from Iona, in Scotland, holds a high position as a Government engineer. Until very recently it was not permitted for foreigners to enter the precincts of the Temple of Shiba and the surrounding and gorgeous tombs of Tycoons and their wives of the past 250 years. Yesterday my party walked freely through and round about these indescribable buildings at Yedo, which for richness in carving, gilding, and decoration surpass all that I have seen in any land. Only a year ago an escort would have been required to conduct a party like mine through Yedo. Yesterday in 13 *Gin-rick-shas* we were drawn by two coolies to each machine through miles of streets, the people laughing and cheering us as we rattled through the great thorough-fares, and crowding around us when we stopped at a shop, an exhibition, or a temple. Not a solitary unfriendly disposition was manifested in that great city of nearly a million of inhabitants. I was astonished to see the great number of book and picture shops in the best business quarters, and I was told that the

Japanese are a great reading people, and fond especially of story. It is easy to see that they are very sagacious, and ready to adopt whatever is likely to contribute to their interest. It is quite expected that an ordinance of religious toleration will soon be published.

In coming over the Pacific I had a report of a most interesting lecture on the great changes in Japan, delivered in Dr. Landell's chapel, Regent's Park. I lent the report to an intelligent attendant on the Prince, and he kept it till the very last hour before landing, and, in thanking me for the loan of it, said how interested the party had been. The Prince and his party sat to hear one of Dr. Ward's lectures on India and Indian Missions.

We are really all delighted with Japan, and 12,000 miles from London, surrounded with endless foreign objects of interest, has in it so much of home life that it is almost like being at home. Permit me, in conclusion, to acknowledge the great kindness of one well known in military, naval, and diplomatic circles, Mr. W. H. Smith, manager of the Yokohama Club, who has been my 'guide, philosopher, and friend' in our pursuits of pleasure in Japan.

To-morrow we embark for Shanghai, going through the inland sea of Japan, which is said to combine all the beauties of all the English and Scotch lakes. Then we go to Hongkong, Canton, and other Chinese cities, after which our programme includes Singapore, Penang, Galle, and parts of Ceylon, Calcutta, and a run over 2,000 miles of Indian railways to Benares, Agra, Cawnpore, Lucknow, Delhi, and thence to Bombay, where we embark for Egypt, the Nile and Palestine, from some of which places I may again trouble you.

Notes

One: Religion, Railways and Respectability

1. Robert Ingle's excellent *Thomas Cook of Leicester* (Bangor, Headstart History, 1991) is only 67 pages long (hereafter referred to as Ingle). Piers Brendon's *Thomas Cook: 150 Years of Popular Tourism* (London, Secker & Warburg, 1991) (hereafter referred to as Brendon), published on the 150th anniversary of the firm, gives a detailed account of Cook, his son John, and the progress of the firm. Edmund Swinglehurst's illustrated *The Romantic Journey: The Story of Thomas Cook and Victorian Travel* (London, Pica Editions, 1974) (hereafter referred to as Swinglehurst) gives detail about the firm right into the twentieth century, with emphasis on the places they visited. John Pudney's *The Thomas Cook Story* (London, Michael Joseph, 1953) (hereafter referred to as Pudney) again tells the extraordinary story of the man *and* the firm.
2. Albert Bishop's notes of memories of Thomas Cook sent to Thomas Budge in 1952.
3. Brendon quotes J.C. Parkinson's article in 'Tripping It Lightly', *Temple Bar*, 12 August 1864.
4. Owen Chadwick, *The Victorian Church* (London, Adam & Charles Black, 1971).
5. Max Weber's treatise *The Protestant Ethic and the Spirit of Capitalism* (German edn 1904–5, English trans. Talcott Parsons, New York, Allen & Unwin, 1930) describes the relationship between religion and economic forces – that the doctrines of Calvinism resulted in socio-psychological responses that pushed forward 'the Protestant work ethic'. It would be appropriate if it was known as the 'the Nonconformist work ethic'.
6. Peter T. Marsh, *Joseph Chamberlain, Entrepreneur in Politics* (New Haven, Yale University Press, 1994).

Two: A Nonconformist Childhood

1. G.E. Mingay, *Rural Life in Victorian England* (London, Futura, 1977).
2. *The Oxford Companion to British History*, ed. John Cannon (Oxford, Oxford University Press, 1997), states that more than 4,000 enclosure acts were passed through parliament in those 80 years, affecting roughly 21 per cent of the land area of Britain. The process continued throughout the nineteenth century.

3. John Cook was born in 1785.
4. The Marriage Act of 1753.
5. Derek Beales, *From Castlereagh to Gladstone* (New York, Nelson, 1969).
6. Thomas Cook, in *Birthday Reminiscences*, said that his mother 'lived to the age of 64 and died in 1854', so she would have been born in 1789 or 1790. Pudney contradicts: she 'could not have been more than five or six years old' at the time of her father's death in 1792, implying that she was born between 1785 and 1787.
7. *Dictionary of National Biography*, quoted by Brendon.
8. France declared war on England on 1 February 1793.
9. According to the historian and soldier Sir Archibald Alison, the French Government never sent any money to maintain these prisoners, leaving them 'to starve or be a burden on the British Government, which, on the contrary, regularly remitted the whole cost of the support of the English captives in France to the imperial authorities'. At least 10,000 French out of the whole 122,000 died. Between April 1814 and the end of August 1814, about 67,000 of the French prisoners crossed the Channel back to France.
10. The south coast was dotted with seventy-four circular Martello towers, each with walls 9 feet deep, armed with swivel guns and howitzers.
11. Charles Dickens's description of a death in *Dombey and Son* (London, Bradbury & Evans, 1858).
12. Brendon.

Three: The Protestant Ethic

1. There is now a Baptist chapel on the site.
2. The Baptists split in 1633 when a number of members withdrew and formed the Particular or Strict Baptists. The remainder became known as General Baptists.
3. The Roman Catholic Church did not encourage people to read the Bible themselves until 1944 and then not fully until Vatican II in the 1960s.
4. One drawback was that if one monitor taught incorrectly, so did their 'students' who in turn became teachers. Errors snowballed.
5. Carl Stephenson and Frederick George Marcham, *Sources of English Constitutional History* (New York & London, Harper & Brothers, 1937).
6. The Congregationalist Union of England and Wales was established later, in 1831, although they date back to a sect called the Brownists (also known as Independents) who began in 1580.
7. An earlier group, the Independents, later boasted Cromwell as a member, but they were absorbed by the Congregationalists, and in a similar way many Presbyterians became Unitarians.

8. Howard Brinton, *Friends of 300 Years: Beliefs and Practice of the Society of Friends since George Fox Started the Quaker Movement* (London, George Allen & Unwin, 1953).
9. Chadwick, *The Victorian Church*.
10. William also laid the foundation for the Bank of England and Lloyd's Insurance.
11. This reform was necessary because the new king was a Calvinist from Holland.
12. Lord Macaulay, *The History of England from the Accession of James the Second*, 6 vols (London, Longman, 1849–51 [1913–15]). Unitarians and Quakers were excluded as they did not accept thirty-four of the Thirty-Nine Articles which had been in force since 1571.
13. England became a 'confessional state'; those who wanted any office, civil or military jobs had to take the oaths of allegiance to the established church.
14. W.J. Reader, *Victorian England* (London, Batsford, 1964).
15. Benjamin Disraeli, *Sybil, or the Two Nations* (London, Henry Coburn, 1845, repr. 1925).
16. G.M. Trevelyan, *Illustrated English Social History* (London, Penguin, 1964).
17. R.H. Tawney, *Religion and the Rise of Capitalism* (London, Pelican Books, 1938).
18. Reports of the Leicester Domestic Mission in Leicester City Reference Library, quoted in Jack Simmons, *Leicester Past and Present* (London, Eyre Methuen, 1974), vol. 1: *Ancient Borough to 1860*.
19. *Ibid*.
20. Richard William Church, Dean of St Paul's, *The Oxford Movement: Twelve Years, 1833–45* (London, Macmillan, 1891).
21. In *Clergymen of the Church of England*, Anthony Trollope argued the need for church reform and the urgency to balance the lopsided pay structure of ridiculously low pay for curates and the disproportionate incomes for higher positions. Bishops, the clergy and his critical ideas on the Church as an institution again became the theme of his six-novel Barsetshire series, which was seen as a piece of satire.

Four: A Spade! A Rake! A Hoe!

1. The most famous are in Derby, Stoke-on-Trent and Belper – with such brands as Royal Crown Derby, Spode, Royal Doulton, Denby and Wedgwood.
2. Cook, *Birthday Reminiscences* (privately printed pamphlet, Thomas Cook Archives, 1890).
3. In the decade between the 1821 and 1831 censuses, Melbourne's population, despite the increasing birth rate, only rose from 2,027 inhabitants to 2,301.
4. For a while these immigrants voluntarily came to Australia, travelling free in sailing ships chartered by the Colonial Office.

5. *Temperance Mirror*, 1889, quoted by Pudney.
6. J.J. Briggs, *The History of Melbourne, in the County of Derby* (Derby, Bemrose & Son; London, Whittaker & Co., 1852).
7. BBC script of *Great Britons: Thomas Cook and His Son*, produced by Harry Hastings in 1978. The others who were proposed were James Baker, Adele Taylor and Hannah Shore – from the Minute Book of Melbourne Baptist chapel, 1825.
8. Ingle.
9. There is no evidence that Cook was indentured as an apprentice, but his printing is not the work of an amateur.

Five: A Long Way from the River Jordan

1. Ingle's papers.
2. The first chapel, the chapel in which Cook was baptised, was built in 1750, and some of the original masonry is still visible in a side wall. In 1832 rebuilding and enlargement, with galleries, took place; the extension for the choir and the organ loft was added in 1856.
3. Winks converted to Baptism when working as a draper's apprentice at Retford. He returned to Gainsborough as a draper's assistant and preacher, and his first appointment was at Killingholme and then Melbourne.
4. *General Baptist Magazine* (1876), quoted by Brendon.

Six: Lay Preacher

1. Wellington was prime minister for just three years.
2. In May 1778 a bill repealing some of the harsher laws against Roman Catholics had been introduced, and in 1780 there was protest against legislation giving relief to them (Andrew Barrow, *The Flesh Is Weak* (London, Hamish Hamilton, 1980)).
3. Chadwick, *The Victorian Church*.
4. Thomas J. Budge, *Melbourne Baptists* (London, Carey Kingsgate Press, 1951).
5. *Ibid.*
6. *Ibid.*
7. Swinglehurst.
8. Thomas Cook Archives.
9. Harry Blamires, *The Victorian Age of Literature*, York Handbook (Harlow, Longman Press, 1988).
10. R.W. Harris, *Romanticism and the Social Order, 1780–1830* (London, Blandford Press, 1969).
11. White's *Directory of Lancashire* (1846), quoted by Derek Seaton in *The Local Legacy of Thomas Cook* (Botcheston, Leics, self-published, 1996).

12. Quote by Albert Bishop from a letter to Budge.
13. Richard Heath, *Thomas Cook of Melbourne, 1808–1892* (privately published in Melbourne, 1980).

Seven: Another New Career

1. Pudney – the *Daily Reporter* 'of the eighteen-seventies'.
2. Thomas Cook, *Memoir of Samuel Deacon* (privately published pamphlet, Leicester, 1888).
3. On the first trip the locomotive ran over and killed the MP for Liverpool, William Huskinsson.
4. In 1819 Stephenson drove at twelve miles an hour on the Stockton to Darlington railway.
5. Christopher Hibbert, *George IV, Regent and King* (London, Allen Lane, 1975).
6. Barrow, *The Flesh Is Weak*.
7. *Ibid.*
8. Hansard, II, 204, 7 February 1831, quoted by Chadwick, *The Victorian Church*.
9. Seaton, *Thomas Cook*.
10. Stephen J. Lee, *Aspects of British Political History, 1815–1914* (London, Routledge, 1964): ten counties in southern England with a combined population of 3.3 million had 156 seats; Middlesex, Lancashire and West Yorkshire had 3.7 million people but only 58 seats.
11. T.A. Jenkins, *The Liberal Ascendancy, 1830–1886* (London, Macmillan, 1994).
12. Asa Briggs, *A Social History of England* (London, Penguin, 1983).
13. Salford is so close to Manchester that they are now administered together.
14. Sheffield – opened by Queen Victoria and Prince Albert.
15. Buckingham was the founding editor of the *Athenaeum* magazine; his travels had taken him to America, India and to the Middle East. He published many books, including *Travels in Palestine through the countries of Bashan and Gilead, east of the River Jordan* (London, Longman, 1821), *Travels in Mesopotamia: including a journey from Aleppo, across the Euphrates to Orfah, through the plains of the Turcomans, to Diarbekr, in Asia Minor from thence to Mardin, on the borders of the Great Desert, and by the Tigris to Mosul and Baghdad* (London, Henry Coburn, 1827) and *Travels in Assyria, Media, and Persia* (London, Henry Coburn, 1829).
16. Robert Curzon, Baron Zouche, *Visits to Monasteries in the Levant* (London, John Murray, 1849).
17. John Greenaway, *Drink and British Politics since 1830* (London, Macmillan, 2003). He quotes *Report from the Select Committee appointed to inquire into*

the extent, causes, and consequences of the prevailing vice of Intoxication among the Labouring Classes of the United Kingdom.

Eight: A New Life in an Old Town

1. Ian Levitt (ed.), *Joseph Livesey of Preston: Business, Temperance and Moral Reform* (Preston, University of Central Lancashire, 1996).
2. Brian Harrison, *Drink and the Victorians: The Temperance Question in England, 1815–1872* (Keele, Keele University Press, 1994). Unfortunately, this excellent book, the best on the subject of temperance, is out of print.
3. The ancestor of the AA – Alcoholics Anonymous.
4. The London Temperance Society started in June 1831.
5. A study in the 1880s showed that 2,500 out of 3,000 Congregational ministers had signed the pledge.
6. Carey had been vicar there since 1795.
7. Rolls Royce and Thomas Cook & Son are connected by marriage.
8. *Pigot and Co's National Commercial Directory for 1828–9*; comprising a directory . . . of the merchants, bankers, professional gentlemen, manufacturers and traders in the cities, towns . . . and principal villages in . . . Cheshire, Cumberland, Derbyshire, Durham, Lancashire, Leicestershire, Lincolnshire, Northumberland, Nottinghamshire, Rutlandshire, Shropshire, Staffordshire, Warwickshire, Westmoreland, Worcestershire, Yorkshire and the whole of North Wales . . . With a large map of England, and sixteen . . . county maps. (London, Pigot, James & Co., 1828)
9. Tennyson, *The May Queen*, Part One.
10. *Brief Notes on the Life, Labour, Sufferings, and Death of Mrs Marianne Cook* (1884), Thomas Cook Archives.
11. R.J. Mitchell and M.D.R. Leys, *A History of the English People* (London, Longmans, 1950).
12. Thomas Cook, *The Temperance Jubilee Celebrations, 1886*.
13. *Great Britons*, BBC film.
14. Cruickshank described his riotous youth and conversion in the *Bottle* magazine in 1847.
15. The *Bottle* (1847), *The Drunkard's Children* (1848) and *The Worship of Bacchus* (1862).
16. *Great Britons*, BBC film.
17. 'John Cook', *Blackwood's Magazine* August 1899.
18. *Ibid.*
19. W.G. Hoskins, *The Making of the English Landscape* (London, Hodder & Stoughton, 1955). Smyth made a fortune in Elizabethan London, leaving money for the poor in the parishes around his native town.

20. William Fraser Rae, *The Business of Travel: A Fifty Years Record of Progress* (London, Thos. Cook & Son, 1891).

Nine: Total Abstinence

1. Unlike his birthplace in Melbourne, the house still stands.
2. An entry in *Historical Notes of the Market Harborough Baptist Church.*
3. No copies of this magazine survive, not even in the British Library.
4. The *Harborough Advertiser* in June 1941 quotes a long-time resident, Mr E.A. Goward, as saying that in 1841 Thomas Cook was 'hard up'.
5. Ingle.
6. Charles Edwards, Lester, *The Glory and Shame of England* (London, 1841), republished in New York (Harper & Brothers, 1842) – an exposé on factory life.
7. Cooper's name was linked with Thomas Cook in the oration of Revd William Bishop at Cook's funeral.
8. Lee, *Aspects of British Political History.*
9. Pudney.
10. *Ibid.*

Ten: 'Excursions Unite Man to Man, and Man to God'

1. Eliza Cook, a Victorian poetess, who was no relation.
2. The first stamp was a Penny Black.
3. Now on the A6 between Peterborough and Leicester (Seaton, *The Local Legacy*).
4. Substantial repasts at the end of a journey had been popular with all classes for many years, especially by Jane Austen's characters.
5. Ingle.
6. Thomas Cook, 'Travelling Experiences', *The Leisure Hour* (1878).
7. Although the number of 571 passengers has been given in publications, this figure was first printed in 1891. Thomas Cook had only ever written 'about 500'.
8. Campbell Street Station was demolished and replaced by London Road Station in 1892.
9. *Leicester Chronicle*, 10 July 1841.
10. *Great Britons*, BBC film.
11. B. Harrison, *Dictionary of British Temperance Biography* (Coventry, Society for the Study of Labour History, 1973), quoted by Brendon.
12. Ingle.
13. *Excursionist*, 11 July 1863.

14. Cook, 'Travelling Experiences': 'It was mine to lay the foundations of a system on which others, both individuals and companies, have builded, and there is not a phase of the tourist plans of Europe and America that was not embodied in my plans or foreshadowed in my ideas. The whole thing seemed to come to me by intuition, and my spirit recoiled at the idea of imitation . . .'

Eleven: Leicester: Printer of Guides and Temperance Hymn Books

1. From the 1950s onwards Leicester became a most popular city for immigrants from India; in the early 1980s the front of the main Congregational chapel was clad in white marble and converted into a Jain temple, the main Jain place of worship in Europe. The Sikh Gurdwara is converted from an old commercial building (Robert van de Weyer, *Heart of England, a Guide to Places of Spiritual Interest* [Alresford, Hampshire, John Hunt Publishing, 2002]).
2. Hoskins, *English Landscape* quotes 'the commissioners' who reported in 1845.
3. *Ibid.*
4. Jack Simmons, *Leicester Past and Present* (London, Eyre Methuen, 1974), vol. 1: *Ancient Borough to 1860*.
5. Belgrave Hall Museum and Gardens, Church Road, off Thurcaston Road, Leicester, said to be haunted by 'the Belgrave aunts', the seven daughters of John Ellis. Max Wade-Matthews's CD-ROM *Walk around Leicester* (Heart of Albion Press, Wymeswold, 2004) and his website http://www.leicesterandleicestershire.com/whos_who4htm.
6. Asa Briggs, *Victorian Cities* (London, Penguin, 1983).
7. 1848.
8. Brendon.
9. General Baptist Repository, September 1844, p. 312.
10. Copied by Budge from notes by F.C. Atton, Thomas Cook Archives.
11. They lived in Belgrave Hall until 1923. Andrew Moore, *Ellis of Leicester: A Quaker Family's Vocation* (Laurel House Publishing, Leicester), gives a thorough portrait of the life of Ellis, his involvement with the railways and other business interests.
12. Also one of the earliest steam railways in the world (Seaton, *Local Legacy*).
13. No surviving copies can be found. Dr Brent Elliott, the archivist and librarian of the Royal Horticultural Society said: 'The magazine *The Cottage Gardener*, the only one of that title of which we have a record, was founded by George William Johnson (1802–86) in 1848. An account of Johnson's life, and the founding of the magazine, was published in the *Journal of Horticulture* (to which the title had been changed in 1861) for 7 July 1881, pp. 11–14; Cook's name is not mentioned.

    'Possibility 1. Cook was employed by Johnson as a sub-editor. Johnson never published a staff list . . . and there is no record known to me of anyone else acting in an editorial capacity until Robert Hogg became involved with the title in the 1850s. Johnson presumably had assistance from the outset, but does not mention anyone. Possibility 2. Cook was involved in printing the magazine rather than editing. But the first printer of the magazine was Harry Wooldridge, Strand, and its publisher William Somerville Orr, also Strand; and Cook's DNB entry does not suggest any association with either. Possibility 3. Cook was falsely claiming credit. Possibility 4. There was another magazine called *The Cottage Gardener* which we have not come across, and is not listed in *Botanico-Periodicum Huntianum*. Possible, but not likely, esp. as he describes it as "a periodical of considerable size".'

14. Brent Elliott, *Victorian Gardens* (London, B.T. Batsford, 1986).
15. Ray Desmond, 'Victorian Gardeners' Magazines', *Garden History*, 5 (1997).
16. Domestic outworkers, including the framework knitters around Leicester, often outnumbered agricultural laborers as allotment holders.
17. Ingle.
18. Between 1860 and 1862 he had worked in Market Harborough as a Baptist minister. Winks stayed in Leicester for twenty-one years until he died. A Poor Law Guardian, he was the first Dissenting minister given permission to preach in the workhouse.
19. Like Wesley, Thomas saw hymns as a powerful way for people to express devotional feelings.
20. Pudney.
21. Briggs, *A Social History of England* (London, Penguin, 1983).
22. Naomi Shepherd, *The Zealous Intruders: The Western Rediscovery of Palestine* (London, Collins, 1987).
23. Trevelyan, *Illustrated English Social History*.
24. Cigars, originally called 'tobacco sticks', were relatively new; the first were manufactured in Hamburg around the time of the French Revolution.

Twelve: 1845: The Commercial Trips, Liverpool, North Wales and Scotland

1. Thomas Cook Archives.
2. *Excursionist*, September 1861.
3. Ingle, in conversation.
4. T.M. Devine, *The Scottish Nation, 1700–2000* (London, Allen Lane, 1999).

Thirteen: Scotland

1. Ingle.
2. Rousseau's descriptions of nature and man's feeling for it are in many of his books, including *Les Rêveries du promeneur solitaire* (Reveries of the solitary walker).

3. Gilpin, William, *Observations on the river Wye* (London, R. Blamire in the Strand, 1782), *Observations relative chiefly to picturesque beauty made in . . . 1772, on several parts of England; particularly the mountains and lakes of Cumberland and Westmoreland* (London, R. Blamire, 1789); *Remarks on Forest Scenery, and other Woodland Views (relative chiefly to Picturesque Beauty)* (London, R. Blamire, 1791); *Observations on the Western parts of England, relative chiefly to picturesque beauty. To which are added, a few remarks on the picturesque beauties of the Isle of Wight* (London, T. Cadell and W. Davies, 1798); *Observations relative chiefly to Picturesque Beauty, made in . . . 1776, on several parts of Great Britain; particularly the Highlands of Scotland* (London, R. Blamire: London, 1789).
4. Mavis Batey and David Lambert, *The English Garden Tour* (London, John Murray, 1990). Numbers lessened after Waterloo; the *Annual Register* described 'a vast exportation of English tourists' to the continent from which they had been debarred for so long.
5. Hibbert, *George IV.*
6. 'Pleasure Trips Defended', *Excursionist*, June 1854.
7. *Ibid.*
8. Devine, *The Scottish Nation.*
9. *Leicester Chronicle*, 4 July 1846.

Fourteen: Corn Laws: 'Give Us Our Daily Bread'

1. Jacques Droz, *Europe between Revolutions, 1815–1848* (London, Fontana, 1971).
2. Gillian Avery, *Victorian People in Life and Literature* (London, Collins, 1970).
3. Trevelyan, *Illustrated English Social History.*
4. Over forty years later, in his *Birthday Reminiscences* (November 1891).
5. Norman McCord, *The Anti-Corn Law League, 1838–1846* (London, Unwin University Books, 1958).
6. Horse-drawn buses had been introduced in 1825.
7. A.W. Palmer, *A Dictionary of Modern History, 1789–1945* (London, Penguin, 1962).
8. For the next forty years there were no restrictions on imports and exports.

Fifteen: Bankruptcy and Backwards

1. *Temperance Magazine*, August 1846 (Brendon).
2. Samuel Smiles began his career in the railways in 1845.
3. Opus 26, December 1830; first performance May 1832, in London.
4. *Betula nana.*
5. *Salix herbacea.*

Sixteen: *1848: Knowing Your Place in Society and Respecting Your Betters*

1. Henry Tudor ascended the throne as Henry VII.
2. Strawberry Hill was significant in the Gothic Revival.
3. Ian Ousby, *The Englishman's England* (Cambridge, Cambridge University Press, 1990).
4. Howard Usher, *William Lamb, Viscount Melbourne, Prime Minister* (Melbourne, Melbourne Hall Publications, 1988).
5. Designed by Augustus Welby Pugin.
6. Ingle.
7. In 1870 Napoleon III was the third French king to be a refugee in Britain in seventy-eight years. Louis XVIII and Charles X had created precedents.
8. Seaton, *Thomas Cook*.
9. Howard Usher, the archivist at Melbourne Hall, *William Lamb, Lord Melbourne*, 1988; *Fatal Females*, 1900, reprinted 2000; *Owners of Melbourne Hall*, 1993, reprinted 2003.

Seventeen: *The Great Exhibition*

1. David Daiches and John Flower, *Literary Landscapes of the British Isles* (London, Paddington Press, 1979).
2. These first appeared under the *nom de plume* of Michael Angelo Titmarsh.
3. William Makepeace Thackeray, *Notes of a Journey from Cornhill to Grand Cairo, by way of Lisbon, Athens, Constantinople and Jerusalem* (London, Chapman & Hall, 1846).
4. Yehoshua Ben-Arieh, *Jerusalem in the Nineteenth Century: Emergence of the New City* (Jerusalem, Yad Ishak Ben-Zvi Institute, 1979).
5. *Ibid.*
6. *Ibid.*
7. Paxton was already known as an architect of genius when he was commissioned.
8. *Chambers Biographical Dictionary*, ed. Magnus Magnusson (Edinburgh, Chambers, 1990).
9. Albert, with his strict moral sense from his Lutheran childhood, showed concern for the poverty, housing, unemployment and malnutrition in Britain; he was particularly disturbed to hear that over 4.5 million people (about one-seventh of the population) were receiving Poor Relief. Wanting to help 'that class of our community which has most of the toil, and least of the enjoyments, of this world', he had much in common with Lord Ashley, who steered him to become the president of the Society for Improving the Conditions of the Labouring Classes for four years.

10. By 1815 the clubs collectively boasted over half a million members.
11. The average weekly wage for men on farms rose from 9s 7d in 1850–1 in 1850–1 to 13s 9d in 1879–81, but there were wide variations between north and south and from one district to another, G.E. Mingay, *Rural Life in Victorian England* (London, Futura, 1977).
12. The monthly issues of this publication were eventually issued in thirteen separate editions around the world.

Eighteen: Paxton, Prince Albert and the Great Exhibition

1. Stephen Halliday, *Making the Metropolis: Creators of Victoria's London* (Derby, Breedon Books, 2003).
2. Avery, *Victorian Times*, figure for the year 1848.
3. Jeffrey A. Auerbach, *The Great Exhibition of 1851* (New Haven, Yale University Press, 1999).
4. Derek Beales, *From Castlereagh to Gladstone* (London, Nelson, 1969).
5. Chadwick, *The Victorian Church*.

Nineteen: Building Houses

1. Ingle.
2. Pudney.
3. Long since gone, but it ended up as a theatre and finally as a cinema.
4. Ingle.
5. J.D. Mackie, *A History of Scotland* (London, Penguin, 1991).
6. *Excursionist*, 1854 (Brendon).
7. Fairs had been popular in Birmingham from 1529; two of them, the Pleasure Fair and the Onion Fair, were held annually.
8. Quoted on the website www.chaddesley-corbett.co.uk.
9. Cook posters of the Birmingham Onion Fair in the 1890s are collector's items.
10. Ingle.
11. Now a camping shop with rented offices above.
12. Arthur Herman, *The Scottish Enlightenment* (London, Fourth Estate, 2002).
13. Including the Act for Setting Schools in 1696.
14. St Andrews (1412), Glasgow (1451), Aberdeen (1495) and Edinburgh (1582).
15. *Ibid*.
16. Pudney.

Twenty: Crimea

1. Seaton, *Thomas Cook*.
2. Napoleon was buried in St Helena in 1821, but in 1840 his remains were returned to Paris.
3. David Roberts R.A., *The Holy Land, Yesterday and Today, Lithographs and Diaries*, texts by Fabio Bourbon (Shrewsbury, Swan Hill Press, 1997).
4. Ingle.

Twenty-one: The Second and Third Decades

1. Ingle.
2. F.M. Leventhal, *Respectable Radical: George Howell and Victorian Working Class Politics* (London, Weidenfeld & Nicolson, 1971).
3. Brendon.
4. Mitchell and Leys, *A History of the English People*. Horace Walpole wrote a four-volume *Memoirs of the Reign of King George III*.
5. Brendon, quoting *Excursionist*.
6. It had been moved to Sydenham.
7. Sir Gilbert Scott, 1811–78, leading architect of the Gothic Revival, including the India Office, St Pancras Station and Glasgow University.
8. Completed and unveiled in January 1867.
9. Seaton, *Thomas Cook*.
10. *Excursionist*, September 1862.
11. *Excursionist*, April 1862.
12. Edmund Swinglehurst, *The Story of Popular Travel* (Poole, Blandford, 1982).
13. Pudney.
14. *Ibid*.
15. Thomas Cook Archives.

Twenty-two: A Leap in the Dark

1. Later pulled down to make way for some large mansion flats.
2. In the eighteenth century audiences sometimes broke into disorder, so iron spikes were erected in the front of some stages to protect actors from their hostility.
3. St Pancras was built in 1868.
4. Steven Marcus, *The Other Victorians* (London, Weidenfeld & Nicolson, 1966).
5. London University received its charter in 1836; Lord Burlington was its first chancellor.

6. Peter Sorensen in a footnote to his essay 'New Light on Shelley's "Ozymandias": Shelley as Prophet of the "New Israel"' (*The Keats-Shelley Review*, 16, The Keats-Shelley Memorial Association, Berkshire, 2002) quotes from the *Norton Anthology of English Literature* (7th edn, Norton, New York, 2000) and notes that according to Diodorus Siculus the statue was 'the largest in Egypt'. He also quotes from Duncan Wu's *Romanticism, an Anthology* (Malden, Mass., Blackwell, 1998): 'Horace Smith and Shelley wrote competing sonnets to celebrate their having seen and admired the statue at the British Museum.'
7. Built by Robert Smirke.
8. Gay Daly, *Pre-Raphaelites in Love* (London, Collins, 1989).
9. Ingle.
10. Brendon.
11. *Great Britons*, BBC film.
12. Other clubs included the Oesterreichischer Alpenverein (Austrian Alpine Association), 1862; the Club Alpin Suisse (Swiss Alpine Club) and the Club Alpino Italiano (Italian Alpine Club), 1863; the Deutscher Alpenverein (German Alpine Association), 1869; the Club Alpin Français (French Alpine Club), 1874.
13. President between 1865 and 1868.
14. Sole editor of twenty-one volumes, he contributed 378 entries in the first edition.
15. Leslie Stephen, *Playground of Europe* (London, Longman, Green, 1871).
16. Lynne Withey, *Grand Tours and Cook's Tours: A History of Leisure Travel, 1750 to 1915* (London, Aurum Press, 1998).
17. *Ibid.*
18. Garibaldi's name in England is now associated with the currant-filled biscuit commonly called the 'squashed fly' biscuit.
19. Verdi was then riding high, having won international acclaim for his operas *Rigoletto*, *Il Trovatore* and *La Traviata*.
20. Robert Blake, *The Conservative Party from Peel to Churchill* (London, Fontana, 1972).
21. 'De Gustibus', by Robert Browning, quoted by L.C.B. Seaman, *Victorian England: Aspects of English and Imperial History, 1837–1901* (London, Methuen, 1973).

Twenty-three: America at Last!

1. Many restaurants in the Far East, including Singapore, still do so.
2. *Daily News*, 5 August 1869.
3. Swinglehurst.
4. Ingle.
5. Pudney.
6. Swinglehurst.

7. Brendon.
8. This is the only item in the Thomas Cook Archives from John Bright. They were not acquainted at this point, and Bright begins his letter with the formal 'Dear Sir'.
9. It took thirty-five years from the time of Thomas's visit for the trends of Temperance to come to a head. In 1900, thirty states allowed local governments to decide whether or not to allow the manufacture and sale of alcohol. By 1916, nineteen states had banned alcohol altogether. By 1919, the 18th Amendment to the Constitution of the United States was ratified, forbidding 'the manufacture, sale, or transportation of intoxicating liquors therein, the importation thereof into, or the exportation thereof from the United States'.
10. Robert Dale, *Dale on the Ten Commandments* (London, Hodder & Stoughton, 1871).
11. Thomas Cook Archives.

Twenty-four: For 'All the People!'

1. *The Complete Poetical Works of William Wordsworth* (London, Macmillan, 1888).
2. Ousby, *The Englishman's England*.
3. Henry James, *English Hours* (London, Heinemann, 1905).
4. Lynne Withey, *Grand Tours*.
5. Laurence Sterne (1713–68).
6. Frances Trollope, *A Visit to Italy*, vol. 2 (London, Richard Bentley, 1842).
7. Withey, *Grand Tours*.
8. The *Pall Mall Gazette* was edited by W.T. Stead.
9. His reputation has been revived by Stephen Haddelsey's *Charles Lever: The Lost Victorian* (Gerards Cross, Colin Smythe, 2000); contemporary notices favourably compared Lever with his rival, Charles Dickens.
10. Rae, *The Business of Travel*.
11. Disraeli's Act of 1875, Trevelyan, *Illustrated English Social History*.
12. Brendon qualifies this figure from John Mason – it may be excessive.
13. *Great Britons*, BBC film.
14. David Duff, *Eugenie and Napoleon III* (London, Collins, 1978).
15. Pudney.

Twenty-five: The Holy Land

1. Words from a Band of Hope song.
2. Now an international hotel.

3. Now the Mena House Hotel.
4. This mummy was part of a group of coffins and mummies presented to the Prince of Wales by the Egyptian Government in 1869 which he passed to the British Museum. The museum's Department of Ancient Egypt and the Sudan's collection numbers over 110,000 objects, most of which came from private collectors in the nineteenth- and early twentieth-century excavations.
5. Anthony Sattin, who earlier edited Florence Nightingale's letters of her trip down the Nile, in his book *Lifting the Veil* (London, Dent, 1988).
6. William Howard Russell, *A Diary in the East During the Tour of the Prince and Princes of Wales* (London, Routledge, 1869).

Twenty-six: Jerusalem, Jerusalem

1. 1876 edition.
2. *Great Britons*, BBC film.
3. There is much dispute whether the site is on the west or east bank of the Jordan, i.e., in Jordan or Israel.
4. *Excursionist*, October 1873.
5. *Stamford Mercury*, 26 April 1872, quoted by Brendon.
6. Charles Dudley Warner.
7. Swinglehurst.

Twenty-seven: The Opening of the Suez Canal

1. Anonymous letter quoted in Gary Hogg, *Suez Canal: A Link between Two Seas* (London, Hutchinson, 1969).
2. Duff, *Eugenie and Napoleon III*.

Twenty-eight: Paris: War, 1870

1. A Catholic branch of the House of Hohenzollern which had already supplied Romania with a king in 1866.
2. Duff, *Eugenie and Napoleon III*.
3. William Carr, *A History of Germany, 1815–1985* (London, Edward Arnold, 1987).
4. For train lovers like Thomas, it was fascinating to discover that one of the reasons for the German success was its systematic use of the railway system.
5. In Oberammergau Cook's early parties were setting the pattern of being 'an overwhelming majority among foreign guests'.
6. Carr, *A History of Germany*.

7. Pudney gives long extracts from John Mason's long typed description of his journeys.
8. Roman Catholic services were in Latin until Vatican II in the 1960s.
9. Dr John Clifford wrote in the centenary volume of the *Baptist Missionary Society*, 'Stirred by the earnest appeal of the veteran traveller, Thomas Cook, our Society started a Mission in Rome in 1873.'
10. Cook, *Memoir of Samuel Deacon*.
11. The wife of the former Baptist minister in Rome, Helen Crutch, has shared her research with me.
12. Cook, *Memoir of Samuel Deacon*.

Twenty-nine: Around the World

1. *Jerusalem*, compiled from material originally published in the *Encyclopaedia Judaica* (Jerusalem, Ketter Books, 1973).
2. Now the Beit Immanuel Guest House, Youth Hostel and Museum.
3. The handbook soon became a regular publication, and now, more than 130 years later, *Thomas Cook's European Timetable*, still produced monthly, is a sought-after volume. A companion volume, *Thomas Cook's Overseas Timetable*, is also published six times a year.
4. Cook did not invent – nor did he claim to have invented – the circular note. The credit goes to Robert Herries, a London banker in the 1770s.
5. Lee, *Aspects of British Political History*.

Thirty: Grandeur

1. The unpublished diary of George Jager, *Palestine and Egypt, 1875–80*, quoted in Shepherd, *The Zealous Intruders*.
2. In 1881.
3. Yehoshua Ben-Arieth, *Jerusalem in the Nineteenth Century*.
4. F.F. Fox (Melbourne Hall Agent) to Earl Cowper, 17 August 1874, Melbourne Hall archives, 260/5/25, supplied by Howard Usher, the archivist.

Thirty-one: Egypt

1. Stanley Weintraub, *Charlotte and Lionel: A Rothschild Love Story* (New York, Simon & Schuster, 2003). Shares purchased at £19 soon rose to £34 and at their maximum in 1935 would be valued at £528. Rothschilds earned nearly £100,000 from the deal.
2. Gertrude Himmelfarb, *Marriage and Morals among the Victorians* (London, Faber & Faber, 1986).

3. Swinglehurst.
4. 1 November 1882.
5. Brendon.
6. *Excursionist*, 1 November 1882.
7. Gordon had resigned as governor-general of the Sudan in 1881.
8. R.C.K. Ensor, *England, 1870–1914* (Oxford, Oxford University Press, 1936).
9. J.A. Spender, *A Short History of Our Times* (London, Cassell, 1934).
10. There had been atrocities in Bulgaria ten years earlier. (Robert Rhodes James, *The British Revolution: British Politics, 1880–1939* [London, Methuen, 1976]).
11. Lytton Strachey, *Queen Victoria* (London, Chatto & Windus, 1921).
12. Mingay, *Rural Life in Victorian England*.
13. Now the headquarters of the Leicestershire branch of the British Red Cross. A blue plaque was unveiled in May 1978.
14. Bishop to Budge, 1952 (Ingle).
15. *Ibid.*

Thirty-two: 'My God, My God, Why Hast Thou Forsaken Me?'

1. The Arts & Craft Movement was founded after an exhibition of that name in 1887.
2. Swinglehurst.
3. Seaton, *Thomas Cook*.
4. Ingle's research on Leicester.
5. In 1937 it was scheduled as part of a slum area, and during the Second World War was used as a warehouse. In 1946 the charity commissioners offered it for sale for £4,000 and was acquired by the Corporation of Leicester (Pudney).
6. The bust is in the custody of the Buckminister Road Baptist chapel, Leicester.
7. Ingle.
8. Cook, *Birthday Reminiscences*.
9. Sattin, *Lifting the Veil*.
10. Vesuvius erupted in 1903, destroying much of the railway, and again in 1906 and in 1929.
11. The 1841 trip to Loughborough was the beginning of Thomas Cook's venture into the travel world, but he did not set up the firm for another three years.
12. The most respected of them all, George Adam Smith's *Historical Geography of the Holy Land*, 13th edn (London, Hodder & Stoughton, 1907).
13. Cadbury's did not start building the village of Bournville on the outskirts of Birmingham with its 143 cottages for another four years.
14. G.R. Heath, *Thomas Cook of Melbourne* (Derbyshire, 'Penn-gate', 1981).
15. April 1891 (Seaton, *Thomas Cook*).
16. Mr Logan.

17. Thomas Cook Archives.
18. Seaton, *Thomas Cook.*
19. *Ibid.*
20. Moore, *Ellis of Leicester: A Quaker Family's Vocation.*
21. David Cannadine, *Aspects of Aristocracy* (London, Penguin, 1994).
22. *Excursionist*, 15 June 1897, during the year of Queen Victoria's Jubilee.
23. The only future Liberal prime minister missing from the cabinet was David Lloyd George, who was then just a backbencher, having arrived in London in 1890 as the Liberal member for Caernarvon Boroughs.
24. Thomas Cook Archives.
25. Clement E. Stretton, *The Development Locomotive, a Popular History* (Newbury, Bracken Books, 1989).
26. Sir Roy Strong, *The Story of Britain* (London, Hutchinson, 1996).
27. The newly formed Birmingham University.

Epilogue

1. Sue Seddon, *Travel* (Stroud, Sutton, 1991).
2. Rae, *The Business of Travel.*
3. *Ibid.*
4. Ben-Arieh, *Jerusalem.*
5. In 1972 Thomas Cook & Son was purchased by a consortium headed by the Midland Bank. Twenty years later it was purchased by the German Westdeutsche Landesbank and the LTU Group.
6. The grave was redone by Thomas Cook & Son.

Select Bibliography

Books

Brendon, Piers, *Thomas Cook: 150 Years of Popular Tourism*, London, Secker & Warburg, 1991

Budge, Thomas J., *Melbourne Baptists*, London, Carey Kingsgate Press, 1951

Burns, A. Dawson, *Temperance History*, London, National Temperance Publication Depot, 1889

Cook, Thomas, *A Memoir of Samuel Deacon*, London, Thos. Cook, 1888

Ellis, I.C., *Records of Nineteenth Century Leicester*, St Peter Port, self-published, 1935

Ferneyhough, F., *The Liverpool & Manchester Railway, 1830–1980*, London, Robert Hale, 1980

Ingle, Robert, *Thomas Cook of Leicester*, Bangor, Headstart History, 1991

Leighton, William Henry, *A Cook's Tour to the Holy Land in 1874*, London, Francis James, 1947

Patterson, A. Temple, *Radical Leicester*, Leicester, Leicester University College, 1954

Pudney, John, *The Thomas Cook Story*, London, Michael Joseph, 1953

Rae, W. Fraser, *The Business of Travel: A Fifty Years Record of Progress*, London, Thos. Cook & Son, 1891

Seaton, Derek, *The Local Legacy of Thomas Cook*, self-published in Botcheston, Leics, 1996

Stretton, Clement, *The History of the Midland Railway*, London, Methuen, 1901

Swinglehurst, Edmund, *Romantic Journey: The Story of Thomas Cook and Victorian Travel*, London, Pica Editions, 1974

——, *Cook's Tours: The Story of Popular Travel*, Poole, Dorset, Blandford Press, 1982

Thomas, R.H.G., *The Liverpool & Manchester Railway*, Newcastle upon Tyne, A. Reid, 1915

Williams, R.A., *The London & S.W. Railway*, Newton Abbot, David & Charles, 1968

Main Sources of Thomas Cook Quotations

Testimonial to Mr T Cook of Leicester (September 1850)

'Twenty-Six Years on the Rails', appendix to *Cook's Scottish Tourist Practical Directory* (1866, much of it reprinted from 1860)

'Travelling Experiences', *Leisure Hour* (1878)

A Retrospect of Forty Years (July 1881)

Temperance Jubilee Celebrations at Leicester and Market Harborough (November 1886)

'My Own Memorial', *Memorial Cottages* (May 1890)

Birthday Reminiscences (November 1891)

Articles in over a hundred issues of the *Excursionist* (1851–78)

Acknowledgements

This book is about journeys and it has been a long journey, made possible with the help of dozens of people – everywhere from Britain to Jerusalem, from Rome to Australia. A bouquet of thanks goes to my sister, Margaret Morrissey, in Brisbane, who gave me daily assistance. I could never have pulled all the strands together without the patient help of Paul Smith, the archivist at the Cook Archives in Peterborough. Robert Ingle, who wrote an earlier biography, spared me much time in Leicester and in London, steering me through many complexities. Piers Brendon, who wrote a significant book on the firm Thomas Cook, also helped and gave me much insight, as did Edmund Swinglehurst, a former archivist at Thomas Cook. Harry Hastings, who made the BBC film in 1976, kindly lent me the script. In Melbourne itself I was helped by the Baptist minister, the Revd J. Birnie, Richard Heath and Howard Usher, the archivist at Melbourne Hall. In Rome, Father Alexander Lucie-Smith was tireless in following the footsteps of Cook, as was Dave Hodgdon, the Pastor of the Rome Baptist Church at Piazza Luciano, and his wife, Cathy. Nonstop emails full of history and guidance came from Helen Crutch, the wife of the former minister. In Jerusalem, while staying at the guest house attached to Christ Church in old Jerusalem, just near the Jaffa Gate, where Thomas Cook had his first office, I was helped by the Revd Neil Cohen and the untiring Kelvin Crombie and David Pileggi.

There is, alas, not room to list all the people who helped and guided me on this long trail, but special thanks also go to Jane Dorrell and Maureen Sherriff, who read through different versions of the manuscript; to Antonia Eliot, who runs the Ernest Cook Trust, and to Mavis Batey, George Carter, Joelle Fleming, Penny Hart, George Haynes, Caroline Lockhart, Elizabeth Muirhead, Tom Pocock, Miriam Rothschild, Ross Steele, Barry Tobin and Alan Ventress. I especially thank Guy Penman at the London Library, who gave me much help. As always, the happiest times while researching and writing this book have been in libraries or in bookshops. I am grateful to the State Library of New South Wales, the British Library in London, especially the staff in the Reading Room, where I spent weeks writing and researching, my local library, the Chelsea Library, the library at the School of Oriental and African Studies at London University and Brent Elliott at the Royal Horticultural Library.

270

Index

Index

Index